THE CRUSADES

BOOKS BY

HAROLD LAMB

THE CRUSADES

GENGHIS KHAN

TAMERLANE

HOUSE OF THE FALCON

MARCHING SANDS

WHITE FALCON

MUHAMMAD THE CONQUEROR

THE CRUSADES

Iron Men and Saints

BY HAROLD LAMB

WITH NUMEROUS ILLUSTRATIONS

DOUBLEDAY, DORAN & COMPANY, INC.

GARDEN CITY MCMXXX NEW YORK

DEDICATED
TO THE UNCOUNTED THOUSANDS
WHO DIED IN THE CRUSADES

FOREWORD

*A*T THE *end of the night of the Dark Ages a multitude of our ancestors left their homes. They started out on what they called the voyage of God.*

It was a migration, and a journey, and war. All kinds of people joined the marchers, lords and vagabonds, weapon men and peasants, proud ladies and tavern drabs. "A thing un-heard of," said a chronicler of the day, "that such divers people and so many distinguished princes, leaving their splendid possessions, their wives and their children, set forth with one accord and in scorn of death to seek the most unknown regions."

They were marching out of the familiar, known world into Asia to set free with their own hands the Sepulcher of Christ. They wanted to live there, in the promised land, ruled by no king but by the will of God. On the shoulders of their jackets they wore a cross, sewn out of cloth, and because of this they were called the cruciati, *or cross-bearers. So we, to-day, call them the crusaders.*

Most of them died on the way. But they went on, and after three years some of them reached their destination, Beyond the Sea. Here their journey ended, but other cross-bearers came out to join them. For the first time all the peoples of Christendom, speaking different languages and separated from each other until now, were united in a common enterprise. Christendom had taken up the sword against Islam, and the war went on for more than three centuries and some two million human beings perished in it.

Historians have picked out six of the crises of this conflict and have named them the six crusades. In reality it was all just the ebb and flow of the conflict begun by these crusaders.

In this volume is told the story of the first crusaders. It begins with their setting out, and it ends with the death of the last survivor. Eight hundred and thirty-five years have passed since then, and the lives of these men are known to us only by the chronicles of their day.

Several of these chronicles were written by men who marched with the crusaders, by two chaplains and an unknown soldier. Two other narratives were finished in Beyond the Sea after the march, and we have the accounts of others who saw the crusaders pass, a princess of Byzantium, an Armenian patriarch. There is also the testimony of Arab travelers and historians of the period, and the notes of Genoese sea traders, and the saga of a Norse king.

Upon these original chronicles the story in this book is based. It does not deal with the legends that grew up after the crusades. It is not history rewritten.

It is the story of a dozen men, most of them leaders, who started out on that long journey—what they saw on the road, and what they did, and what befell them at the Sepulcher of Christ.

H. L.

CONTENTS

CONTENTS

CONTENTS

ILLUSTRATIONS

PART I

I

BARBARIANS

ROME was dead. A white-faced boy emperor had seen his crown handed to a bearded chieftain, standing on the marble steps of the Ravenna palace, in the year of our Lord 476.

For centuries Rome had rotted, growing impotent. The last scene passed almost without notice. By then the old civilization had vanished. The future belonged to the young peoples thronging in from the north.

They came from ice-filled fiords and wind-swept steppes, but always from the north, pressing toward sunny lands and fertile soil. Some of them arrived overseas in dragon ships, and others in the covered wagons of the nomads, driving their cattle. They made camp along the marble road posts of the Caesars. The Mediterranean was their objective, for here Rome had gathered its wealth.

Wandering and fighting, they bred chaos among the ruins of imperial cities. Untaught, they fared badly. In time they were scattered or harried along by new waves of barbarians from the north and the east. Roman law was forgotten, the strongest held power. Clan traditions governed the masses, and the priests of Odin filled bowls with steaming blood, while horsemen watched who had been weaned in the barren Gobi.

For five centuries the Mediterranean world became a wandering ground of the clans. The barbarians had forsaken the old clan life, and as yet they had learned little from the ruins of Greek-Roman culture.

There were two interludes. An orphan of the Khoraish Clan in the desert near the Red Sea preached a new faith. He harangued the Arabs, telling them that there was no more than one God—they had worshiped until then many gods and demons and a great black stone—and they believed him. His name was Muhammad, son of Abdullah, and he made a multitude tremble at his description of the day of judgment. When Muhammad died the multitude accepted *Islam*—submission—and the *Koran*—the recitation. There was one God, and Muhammad, the son of Abdullah, had been His Prophet.

What this man of the Khoraish had not accomplished in his life came to pass after his death. Desert men wearing motley helmets, mounted on little horses and thin camels, went out to conquer. The fire of fanaticism burned in them, and spread from land to land with amazing speed.

Under the Companions, who had been the comrade-disciples of the Prophet, the rush of conquest began. In less than a century the banners of Islam had been carried east as far as the Indus and the outposts of Cathay. The swords of Islam were flashing in the deep gorges of the Caucasus. Egypt had fallen to them, and all the north of Africa, and Andalus—modern Spain.

Almost at its outset, the tide had swept over the rock-strewn valleys of Jerusalem, and the sepulcher of Christ.

Two obstacles checked the rush of the Muhammadans upon Europe. A certain Charles the Hammer, king of the Franks, withstood them in the west. And in the east they were flung back from the walls of Byzantium. But the real reason for the ebbing of the tide was that the Muhammadans had split up into different factions, each holding to its portion of the conquered lands.

Their conquests brought them face to face with the barbarians who had quartered themselves on the ruins of the Roman Empire and had become Christians. Europe became the neighbor of near-Asia. The front line of Christendom could look across at the advanced posts of Islam. No-man's land had disappeared.

In the west, where Spain was the battleground, the Christian Franks retook the passes of the Pyrenees and gained ground steadily. In the east the Muhammadans gradually edged across Asia Minor.

It was in the center that the Muhammadans held the upper hand—in the sea itself. The Arabs took kindly to the sea. They built ships and changed slowly from warriors to warrior-merchants. They made themselves at home on the islands, especially Sicily, and they sailed up the Tiber almost to the walls of Rome.

Meanwhile the Arabs and the conquered peoples of Islam gained in culture. Caravans came over the passes from India; the riches of Cathay appeared in the *serais* of Aleppo and Alexandria. Academies and palaces made Córdoba and Cairo beautiful, and Haroun al-Raschid reigned in Baghdad.

The long frontier quieted down, but the Muhammadans were now more intelligent as well as more powerful than the barbaric Christian peoples.

About this time, in the beginning of the Ninth Century, the second interlude held the stage of Europe. Charles the Great—Charlemagne—king of the Franks, played the chief part in it. Downright hard fighting and simple one-man rule established a brief empire for a generation. Charlemagne and his peers rode from the Pyrenees to the east, almost within sight of Byzantium.

To the wiser heads this seemed the beginning of order and law. The only government they knew was what they remembered of the Roman Empire. Only an emperor could rule. Charles died, and the sturdy dominion broke up.

And with its passing the real darkness of the ages settled down upon western Europe. The nations lived apart, without knowledge of how to do otherwise. They fought as their ancestors had done, like wolves. And new barbarians came raiding from the north, this time by sea. Danes and North-men—as the Normans were called at first.

They emerged from the mist-shrouded seas with a thirst in them for the fertile green lands of the south. Untamed, clad in wolfskin and sealskin, wearing gleaming gold, wielding their long swords and axes, they harried and burned and then settled themselves along the coasts.

A good many credulous fellows believed, after this, that the world would come to its end in the year 1000. They sat up all night to await the sounding of the horn that would summon them to judgment. But the sun rose again in silence, and the earth had not changed.

Nor had that part of it known as western Europe changed very much in the year of our Lord 1095.

II

DARKNESS

THE damp forests were there as before, and the gray ruins where owls glided from the vines. The wolves hunted in packs as usual. Only small patches of land were cultivated, in stony ground, near the hamlets. Clay and stone huts, roofed with thatch, clustered below the hewn logs of a lord's hall and a stone tower.

Cow-herders slept by the beasts in the outer fields, and sheep crowded the narrow forest trails. Here and there could be seen the white dust and broken stones of a Roman road. Sometimes a Jew passed along the highroad with his pack horse, or a merchant with his guard of spearmen. More rarely the cavalcade of a baron—a master—raised the dust, and the men in the fields thronged around to stare at the powerful chargers and the dark, oiled chain mail and the fur-edged cloaks.

Few of them ever saw more than this—except perhaps the great cross where the roads met at the end of their valley. What lay beyond the hills was unknown, and hostile. Only the black-robed monks, wandering barefoot from abbey to abbey, could give them news of the outer world, or a rare troubadour, hastening to the hall for his dinner.

The men of the Dark Age often were buried in the valley of their birth without having seen any other. And they labored without ceasing.

When day breaks I go out at once [these words of a ploughman have come down to us] driving the oxen to field, to yoke them to the plough. I must plough a whole field as a day's work. I have a boy who is now hoarse with cold and shouting. After that I fill the bins with hay, water the cattle and carry out the dung. Yea, truly, this is great labor, because I am not free.

Famine took toll of them. Rain at seed time—smothering crops, and rotting wheat in the ear—drought or war might bring on a time of hunger. The four horsemen of the Apocalypse rode with a loose rein over the land at such times.

Chalk was taken from the earth and mixed with flour to make bread. Their faces grew lean, and they had not strength to drag themselves around. Pits were dug in the ground, and the dying were dragged into them. Another calamity followed. Wolves, finding so many bodies on the roads, began to grow bold and to attack living men. Nourishment was kept for the strongest, in order that the fields might be cultivated.

A man was seen in the market place of Tonnere carrying cooked flesh to sell. He pretended it was the meat of an animal. He was taken and judged, and did not deny his crime. They burned him, and the human flesh he had brought to sell was buried by order of justice. But another man went and dug it up and ate of it. He also was condemned to flames.

At such times plague visited the living. Crowded in the hamlets, whole families were stricken, until the survivors often fled in terror from the buildings. The sick were carried to the churches in the hope of a cure, and contamination spread to the throngs who had come to pray.

Death raged [said Ordericus Vitalis, a priest-chronicler] and emptied many homes of inhabitants, and great hunger troubled the sufferers. When fire and waste devastated the land, many were driven out, and, the parishes being obliterated, they fled from the empty churches of the Presbytery.

They had the patience of sufferers, and they had their joys. A juggler might wander in, leading a bear upon which sat a strange and amusing animal, a monkey. The good people of the hamlets would watch merrymaking by the hour, when tumblers balanced cartwheels on their shoulders, or daggers upright on their palms. When two blind men, armed with wooden swords, belabored each other, the crowd roared its appreciation.

When the lord's courtyard was opened to them, upon rare feast days, they fed hugely from spiced pigs' heads, washed down by honey mead or beer. They climbed the rafters to watch pirouette dancers who circled slowly to the twanging of a viol. And they stared at tumblers with red beards and wigs, who stood on their hands upon the table and forked their legs in the air.

They were insatiably curious, these people of the hamlets, and restless. In them lurked a craving to wander, as their ancestors the Northmen had roved along the edges of the sea. They would walk, carrying their young children, to the yearly gathering of the nobles at a town. Although the towns were poor affairs—an abbey or a lord's castle on the height, both fortified and garrisoned by armed men, and a straggling of skinners' and carpenters' and silver workers' shops.

The homestead of the barbarians had grown into this feudal *fief*. It was larger, but still the same abiding place of the clan. The head of the clan was the chieftain of the fighting men, the master—the baron. He belonged to the class of *gentils hommes*, gentle men. Below him existed the *prud' hommes*, the stout fellows, the fighting men. And then the *bonhommes*, the good men—merchants, or well-to-dos.

These last were also the residents of the slopes that led up to the castle, upon the height, or *bourg*. So they were known as *bourgeoisie*. But all power and all responsibility lay in the hands of the lord. He might be a liege lord, if the men had done homage to him—pledged their bodies to his service. Or a land lord, if they held their lands from him.

In this age of unceasing war, the fighting man held the mastery. His household lived in a stone or wooden citadel, built to stand siege. More often than not he kept his horse and arms in the room where he slept with his wife.

He rode abroad in chain mail, with a long shield ready to hand, and sword and ax hanging from his belt. Helmeted, skilled in arms, he was a match for a dozen common men on foot, and that was his title of nobility. He was justice-in-chief, counselor, and tax assessor for his people—and plunderer extraordinary.

Their quarrels were decided at his pleasure; he might seize their cattle for his table, or require their daughters to be sent to his bed on their first bridal night; at other times he would open his granaries to relieve their hunger, or carry fire and sword through a neighboring fief to supply them with goods. He plundered for them as well as for himself. Money—silver —was rare indeed, and his men paid their taxes to him in grain, meat, woven cloth or leather, or such-like. All this went to the people of his household and his armed men. Real wealth, fine cloth, gold tissue, silver, he was forced to pillage afield, and he did so.

So feud was built up on feud. The lord of the manor saw his sons die in a cattle raid, or in the great wars. There was no truce in the struggle, when famine came on the heels of pestilence. Hard as were the ties that held bondsmen and serfs to the will of their lord, life itself was harsher: the stagnation of the forests and fallow land—the misery of isolation, when men could only gain advantages by the deaths of others.

The age of iron, we have christened it. Untaught, scarred by hidden lusts, unthinking, and cruel beyond our conception, it was ruled by iron weapons and the arms of mighty men. But in this night of the Middle Ages men were already laboring at the stones that would build the great cathedrals. It was an age of blind, unreasoning faith.

III

THE IRON MEN

CHIVALRY was still young. Even so, it dominated the lives of the men. It was an order, to enter which a man need be qualified; and it bound him to lifelong duties.

He was required to abide by his spoken word, to say nothing that he was not ready to maintain at risk of his body, to keep faith with his lord, to protect the weak, and to fight against injustice. His courage must be proof. A baron—a master of land and dwellings—did not necessarily become a knight. Likewise a knight did not always own property, although he was usually given sufficient to support himself, a few horses, and his esquire, with some men at arms.

He could not inherit knighthood. He had to acquire it by long service. A boy of six or eight years would be sent away from his home to be reared and trained by another lord. In his new household he was dismissed at once to the kitchen, to be ordered about and cuffed by the older esquires and attendants. He could not eat white bread or sweets, and he had to clean the spits and watch the fires.

These youthful bachelors, as they were called, had few

diversions. They played with sticks and dogs in the court-yards around the donjon tower, where sentries always kept watch. They listened to the smiths and bowyers singing interminable chants in the penthouses.

When they were nine years of age they devoted themselves to the horses and the play of wooden weapons. Staging mimic hunts, followed by their motley dogs, cleaning out the stables, riding to neighboring hamlets with a letter from their mistress, they longed for the day when they would be recognized as esquires and shield-bearers.

And when this came, it proved to be an arduous day. No longer, after vespers, could they sit by the hearth in the vaulted hall and watch the master of the castle finishing his wine upon the raised platform, or playing at chess with his guests.

They were no longer curly-headed bachelors, bent on mischief. The esquire was *armiger*—arms-bearer, attendant and pupil of his master. He rose early in the day, to groom and feed the horses. Then to the armory, to clean, oil, and wipe the helmets, weapons, and mail of his lord. Perhaps in the forenoon he had the joy of riding to hunt, to attend the older men.

Returning, he looked to the horses, and hastened to the hall where, silent and watchful, he served bread and meats and poured the wine. After the evening he must needs make his lord's bed and undress him. Before he could sleep the stables must be visited again, and the round of the castle made with the guardsmen.

Colts were given him to break in, until he became "steady on a horse, and fit to carry knightly arms." Fit, but forbidden that most-longed-for privilege. For the long sword was sacrosanct—only to be borne by a belted man—its hilt the shape of a cross, its pommel enclosing a holy relic.

The esquire might be a master of sword play, with wooden weapons, or skilled in handling the ten-foot lance. He might be able to spring in full armor from a running horse, or to leap ditches with the weight of mail upon him; but even when he followed his lord to battle, he was not permitted such weapons. Bare-headed and unarmed, he watched the paladin, his master, throughout the turmoil of hand-to-hand fighting, ready to help him off the field if he was hurt, or to lead up a fresh charger. Often these headstrong young ones cast off restraint and plunged into the battle empty-handed —to come out bleeding, flushed, and triumphant, a captured sword in hand.

Youth and mighty sinews made light of obstacles. This was before the time of mincing pages and sanctimonious heralds, and all the peerages. A great name must be won by deeds, and a strong fief had to be held by courage and watchfulness.

Esquires and young girls alike hung upon the talk of their elders, to glean the tidings of events—who had gone forth against the Moors?—what lands had been won?—what gentlemen had fallen? Their mothers, mistresses of the castles, governed a milder world within the dark walls. They managed the maids at the spinning, and watched the slow progress of the embroidery looms. They heard the seneschal's tale of wine stocked in, and white flour brought up from the mill. And when the men rode out, upon a summons to arms, the women must needs smile and cry good fortune to them— and turn back to manage a masterless fief, with its poor and its sick and its garrison idle upon their hands.

Stout-hearted women, these, of the feudal years, pent up and shut off from the outer world no less than the serfs who labored for them.

The tapestries they wove made clear their story—of hunting and armed men, banquet and siege. The crude paintings on the chimney pieces, the illuminations of the few manuscripts treasured in a chest, told the same story of long-dead saints or warriors. Rare indeed was the jongleur who could sing of love in the gay Andalusian way—the favorite song of the time was the "Song of Roland," with its melody of ivory horns and the neighing of horses and clash of armed hosts.

To these youths of Normandy—or France, or Burgundy, or Saxony—only two careers were possible, knighthood or the Church. Other professions did not exist for them. A merchant's counting house opened its doors to them in vain.

One boy, manor-born, was fostered by a trader who tried to teach him the virtues of calculation and the arts of buying. The lad had eyes only for passing horses until the worthy *bourgeois* determined to try him in his new profession and gave him several marks of silver—a large sum—to go to the market and purchase stock-in-trade. And the protégé came back without the silver but with a pair of hunting dogs.

"Thou hast been defrauded," the merchant cried, "and I have lost my silver."

"Not so," the boy maintained stoutly, "for these dogs are skilled at worrying boars or tracking wolves."

For such as he, only one course lay open, and one hour, when he would remain prostrated with his arms extended as if upon a cross, before the altar, and would rise to take up a sword for the first time and go forth as a man among warriors.

At dawn, after the end of his watch at the altar, friends came in and greeted the knight-to-be. He bathed and clothed himself in white. Then, after making confession and taking the sacrament of communion, he was led before the seigneur who awaited him with other knights.

Women came forward and put on him the pieces of armor: the heavy mesh shirt of iron chain-work—this he had been privileged to wear as an esquire—the coif, or hood, of similar mesh, and, for the first time, the sleeves and gloves and hose of mail. So he stood encased in iron, and the seigneur asked if he was ready to give obedience to the Church and to the laws of chivalry.

Then he knelt, after making his vow, to be struck upon the base of the neck with the flat of a sword, and to hear:

"In the name of God, I make thee knight."

The seigneur lifted him to his feet and said, "Be proud!" With that the lord who had given the accolade girdled him with a belt and thrust his new sword into its sheath. Others fitted gold spurs upon his heels, presented him with the long kite shield that he would carry henceforth and the conical steel cap with the nasal piece, that was called a helm.

So equipped, he was conducted out to where a powerful charger waited, and the ten-foot lance was put into his hand.

He rode a few courses with the lance, and the ceremony was ended, except for the feasting.

The new knight was now privileged to take his place in the tournaments. And these were not the ceremonious affairs of later centuries. In fact, only the Franks—now called the French—and the Provençals and Normans held them.

They made grim test of the strength and hardihood of novice knights. The combatants formed on two sides, several score strong, and rode against each other in an open field. Their weapons might be seasoned wood or blunted iron, but that did not save the riders from broken bones and blood-letting. When they bore weapons of sharpened steel, some of them would die. The lists, instead of housing a colorful assembly to watch the conflict, were in reality spaces fenced off, whither wounded or wearied fighters could withdraw and be safe. So, outside the lists, the tournament was actual combat.

IV

CHIVALRY

IN WAR the knights formed the heart of the army, the shock division. The men at arms, the sergeants, who accompanied them might carry crossbow or long bow, but not they. The sergeants were liegemen, who had been given homesteads or pay by the knight, in return for military service. Skilled fighters, often more experienced than the young lords they followed, they made up the bulk of the combat division.

The rest of the army was recruited from the peasantry and masterless men. These levies were equipped with the long bow,[1] the javelin, and the pike. They formed the infantry and their task was to annoy the enemy cavalry and to follow up a charge of their own mailed riders.

Skilled workmen served in the engineer's division of the

---

[1] The five-foot long bow of the English archers did not become destructive until two centuries later. Sir Walter Scott and many other writers err when they place it in the time of Coeur de Lion. Their mistake is due to the fact that the early chroniclers speak of the "long" bow meaning merely the plain bow, as distinguished from the crossbow. The European archers of the Eleventh Century carried three-foot bows, much less effective than the Moslem bows. And they used few crossbows.

The levy of infantry was known as the *posse* and its character may be judged from the fact that the word survives in our sheriff's posse. The word "sergeant" comes from the Latin *servientes*—helpers—which was altered to *sergents*.

army, to put together siege engines, when required—catapults for shooting iron darts, *ballista,* and mangonels for casting the heavier barrage of great stones. These "gyns," as the men called them, were constructed out of beams of seasoned wood, a long arm with a counterweight giving the propelling force.

Sometimes the engineers had to build "sows" or rams, swinging from ropes attached to a framework of beams, and covered by a shed to protect the men working them. Rarely— because the walls of that day in western Europe were crude affairs of wood and dirt with some stonework—did the besiegers find it necessary to construct one of the great wooden towers called *belfrois,* mounted on wheels so that they could be pushed up to a city or castle wall and the armed men could pass over planks from the summits of the towers to the ramparts. Still more rarely did they resort to sapping, or tunneling, beneath the walls.

The knights planned the engines and directed the siege work. They made the attack on foot when they had opened a breach in the walls, and they manned the moving towers.

In later centuries, when men were somewhat less powerful physically and wore defensive armor of elaborate steel plates, a knight dismounted or thrown from his horse was practically helpless. The horses also carried plate armor then, so that a man and his mount went into battle like a small, animated tank, which was out of action as soon as anything overturned either horse or rider. Weapons as well differed then, being adapted to smash steel plates—massive lances, sledge hammers.

But in this Eleventh Century, at the dawn of knighthood, men had the immense physical strength needed to bear the weight of their iron mesh through a battle. The pliant iron rings allowed them freedom of movement. And they favored the long sword. In their hands the three-foot steel blade, almost as broad near the point as at the hilt, became a thing of terror.

It had a ball of iron for a pommel, to balance the weight of the blade. Few men, to-day, could lift such a sword from the ground without using both arms. The iron men could swing the swords like staves, and a single stroke might cut a foeman's arm and shoulder from his body, or slash his body in halves. When the impetus of a charging horse was added to the blow, the effect was terrible. Dismounted, the knight would be little less dangerous, as long as he had his sword.

The knights were the officers of the army and the shock division, and the inspiration of all the others. The tactics of the day sought for one end, the most effective charge of the mailed riders. No arrows or crossbow bolts could check them, and rare indeed was the infantry that dared stand their charge. Usually the archers and javelin throwers remained on the wings, while the knights and mounted men at arms advanced in the center. Sometimes they charged in a solid wedge, sometimes in double or triple ranks with intervals between.

The only effective answer was a countercharge of the hostile chivalry.[1] Maneuvering played its part then, and a battle was often won or lost by the skill with which the mounted divisions were thrown into the conflict. Unless one side gave way under the first shock, the fighting changed in a moment to a *mêlée* of individual combats wherein the prowess of the leaders and champions might decide the issue.

In the end, everything depended upon the individual. A matchless champion might disable twenty men of less power in as many minutes. A single swordsman might hold a bridge or the gut of a breach against the attack of fifty inferior fighters. Naturally, foemen often drew back before the onset of a well-known champion who could lick the lives from their bodies with a slash of his sword. And the death of such a leader disheartened in equal measure the men who followed him.

These champions of the iron men had been trained to war almost from their birth, as were the Spartans. The battlefield was their place of work, and the charger—the great horse equally trained to conflict—became their companion, to be groomed and tended and nursed as carefully as any woman.

---

[1] The word "chivalry" is derived from *cheval*, horse. The chroniclers of this day used the word to signify the mailed horsemen, led by the knights—the *cavalry* (*chevalerie*). Not until later did it come to mean an abstract ideal of courtesy.

Such war horses were chosen for their courage and size and strength. If possible, they were never mounted except in the tournament or battle. On the march, or in hunting, their masters would ride other less cherished mounts, sometimes called palfreys.

Tales have come down to us of great chargers who fought with teeth and hoof in a *mêlée*, to aid their masters.

The iron man, their master, was also schooled in courtesy. He must stint not, in his love of God and of his lady. He passed from the field of war to the chapel; he washed his hands of blood, and prayed. His life became one of conflict, with his foes and with his inward conscience. The legendary Galahad, never failing in courtesy, spends his life in search of the Grail. Happy is the one who has made his peace with God. Roland, dying, takes the gantlet from his right hand and holds it toward the sky: "God, I confess me guilty. I ask Thy power, to cleanse me of the sins from the hour in which I was born, to this day when death comes to me." Not in mockery were the best of them called gentle men—because they had such power that it behoved them to be mild in speech and courteous in action. No law court had control over them because they themselves were judges and executors; nothing could very well bind them except their own pledged word.

The ideal of chivalry was the fearless man who gave the benefit of his strength to others and who kept his word.

To distinguish them in the *mêlée* of battle, the leaders of the armed hosts sometimes had gold-work on their helms, or crests. They also had a war shout, known as the battle cry. This helped a leader to make his position known to his men, to rally them or lead them where he wished.

The great leaders, kings or powerful barons, had their different standards—poles bearing a lion's head in effigy, a raven, or even a complete dragon. Often these devices were painted or embroidered on banners which were called gonfanons. And the standard bearer must needs be a man of proved courage. Usually picked knights rode around him, forming the standard guard, behind the leader. These banners or devices received more care and honor than any regimental stand of colors to-day. They were the visible sign of the presence of the king or baron. Common men regarded them with superstition mixed with awe.

So the fall of a standard or banner in battle meant not only ill-luck; it usually signified the capture or death of the leader who fought before it. And three times out of four the loss of the leader meant the loss of the battle. Likewise the advance of the gonfanon to the enemy's position was a token of victory at hand. The common soldiers always had half an eye on the gonfanon. They listened, too, for the roaring blast of the chieftain's horn—the olifant.

Beneath the king or baron in rank was the constable—the second in command. He carried a baton as emblem of his office, and transmitted the orders of his lord. He had personal charge of justice in the army, and the keeping of discipline, and was privileged to kill any man not of gentle blood, or to slay the horse beneath a gentle man, as punishment.

The constable ranked the marshal, who combined the duties of adjutant-general and leader of the shock division. Inspection and pay and division of the spoil fell to his hand, also selection of camp sites and routine. In battle he carried the gonfanon when the constable did not, and always charged at the head of the chivalry.

The seneschal had charge of the service of supply, being overseer of the home castle and lands and food.

Such was the army of a king or baron—the only army known in western Europe. It might number five hundred men or five thousand, seldom more than that. Rarely did the barons league themselves together, and then their hosts of armed men fought as separate units. These hosts were the barbarian clans of yesterday; they felt bound by ties of loyalty only to their own chieftains.

As in the army, so at home. The serf worked the lands of his lord, who in turn protected the serf; this lord had been given his lands by a great baron. To the baron he had rendered *homage*, the pledge of his body in the other's defense, and *fealty* or faith, the pledge of his conscience, to the other's benefit. He was then the liegeman or vassal of the baron, who could call upon him for military service. At this call the lord, or knight, must arm himself and ride to the appointed meeting place with a certain number of followers—so many men at arms, so many archers and horses.

In their turn the barons had done homage to some sovereign—king or duke or prince. Like the lesser lords, they were expected to come at call with their hosts of liegemen to form the sovereign's army. They did not always do so. A baron with a strong castle, difficult to take by siege, crowning some steep hill, could do about as he liked.

The king could actually control no more than the castles he held in his own right—where he was baron as well as king.

That, in brief, was the scheme of things called the feudal system, by which men protected themselves from being despoiled and slain by others. The king of France was master only for about two days' ride from Paris. Beyond that, to the north, lay Flanders with its own young count for master. Along the sea lay Normandy, serving its duke, and Brittany. The heart of France rested in the hand of the duke of Aquitaine, and the south of it had long been shared among the Provençals, whose leader was the count of Toulouse. Neither in nor out of France lay Burgundy with its Teutonic swordsmen.

England proper had been conquered a little while ago by William the Bastard, but its Norman barons were occupied with their own troubles under his son, William the Red. Beyond the North Sea the Danes and Northmen prowled the coasts. Only in middle Europe, where the German peoples had spread from Lorraine to Bohemia, did an emperor hold power.

Rome had left to the world two ideals of government—the emperor, who would rule the lands, and the pope, who would rule the consciences of men. So the emperor of the great German Reich was more than only the overlord of the day—he was the candidate for the throne of the Caesars, and universal dominion. He pacified the predatory Danes, and his eastern marches formed a bulwark against the semi-pagans of the Prussian forests and the Lithuanian swamps.

He also came down and entered Rome, by dint of sword-strokes.

The lands of Italy were occupied by peoples of all sorts, the most powerful being the Lombards—the now tamed Long-beards—in the north, and the Normans in the south. These Normans had come in as adventurers, to pillage, and had remained to settle in the sun-warmed hills. They had just made themselves masters of the Arabs in Sicily, and were looking for new worlds to conquer.

So western and middle Europe had become a checkerboard of lands peopled by the descendants of the barbarian clans, ruled by the iron hands of the great barons. These in turn looked for the emperor to become the successor of the Caesars of Rome. Meanwhile they recognized, willingly or grudgingly, only the authority of the Church of God.

Law and order did not exist. Men who had a generous lord fared well, while those who had a mean master fared badly. There were penalties, of course—so much to be paid for slaying a common man, so much for cutting out an eye, or mutilating a hand. But who was to enforce the penalties?

Gentle men were subject only to the judgment of their peers and they could appeal from any judgment to the ordeal by combat. In that case the accused met the accuser clad in red, armed with similar weapons, before witnesses. The victor was vindicated; the loser—if he did not die in the combat—was often hung, or stripped and scourged.

An accused could claim the right to defend himself by champion—that is, to have another man take his place in the combat. But he himself had to be present and to suffer if his champion were worsted.

Like the ordeals by fire or water—in which a man accused of wrong-doing took heated iron in his hands, or walked through flames or was thrown, bound by ropes, into deep water—the ordeal by combat sought to determine the will of God in any controversy among men.

To cleanse themselves of sin, they did penance—fasted or flogged themselves, or went on pilgrimages. These journeys might be to neighboring shrines, or to Rome, but the great pilgrimage was to Jerusalem. That often took from two to three years. A company of pilgrims disappeared upon the Great Sea in ships, and entered the dominion of the Moslems. They were harassed and humiliated, and if they survived to return home with their staff and palm branches and perhaps a precious relic from the Holy City, they were greeted joyfully and hailed as men who had sanctified themselves.

The iron men felt that they must do penance, to make their peace with God. Often they laid aside the sword for the pilgrim staff, or entered the silence of the cloisters.

V

THE ROBED MEN

THE brother of the warrior became the follower of the Church. Perhaps his father had carried him, in years gone by, to the door of the near-by monastery.

"I now offer this my son to omnipotent God and to the Virgin Mary, Mother of God, for the salvation of my soul. I promise for him that he shall follow the monastic life in this monastery, according to the rule of St. Benedict, and that from this day forth he shall not withdraw his neck from the yoke of this service. I promise also that he shall not be tempted to leave by me or by anyone with my consent."

Robed and girded with a cord, the monk passed his hours in the throng of those who had forsaken life with its riches and tumult. His worldly garments had been laid away, never to be put on again, unless he should fail in his service and be cast out. He had the solace of quiet, and the security of ordained hours.

Within the walls he became a laborer, part of a multitude where the lord of twenty towns had less authority than an elder monk. He worked in the gardens, or strained his eyes over the illumination of written parchments. Sleeping in his robe, rising at vigils to add his voice to the low chorus of praise in the first hour of morning—receiving only a rare letter or token from outside, through the hand of his father superior, the abbot, he drew further into isolation, sinking into the silence of the dark cloisters.

If by some chance—perhaps the monastery had become too poverty-ridden to shelter him longer, or he had served so long that he was trusted to carry a missive to a distant abbey—he were sent outside the walls, the brothers of the monastery prayed for his preservation from evil. And, indeed, the unarmed wayfarer went in peril. Packs of dogs worried him, bands of masterless men stopped and searched him for silver. Only in the monasteries on the heights or in peasants' sheds in the lowlands could he find a bed at night. Unless he carried food he had to beg his meals.

Maps of any value were unknown; beyond the crossroads at the valley's end the traveler entered unknown country. Inns were no more than wine shops, and only the bolder merchants or powerful barons or determined pilgrims undertook the journey from Paris to Rome—two months would barely bring them to their destination. To leave western Europe and go by ship or highroad to Byzantium (Constantinople) or Jerusalem would be a mighty undertaking. Only a few curt records of such journeys have come down to us. Not for two centuries would the brothers of the Polo family with young Marco make the great journey to Cathay.

But the doors of the monasteries stood open:

Everyone who knocks, regardless of his station, shall be greeted in the name of God, and thanked for his coming.

Within the doors human beings existed only upon one level, and rigid was the discipline of their hours:

If the brother is ordered by his superior to do a difficult or impossible thing, he shall do his best to obey. If he finds it beyond human strength, he shall explain to the one in authority why it cannot be done. But if, after humble explanation, the superior still insists, he shall still do his utmost to carry out the order, relying upon God, to whom all things are possible.

The monastic rule as to wine drinking is interesting:

"*Each one has his own gift from God, the one in this way, the other in that.*" So we hesitate to determine what others shall eat or drink. But we believe that a half-measure of wine a day is enough for anyone, making due allowance of course for the needs of the sick. If God has given to some the strength to endure abstinence, let them use that gift, knowing that they shall have their reward. And if the climate, the nature of the labor, or the heat of summer, make it advisable to increase this amount, the superior may do so at his own discretion, always guarding however against indulgence and drunkenness. Some hold, indeed, that monks should not drink wine at all. We have not been able in our day to persuade monks to agree to this; but all will admit that drink should be used sparingly, for "*wine maketh even the wise to go astray !*" Where wine is scarce or is not found at all, let those who live there bless God and murmur not. In any case, let there be no murmuring because of the scarcity or the lack of wine.

Strangely enough, these men of the Eleventh Century did not murmur. Life might be a veritable hostelry of pain, but the records they have left us bear witness to their faith in relief to come. We find the traces of rejoicing rather than tears between the lines so carefully inscribed on the hard old parchments. They were young, and they labored and died at an early age. And they hungered for learning. Some of the pages are worn through by the fingers that turned them year after year.

The illuminations of the manuscripts are crude patches of color: red, yellow-gold, and faded blue—stiff figures of well-remembered scenes. Every monastery had gathered together a library. Men thirsted for knowledge. And it needs an effort of the imagination to realize how pitifully meager were the sources of knowledge.

Latin texts on the rules of rhetoric, the dictums of logic. Here, perhaps a Greek volume of Aristotle that no one could rightly comprehend. Everywhere patrologies and hagiologies —lives of the fathers of a day long past.

Not yet had the leavening of Arab culture quickened the minds of the searchers. Not for a century and a half would Marsilius of Padua write his summary of human events, or the wanderer, Dante, write: "Lo, now is the acceptable time wherein are rising the signs of consolation and peace. For a new day glows and reveals in the east the dawn that is to banish the shadows of long-drawn-out calamity."

The exact sciences remained mysteries. How could a man calculate with numbers in the Latin numerals that would serve only up to a hundred? The sign for a million was an adaptation of the Egyptian hieroglyphic—a figure of a man looking upward in astonishment. Astrology formed part of the stock-in-trade of mountebanks or mock priests.

How could disease be studied, when it was the indubitable work of demons entered into the human body? To be sure, there were disciples of Hippocrates, and some who knew of Galen—but medicine could be found only in herbs and concoctions that savored of black magic.

Clerics—priests who served the churches of the outer world—were at the same time the students and dispensers of knowledge. They were summoned to attend the sick, to write letters and read them—to draw up deeds, to give counsel. They listened to the quarrels of kings, and heard the confessions of troubled men. Because travelers frequented the hospitals and guest rooms of the churches, the robed priests learned much of distant lands and kept a record of what they knew. This power of knowledge belonged to them alone.

The Church was in touch with what went on in the various kingdoms and counties. Her servants held the outposts of the Northlands; her bishops often owned domains as large as reigning princes; her messengers crossed the seas. Within her doors a universal language, Latin, was spoken.

The Church had become the only great and centralized force in Europe. Universal spiritual leadership lay in her hands—because her servants were the visible representatives of the Apostles of Christ.

But in these eleven centuries the Church had acquired vast properties. And these must be administered. So, in her other aspect, the Church had become a temporal power, with interests at stake upon the chessboard of politics. Bishops often kept small standing armies, and waged war heartily. Many monasteries were as strongly fortified as the castles of the barons. Some abbots owned slaves.

At the head of the Church there was one man, the Father, the pope. And upon the shoulders of him who called himself servant of the servants of God rested unceasing responsibility and endless care. Never, in the history of the Church, had a leader faced such responsibility as now, at the end of the Eleventh Century.

VI

THE SERVANT OF THE SERVANTS

To UNDERSTAND what followed, it is necessary to remember what the pope was—servant of the servants of God, in very truth. He was the judge, perpetually in the chair—the counselor, who must decide all problems. The tiara weighed upon him, the pallium burdened his shoulders. Himself, as a human being, he must not aid. He should not, for instance, take up the sword on his own behalf. In fact, he was the leader of the new struggle against war.

Some three generations before this the Church had tried to enforce what it called the Peace of God. This decreed that clerics, monks, and nuns were inviolate and must not be harmed. Then shepherds, school children, merchants, and travelers were added to the list. At first asylums were named, places where men could not enter with weapons— the great crosses upon the highroads, and the ground around bell towers, for a distance of thirty to sixty paces. Then, on Sundays, all churches and people going to them and returning were to be inviolate. The Peace of God failed.

After a while a new effort was made, and it took the form of a Truce of God. In the earliest record of it we find this:

All Christians, friends and enemies, neighbors and strangers, shall keep true and lasting peace one with another from vespers on Wednesday to sunrise on Monday, so that during these four days and five nights, all persons may have peace, and, trusting in this peace, may go about their business without fear of their enemies.

All who keep the truce of God shall be absolved from their sins. . . . Those who have promised to observe the truce and have wilfully violated it, shall be excommunicated.

Later on, the truce appears in this fashion:

During those four days and five nights no man or woman shall assault, wound, or slay another, or attack, seize, or destroy a castle, burg, or villa by craft or by violence.

If anyone violates this peace and disobeys these commands of ours, he shall be exiled for thirty years as a penance, and he shall make compensation. Otherwise, he shall be excommunicated and excluded from all Christian fellowship.

In addition you should observe the peace in regard to lands and animals and all things that can be possessed. If anyone takes from another an animal, a coin, or a garment during the days of the truce, he shall be excommunicated unless he makes satisfaction.

If anyone has been accused of violating the peace and denies the charge, he shall take the communion and undergo the ordeal of hot iron.

Some places observed the truce; elsewhere matters went on as before. Councils were assembled in the bishoprics to enforce the decree, and here and there a kind of peace-militia, called *pacata*, was organized. Almost at once the *pacata* found itself fighting with the feudal men at arms.

The Truce of God was failing, in spite of the pope's leadership.

In addition, the apostolic lord had to deal with an internal struggle. Not long ago the papacy had fallen to the lowest level in its history. "As soiled," men said, "as was the loincloth of Jeremiah."

Rome had infected it. Rome, where the night mist hung like a shroud and beggars filled the alleys under the shadow of yellow marble palaces. Rome, a meeting place of all peoples, a journey's end of pilgrims—turbulent, lawless, and greedy. Robbers haunted the empty cellars of the Forum, the nobles waged their feuds from hill to hill, and armed priests guarded the Lateran—the residence of the popes. The once-proud city had become an open sore that contaminated the Church within it.

Dogs and men at arms idled in the monastery courtyards; many nunneries were whore-infested. Trundling wagons carried in wine casks. "Not a priest could be found," said a chronicle of the time, "who was not ignorant and given to women, and a buyer and seller of his rights."

Some of the late popes had passed their lives in luxury that would not have disgraced an emperor. Some built palaces for their women. Young boys were installed as abbots. Finally a youthful pope, Benedict IX, sold the papacy for cash paid down, at the Latin gate of the city in the year 1046.

Then the German emperor used his power to select new popes. They came from outside, and especially from the great monastery of Cluny, from which pure blood was pulsing through the diseased arteries of the churches. They were zealous men of high ideals and they threw themselves into the struggle on behalf of the Truce of God and the cleansing of the clergy.

But they were faced by a third problem. The high prelates of the Church had, in most cases, become virtually sovereigns, heirs to vast properties—lands, serfs, toll rights and revenues, even cities and trade concessions. Thus, these spiritual lords had become temporal lords as well. Church offices, in consequence, were bought and sold. One of the new popes with immense courage tried to end the evil by a stroke of the pen. He decreed that all such possessions be abolished.

Naturally, many of the prelates refused to give up their personal property. Instead, they defied the pope. This conflict soon merged into a greater one.

The mighty German emperor became the open foe of the new popes.

It was a tremendous thing, this breaking apart of pope and emperor. Until then, each had ruled in a separate sphere. The spiritual empire of the apostolic lord, Father of the Church, had embraced the souls of men; the temporal empire of the German[1] monarch had ruled the property of men. The pope had been shepherd of the flock, the emperor had been, as it were, the owner of the same flock.

But now the churches possessed lands of their own. Were these new lands to be administered by the Church—whose head was the pope—or by the empire—whose head was the monarch? One emperor, Henry IV, took the matter for granted and began to appoint bishops for the new lands, without consulting the pope. He gave them their rings and staffs, the symbols of office.

The pope objected. Only the Church itself, he said, could appoint bishops.

Henry maintained, in effect, that the lands and the church buildings lay within his authority. But the pope could not yield the point. He was shepherd of *all* the flock; the lands belonged to the Church itself, and so formed part of his universal, spiritual dominion.

Nor would the emperor yield. He was overlord of *all* the flock, and the lands and church buildings formed part of his dominion.

Two ideas had come into conflict,[2] and two determined men—Gregory VII, the pope, and Henry IV, the emperor, forced the issue to the last, bitter extremity. In the year 1076 Gregory excommunicated the emperor, pronouncing him outcast from the Church and the society of men, releasing his subjects from allegiance to him. And Gregory tried to bring about the election of a new emperor.

---

[1]The Holy Roman Empire. A meaningless title, due to the belief that all power must be an empire, Roman in name, and united to the Church. It was actually the German Reich, or collection, of small states ruled by the emperor as overlord. But it was meant to be, at that time, the successor to Rome, and the city of Rome usually lay within its limits.

[2]The emperor believed that he held authority over men and lands by divine right; the pope maintained that the Church must be free of the authority of the State. Gregory had labored to raise the papacy to the dominion of the world—the old dream of St. Augustine, of God's kingdom on earth. The resulting struggle shaped events in Europe for centuries.

At the time these lines were written in Rome, in the beginning of the year 1929, a report was made public that the king and the government of Italy had agreed to restore to the present pope the full title to the land of the Vatican city, and the Lateran quarter, thus giving the Church a tiny independent dominion within Italy, free from all other authority.

Whereupon Henry assembled a church council that denounced Gregory and elected an anti-pope named Guibert. And he marched on Rome, with spears flashing behind him. Open war raged, and the spears gained the mastery. Gregory called in the dour Normans from the south, and they added flames to slaughter in the city. Borne away by the Normans, Gregory died an exile by the sea. His successor, an aged man, took the tiara reluctantly and yielded still further to the emperor before he also died. The anti-pope reigned in Rome. The Truce of God was ignored, and the churches managed as best they could.

Such was the situation when Urban II was chosen pope by the council of the cardinal bishops. He came out of the silent cloisters of Cluny.

It is known that he was born of a noble French family, in Chatillon-sur-Marne, near Rheims. There he passed his boyhood in the world of chivalry. He studied under able masters and did not enter the monastery until he had been canon of Rheims. At Cluny he became the companion of Hugh, the abbot, a man in touch with the affairs of the world outside the cloister walls. Urban—Eude was his name then—found himself summoned to Rome, where he became Gregory's adviser, and sharer in the conflict. At one time he was imprisoned by Henry in Germany.

Urban, who had been so long a monk, entered upon his pontificate in middle age, a tall and strong man with hair and beard the hue of gold. In manner he was indulgent, even charming. Above all, he had the gift of oratory. "A golden pope" they called him.

He had keen political sense, an unperturbed spirit, and quiet persistence. He took up the struggle where death had forced Gregory to relinquish it. From the first, he sought to add power to the monasteries—to counteract the weakness of the clergy elsewhere. Of the Truce of God, he said, "The Truce of God shall be enforced as it was sworn."

Deprived both of St. Peter's and the Lateran palace, he traveled from place to place, becoming, in fact, an apostolic wanderer. For a while he was quartered on an island in the

Tiber, where he could hear the bells of St. Peter's basilica summoning people to the service conducted by his rival, Guibert, the anti-pope. He lived there by the charity of an old woman who brought him food.

Upon the emperor and Guibert he turned all the resources of an able mind and a fertile pen. Nor did he mince words. "Henry, that sacrilegious seller of churches, the scourge of the Roman Empire." And Guibert—"That standard-bearer of Anti-Christ, Satan's beast of burden."

Guibert, secure behind his armies, essayed a pun.

"Come to thy city," he wrote, "or change thy name."

The struggle became a deadlock, embittered by war. Urban appealed for money to the clergy of France, and bought back the Lateran and the castle of San' Angelo, which guarded the entrance of St Peter's. (That was in 1093.) He visited the Normans in the south, and cultivated their good will. But Guibert, supported by Henry's soldiery, held the fortified places outside Rome.

In the next year pestilence swept the lands from Bohemia to Flanders and famine broke out in Lorraine. An appeal came to the West from the emperor of Byzantium for armed aid against the pagans who were overrunning his frontiers.

Stars were seen falling toward the west. A hard winter set in. The feudal powers were in arms. "The poor plundered the rich, and peasants ate roots from the forests." The Truce of God went unheeded, while men banded together, restless and uneasy.

A simple priest of Chartres, Fulcher or Fulk by name, has this to say of the situation:

The year of our Lord one thousand and ninety-five. Henry, the so-called emperor reigning in Germany, and Philip in France. In all parts of Europe many kinds of evil increased, and faith weakened.

Pope Urban II, a man of blameless life and habits, was prevailing in Rome. Yet he beheld faith being destroyed among Christians, clerics as well as common people, and the princes incessantly at war, while captives were thrown into abominable prisons, and monasteries and towns were given up to fire.

Guibert, supported by the aforesaid emperor and inflamed by

the instigation of many people in Rome, kept Urban a stranger to the church of St. Peter as long as he could. But Urban, deprived of his Church, wandered through the lands bringing back to God the people who had lost faith. Guibert, indeed, was swollen with pride because of his leadership in the Church, and treated sinners indifferently.

So two popes ruled. People did not know which one to obey, or which one would remedy all these ills. Some favored this one, some that one. It grew clear to men that Urban was the more just, while Guibert glittered with all honor and riches.

There could be no compromise. The emperor had acknowledged Guibert. There was constant rioting and fighting, but Urban would not give his consent to a general war. Besides, the balance of military power lay with the emperor. Urban had only the faithful Countess Matilda, the city of Genoa, and the wayward Normans in the south to rely on. Even Rome, remembering the sack of ten years before, was hostile to him.

That summer Urban acted. He assembled his companions and retainers and set out across the Alps toward the west, keeping his purpose a secret. That he had a purpose is quite evident. No vicar of St. Peter had ever journeyed across the Alps, and Urban was leaving behind him the few armed vassals, his supporters. Moreover, he had sent out letters calling church prelates and lay lords to a council at Clermont in Auvergne during the coming November.

Except for that, he remained silent. This silence of the golden pope and the lapse of the centuries have left no clear evidence of his thoughts. It is certain that he had set his mind upon several things—to reform the clergy, to strengthen the monasteries, to enforce the Truce of God, to stop the buying and selling of church properties, and finally to do his utmost to regain the spiritual dominion that the papacy had lost, and that Gregory had sought in vain.

Gregory had been Urban's leader. And Gregory, the dreamer, had talked of uniting the armed powers of Christendom, to march to Jerusalem. But the enterprise had never been clearly planned. There had been pilgrimages of men in masses, several thousand strong, armed for protection on the road. On the other hand, there had been small military expeditions—raids for plunder or to recapture a city—along the shifting frontier that separated the Moslem from the Christian world.

Urban planned a greater thing. He meant to summon the fighting men of Christendom to take up arms, not in any earthly quarrel, but to march into Asia to recapture the sepulcher of Christ.

It would be a pilgrimage, and it would also be a war. Men of all nations would enlist, and by so doing earn the right to absolution from their sins. They had not kept the Truce of God, but they might go forth upon the voyage of God. So Urban spoke of it—the voyage of God—when the time came to speak.

It would also change the feudal strife that was draining the best blood of Christendom. Urban had been born in the feudal castle. He had been in close touch with the men of Cluny, who had their fingers on the pulse of happenings, and he must have known that conditions favored his enterprise. For one thing, a warlike Berber dynasty had taken the place of the more pacific Arabs in Spain, and the Christians there were enduring persecutions. For another, the few pilgrims who had penetrated to Jerusalem in the last years brought back tales of hardship and insult. There also a barbarous race, the Seljuk Turks out of central Asia, had driven out the tolerant Arabs. So in the west and the east, Moslems were crossing the once-quiescent frontier.

No pontiff of Rome had ever voiced such a summons before. Would the people listen to him? Would foemen forget their feuds and agree to march together? How many would go?

Urban could only exhort them. The emperor was his enemy, and the kings—even Philip of France—were excommunicate or antagonistic. He had no treasury to give to the enterprise.

But if the iron men did listen to him, and if they did go, Urban must have reasoned that this would be virtually a victory over Guibert and the emperor. If the host of Christendom, even a few thousand strong, marched under the banner of St. Peter, the conflict in Italy would pause, or even cease.

The schism would remain, but the prestige of the Church would be restored. Urban, as leader of the voyage of God, would be equal in power to Henry, emperor of the Romans, and Augustus.

Urban kept silence until he had crossed the Alps. If Guibert or Henry knew of his purpose nothing was more certain than that they would oppose it, and Urban had so little to build upon that he could not risk opposition of any kind.

The golden pope marched swiftly through Burgundy into Provence, where he had a staunch supporter in the devout and warlike Raymond, count of Toulouse. He stopped briefly at Le Puy—whose bishop Adhemar had been born like himself into the world of chivalry, and had made the pilgrimage to Jerusalem. At Cluny his fellow monks greeted him in procession, and he talked with his former superior, the saintly Hugh, at the consecration of the altar of the new cathedral by the old bell tower that had so often summoned him to his hours. Within the heart of France, men rejoiced at the coming of the French pope. Not until mid-November did Urban hasten at last to Clermont.

November the eighteenth. The council convened, not too well attended. Most of the German clergy failed to appear. For a few days routine questions were settled behind closed doors, the excommunication of Philip of France was confirmed, and Urban stirred the clergy by his sudden, eloquent reproach—"*Ye are the salt of the earth*, and if ye are lacking, by what shall it be salted?" He could sway men by his words, no doubt of that. His tongue lashed the evils he had set himself against, the concubines of the priests, the buying and selling of church offices. The Truce of God *shall* be kept inviolate.

Then the doors of the chapel were opened. Urban went out, to face the public gathering in the field to the east of the town, in the shadow of the great bell tower of Our Lady of the Gate.

VII

URBAN'S SUMMONS

THE autumn sun hung above the mists of the fields. Brown and bare and dry, the foothills swelled in the haze. Through the still, cold air the clanging of the bells sounded. And against the gray wall of Clermont town the throng grew greater.

Nearest the empty platform clustered the purple robes of cardinals. Behind these the gold of the *chapes* of bishops could be clearly seen, and then the black capuchins of monks, the brethren of the monasteries. Here were pilgrims from Normandy, and thin, dark faces from embattled Spain. Beyond them the Frisian cloaks and mantles of laymen—barons and bourgeoisie—with here and there the white kirtle and embroidered hood of some lord's lady, with her maids.

They moved restlessly, staring at the platform under the cloth-of-gold canopy. Two glittering crosses appeared, held by figures in white. Even the gloves were white. Behind them rose a gonfanon, a red and gold and white banner, hanging limp against its staff in the still air. Now a tall man took his stand between the crosses, and the throng stirred like a field of grain under a breath of wind. The man was robed in white, except for the heavy pallium over his shoulders bearing tiny crosses, which was the hue of his thick, curling beard. A gesture, the murmur of a prayer, and he came closer to the edge of the platform. They could see his face now, firm and assured, and a murmur greeted him. For Urban, the pope, had been born a man of France, and his commanding presence and courage roused their admiration. Had he not dared journey over the mountains to them?

His first resonant words brought instant silence. He was speaking in their own Romance, not in harsh Latin:

"O ye men of the Franks, who live beyond the mountains! God hath favored you in many ways, in your happy land as in your steadfast faith, and valor. To you our words are spoken, and by you our message will be passed on. We wish you to know what grievous cause has brought us hither, to your land, and what need has led us not only to you but to all the faithful.

"I speak to you who are present; I announce it to those who are absent, and Christ ordains it.

"From the borders of Jerusalem and the city Constantinople ominous tidings have gone forth. Often, before now, have they come to my ears. An accursed race, emerging from the kingdom of the Persians, a barbarous people, estranged from God, has invaded the lands of the Christians in the east and has depopulated them by fire and steel and ravage. These invaders are Turks and Arabs. They have advanced through the empire of Constantinople as far as the Mediterranean—that is, as far as the strait called the Arm of Saint George.

"The empire of Constantinople is now mutilated and has lost so much land that a voyager could not cross the dismembered part in two months. Until now, this empire has been our rampart. It is in dire straits.

"These Turks have led away many Christians, captives, to their own country; they have torn down the churches of God everywhere, or used them for their own rites. What more shall I say to you? Listen. The invaders befoul the altars with the filth out of their bodies, they circumcize Christians and pour the blood of the circumcision upon the altars or into the baptismal fonts. They stable their horses in these churches, which are now withdrawn from the service of God. Yea, the churches are served, but not by holy men— for only the Turks may use them. And who else now serves the church of Blessed Mary, where she herself was buried in body, in the valley of Jehoshaphat?

"Even now the Turks are torturing Christians, binding them and filling them with arrows, or making them kneel, bending their heads, to try if their swordsmen can cut through their necks with a single blow of a naked sword. What shall I say of the ravishing of the women? To speak of this is worse than to be silent. You, in France, have heard the murmur of agony on the border of Spain. The time may come when you will see your wives violated and your children driven before you as slaves, out of the land.

"Think of those who have crossed the sea, as pilgrims. If they carried wealth, they were forced to pay toll and tribute every day, at the gates of cities and at the entrance to the churches. If they were accused of anything, they were forced to buy their freedom again. And those who had no money, trusting in poverty—what of them? They were searched, and even the calluses were cut from their bare heels to see if they had sewed something there. They were given scammony to drink, until they vomited or burst their bowels—lest they had swallowed coins. More, their bowels were cut open with a sword, their intestines pulled forth and slit, so that what was hidden there could be disclosed. Who can relate this without sorrow? For they are your blood brothers—children of the same Christ and sons of the same church.

"On whom will fall the task of vengeance unless upon you, who have won glory in arms? You have the courage and the fitness of body to humble the hairy heads uplifted against you. I say this to you—and what more must be said? Listen!

"You are girdled knights, but you are arrogant with pride. You turn upon your brothers with fury, cutting down one the other. Is this the service of Christ? Let us hold to the truth, to our shame. This is not the way of life. Oppressors of children, despoilers of widows, man-slayers, wreakers of sacrilege, murderers, awaiting the payment of blood—you flock to battles like vultures that sight a corpse from afar. Verily, this is the worst way. Verily, if you would save your souls, lay down the girdles of such knighthood.

"Come forward to the defense of Christ. O ye who have carried on feuds, come to the war against the infidels. O ye who have been thieves, become soldiers. Fight a just war. Labor for everlasting reward, ye who were hirelings, serving for a few *solidi*.

"Let no obstacle turn you aside, but when you have arranged your affairs and gathered together supplies—enter upon the journey when winter is ended and spring is here again, God guiding you——"

The deep voice had not ceased, but a shout went up that drowned the words. The throng had been stirring, some whispering to others, a few weeping. Men were seen to hide their faces in their hands, and the murmur among them found voice at last.

"*Dieu lo vult!* God wills it!"

Urban was silent, his hands on the railing, his face uplifted. They were all shouting now, standing up, stretching out their arms. Above the roar of voices steel clanged as men jerked swords from sheaths. "God wills it!"

Not until Urban motioned to them did the tumult subside. He had more to say:

"'*Where two or three are gathered together in My name, there am I in the midst of them.*' Unless the Lord God had been here in your minds, you would not have cried out thus, as one. And so I say to you that God has drawn this cry from you. Let it be your battle cry; when you go against the enemy let this shout be raised—'God wills it!'

"And more—whosoever shall offer himself to go upon this journey, and shall make his vow to go, shall wear the sign of the cross on his head or breast.

"Yet the old and infirm should not go, or they who are unfit to bear arms; nor should women set out upon this holy pilgrimage without their husbands or brothers or guardians. For such are a hindrance rather than an aid. Let the rich give help to the poor. Let no possessions detain you, nor the love you may bear to children or parents or homes. Remember what is said in the Gospel. '*Every one that hath forsaken houses or brethren or sisters, or father, or mother, or wife, or children, or lands for my name's sake shall receive an hundredfold and shall inherit everlasting life.*'

"Set forth, then, upon the way to the holy Sepulcher; wrest that land from the evil race, and keep it for yourself. That land which floweth with milk and honey—Jerusalem, fruitful above other lands where rested the Lord. There He died for us; there He was buried. And in the Sepulcher the yearly miracle has not ceased. For—I say what you know well—yearly in the Passion, in the darkened church the lamps were lighted by no human hand, but by divine agency. And now, unattended, with few to see the miracle, these lamps still kindle miraculously. Let them summon you! Who is so hard of heart that he is not moved by so great a miracle?

"Go, therefore, and fear not. Your possessions here will be safeguarded, and you will despoil the enemy of greater treasures. Do not fear death, where Christ laid down His life for you. If any should lose their lives, even on the way thither, by sea or land, or in strife with the pagans, their sins will be requited them. I grant this to all who go, by the power vested in me by God.[1]

"Fear not torture, for therein lies the crown of martyrdom. The way is short, the struggle brief, the reward everlasting. Yea, I speak now with the voice of the prophet, '*Arm thyself, O mighty one!*' Take up your arms, valiant sons, and go. Better fall in battle than live to see the sorrow of your people and the desecration of your holy places.

"Go, with One who lacks not the power greater than wealth to aid you. Lo I see before you, leading you to His war, the standard bearer who is invisible—Christ."

A massive figure uprose and forced its way toward the dais, falling to its knees beneath the holy Father. It was Adhemar of Monteil, bishop of Le Puy, scion of the knightly family of Valentinois. He prayed that he would be given a command in this new army of God.

In his purple robes a certain cardinal, Gregory, stood up, and cried out in a loud voice, "*Confiteor*——" And the throng repeated after him a general confession of sin. At the end the pope made the sign of absolution above their bowed heads.

When he had left the dais they gathered into groups, low-voiced. They repeated to each other the promise of the apostolic lord, an incredible promise. A way was open to cleanse themselves of sin. More than that, here was freedom. In this host, setting out upon the voyage of God, there would be no feudal prince in command. Had not the blessed Father promised that the Seigneur Jesus Himself would lead them?

---

[1] "*Dono tanto investus a Deo*"—Fulcher of Chartres. Urban's speech, as presented here is quoted from portions of four chronicles, that of Robert the Monk, Fulcher of Chartres, Balderic of Dol, and Guibert of Nogent. Probably all of them heard it at Clermont, although they do not seem to have written it down until a few years later. When they did so, their versions differed a good deal, but some points were mentioned by two or three of them. Such points we assume were actually pronounced by Urban. The chroniclers wrote from memory, in Latin, and an effort has been made in this chapter to bring the style of the address closer to the spoken word. Urban spoke in the vernacular, Romance, not in Latin.

Out of their valley, beyond Rome, into the holy land itself? He had said this. They had all heard it.

They dared speak of it only in whispers. They likened Urban to Moses holding his arms uplifted, unwearying, while the host went out against the Amalekites. Some of them cried out that while he was speaking they had seen an apparition in the sky to the east, the phantom city of Jerusalem, taking shape in the thin haze.

Evening fell, the bells resounded a joyful summons to vespers. The throng knelt where it stood, eager and expectant. Little by little it melted away, moving toward hostel and hall and cottage. The fields were dark. Torches came and went through the gates of the town, and light glowed in the embrasures of the abbey where the holy Father rested.

He had done what he set out to do. But, more than that, he had kindled a fire that would spread beyond his control and burn through the ages of men.

VIII

THE crowd at Clermont had been stirred by the pope's summons. This gathering, however, numbered only some thousands, and the rest of France and Europe had heard nothing. No radio would carry the message to listeners; it could not be printed in the morning papers, in fact it could not be printed at all. No machinery for spreading news existed then.

Of course the reigning monarchs had their personal couriers to carry missives, but the three nearest sovereigns were William the Red in Norman England, Philip in France, and Henry in the German Reich—all excommunicate or antagonistic. Urban would have to broadcast his message without their aid. Moreover, when strangers heard his summons they would be amazed. The cynical among them would point out that lions and lambs do not eat together, and feudal enemies do not become brothers-in-arms. Experienced travelers would explain that such a journey of more than three thousand miles was not feasible for an army. Urban had nothing in the way of tangible pay to offer.

And when the first heat of enthusiasm had cooled men would ask how their families were to be protected while they were gone. Guibert, the anti-pope who had heard nothing as yet in his palace at Ravenna, would surely mock the enterprise.

The whole thing hung in the balance. And failure now would place Urban in the position of a leader disavowed. The die was cast, he could not alter it. He had summoned men to a universal, holy war.

Almost certainly, knowing that he had caught the multitude with his speech—had he not heard their answering cry?—he expected many of the barons and fighting men to respond. He had invited them to Clermont, and his words had been directed at them.

Urban set about organizing the expedition he had fathered. Not an hour was wasted. Candles burned in the abbey of Clermont that night, while the council of cardinals and bishops sat again, and the golden pope bade them return to their dioceses and preach the voyage of God. Adhemar of Le Puy was granted the position he sought—papal legate, shepherd of the expedition. A happy choice, for he knew the road to Jerusalem and beneath his robe beat the heart of a soldier.

We have appointed our well-beloved son Adhemar, Bishop of Puy, to be head of this expedition, in our stead. All who may go should obey his commands as if they were from us, and submit to his binding and releasing.

The date for assembling the armed men was fixed upon— mid-May of the coming summer. An open letter explaining all that had happened was addressed to the men of Flanders. Urban himself urged support of the enterprise whenever he spoke thereafter to the masses, at Limoges, Toulouse, and on the very boundary of turbulent Normandy. Envoys hastened to the bishops in Germany who favored his cause.

Urban made use of the Church itself to bear his message afield. Mounted couriers went from abbey to abbey. From the gates of the monasteries barefoot brothers sallied forth in their black robes, halting to give the news wherever peasants were gathered in the fields.[1]

These heralds wore red crosses, and had fresh and heartening tidings to offer. The Truce of God would be invoked to protect the homes and goods of any who might take up arms. Whoever seized their property would be outlawed, and anathema would be pronounced upon any who molested their wives while they were away. And they themselves would be granted for three years' indulgence from all sin—the first plenary indulgence for that length of time to be offered by a pope of Rome.

That was good hearing. The country people saw more and more of the sturdy young men going around with the red cross on their shoulders. Having made the vow to go, and having been given the fine strips of cloth to sew on, these fortunate ones were now absolved from their sins.

O how worthy it was and how pleasant to us when we saw those beautiful crosses of silk or gold stuff on the tunics or byrras of the pilgrims! How fitting it was! They had marked themselves with the symbol in order to seek the reality of the symbol.

To these people of the bourgs and hamlets, the sign *was* real. Written words mystified them. Working with their hands and living among concrete things, they thought of objects, not of ideas. If they thought at all about the struggle going on between Urban and the great emperor, off beyond the mountains, they reasoned that the emperor had tried to take the holy Father's ring and staff away from him. The black-robed clerics knew better; they were aware that the ring and staff were the symbols of a bishop's office. But to the men in tunics and byrras the ring and the staff *made* the pope. If somebody else had the ring and the staff, then he would be the holy Father.

But they did not want anyone else to be the holy Father. Had not the splendid Urban tried in every possible way to bring about peace? And peace was good, because the cattle

---

[1] These speakers appear in the church chronicles of the day as bearers of *excitatoria*—rousings or encouragements. One is reminded of four-minute men.

could graze unmolested, and men could keep more than half their crops and wood for themselves. True, this golden pope had urged them to make war on the pagans. They were vague in their minds about these pagans, who had become enemies of God. But they understood that churches had been torn down, and honest people tortured.

Therefore, since he was trying in every way to exalt all that belonged to God, almost all yielded themselves to his paternal guidance.

The winter set in, bleak and devastating. Whoever had a good supply of food hoarded it up, and watched over it to be certain of it until the coming of grass again, when the cattle would fatten and give more milk. In some places the poorer people ate only chestnuts and roots. They complained more about a sickness that had sprung up around the church of St. Gertrude of Nivelle, an affliction that burned inwardly like fire. Shut in about their fires, men who had let the summons go unheeded until then began to envy the men marked with the cross. They would be faring forth with the first thaws; their ploughing and piling of stones was ended. More than that, their households would be protected, and perhaps nourished in some way.

What a road they would follow! They would march with the iron men, the warriors, and their lords and bishops. Probably they would cross the sea somewhere—it was pretty well agreed that Jerusalem lay beyond the sea—like rich merchants. And at the end of the road they would find the everlasting city, in its paradise of fruit trees, where manna grew. They would walk among gardens and bathe when they wished in the purifying waters of the Jordan.

To these winter-bound souls, discussing the expedition over the fires, it seemed as if the cross-bearers were setting out not to the earthly Jerusalem, but to the celestial city. (The symbol *was* the reality.) They had been told many times about this celestial city, with its walls set with jewels and its streets paved with stones of gold. And they longed for it. It seemed to them, brooding in the damp peat smoke, as if this were their real destination. Except where pilgrims and wiser heads gathered together, they had not heard of any other Jerusalem than this—where the sun always shone and men cast off their sins as if they were furs, to be thrown aside in the time of spring.

The grindstones hummed, as steel sword edges were pressed upon them by strong hands. Forges in the smithies blazed red, and hot iron clanged under tapping hammers. Shields were being shaped, and hand hilts fashioned. The hammers beat out iron stirrups—sharp halberd heads, and massive maces. Arms for the iron men who would ride to the east.

"God wills it!" The smiths laughed in the smoke.

The good men of the cottages sat late at table, while the children slept, clinging together in the straw of the bed, and women stirred the fire restlessly. Old memories moved in their minds.

A hard winter, this. More and more of the good men knelt before the priests, repeating words that were said to them, and rising with the strips of a red cross in their fingers. It was God's war. The idol-worshipers of Satan had troubled Him—the beast Leviathan was rising from the sea. The horde of Anti-Christ had pitched its tents opposite Jerusalem's walls. The heavenly city was calling, and they were going to free Jerusalem.

In the cottages women rocked on the benches, staring into the fire. The children slept fitfully when the wind blast stirred the straw. The men were rising up, they were taking the cross.

And the iron men were riding forth. They were gathering in the castle halls where the great fires leaped and smoke-darkened tapestries swayed along the wall when the wind gusts came—they were listening to the troubadours singing the "Song of Roland" again, while bright-eyed boys poured wine into the goblets, and quiet ladies watched.

In the stables they were grooming the great chargers for the road. The young esquires sang and tossed a merry word to the castle girls. Wooden bridges rumbled under heavy hoofs. Knights rode in to sit with their liege lords and talk of the venture. So many spears—so many bundles of arrows—pack horses must be had—and so the tally would be complete.

Knights of Normandy, chevaliers of the Loire, and barons of the Rhine—they were making ready joyfully. Their olifants sounded the new summons to arms. They were making peace with the neighbors, and choosing a new castle guard —selling cattle and grain for gold to carry in their chests. Spare arms must be bought, and the men mounted in fit style. They borrowed money from merchant and abbot and Jew. They wanted time in which to pay, because the future —why, the future lay beyond Jerusalem.

And between now and then would befall many a fair battle and onset, and a breaking of spears in a good cause.

"God wills it!" they assented.

They rode in to the near-by abbeys, remembering perhaps a raid and a spoiling which had taken them that way not long before. They must make their peace. Bearded men, sitting in the reception rooms, they explained awkwardly in blunt words that they would like atonement, and had thought of making a fitting gift to that end. The robed men heard them gravely, and scribes wrote down upon parchment scholarly and legally binding petitions, which the cross-bearers signed. They could not write, but they made their mark.

I, Stephen of Niblen, aware of the uncertainty of human life, and desiring forgiveness of my heavy sins——

Some of them pledged property to the Church in another way. Among the deeds of the abbey of Cluny there is this:

We, Bernard and Oddo, brothers, setting out for the remission of our sins with the rest on the expedition to Jerusalem, pledge to Master Artald, *decanus* of Lordon, for 100 shillings the following— one homestead with all belonging to it, that is to say buildings, fields, woods, vineyards, shore rights, pastures, watercourses, cultivated and uncultivated land. But, however, we make this condition that if in this pilgrimage upon which we set out—as we are mortal— we should be prevented from returning by death, the mansion itself with all intact shall remain perpetually the property of St. Peter, and Cluny, whose master is the reverend father Hugo.

Who were Bernard and Oddo? How did they fare, after relinquishing their one homestead to this Master Artald of the monastery of Cluny? We will not know, except that upon the margin of the parchment, below the signatures, these words have been written in the same hand, "*In hac autem expeditione ambo defuncti sunt et non reversi*—However, in this expedition, both died and did not come back."

Ordericus Vitalis wrote in his cell by candlelight:

An astonishing desire to go to Jerusalem, or to aid those who were going, animated equally the rich and the poor, men and women, monks and peasants. Husbands were ready to leave their loved wives; these in their turn longed ardently to leave their children—although with tears—and all their cherished belongings, and to follow their husbands on the expedition.

Lands, of great value until now, were sold at a vile price, and everyone bought arms to go to avenge God against the infidels. Thieves, pirates, various criminals were touched by grace, and came out of the abyss of their misery, renouncing their crimes and setting out for the far-off land to expiate them. The wise pope encouraged to go to war all those who were in condition to carry arms against the infidels. He accorded them, by virtue of his great power, absolution from all their faults after the hour when they took the cross.

Urban had prevailed. His expedition was mobilizing.

IX

THE GONFANONS

THE final test lay in the decision of the great barons. If some of them—a half dozen might suffice—joined the movement, it would have the leaders it needed, and the organized fighting men. If the feudal lords held back, Urban's expedition might end in failure. And none of the great barons had appeared at the council.

Urban wrote at once to that old warrior, Raymond, count of Toulouse, down by the Pyrenees. Raymond the Provençal was a devout follower of the Church and he had fought, at the head of his Gascons and Catalans, against the Moslems in Spain. Word came back to the pope that he had taken the cross.

Nothing could have warmed the heart of the southerner more than this summons. For generations his ancestors had waged hearty warfare within sight of the snow peaks of the Pyrenees against Arab and Berber out of Africa. In his veins ran the hot blood of the sun-warmed valleys of the Garonne's headwaters. He was impulsive and swift to anger, and at the same time canny and covetous as his own Gascons and Catalans. Lord of St. Egidius,[1] and count of the rich city

---

[1] They called him "St. Gilles."

of Toulouse, he had wooed many women and married some, always to his gain. By the dower of one he became count of Provence, by another he made himself son-in-law of the Norman duke, Roger of Sicily. Only the previous year he had married again, a fair young thing, Elvira, the out-of-wedlock daughter of Alfonso VI of Leon and Castile.

Scarred, blind in one eye from an old wound, already aged —fifty-three years was advanced old age in this time when lads of fifteen had the strength of grown men—Raymond the Provençal prepared for his last expedition. Being devout, he gave some lands to the monasteries for the good of his soul, and being a lover of silver as well as women, he gleaned every possible penny out of his city treasuries for his war chest. Stalwart, dark-skinned mountaineers flocked in to Toulouse when Raymond issued his call for the feudal levies; they hastened to his blue standard, to talk endlessly about the new expedition, and to eat hugely of his food. They were lazy and quarrelsome and eager for gain, but they had learned courtesy from the Arabs, and their love-singers chanted the songs of the Moors.

When Raymond led them north—a small and stubborn figure with a clipped gray beard, mounted on a black horse of racing stock—they rode with garlands on their spear heads. Dry leaves and scented grass covered the dust in the streets where the cavalcades passed. Their saddles were bright with red brocades and soft crimson leather of Córdoba; gold discs weighed down their reins.

From the balconies above them hung Venetian tapestries and striped silks. Tambourines and gitterns greeted them, and the towers resounded with the chiming of bells. Black-robed priests lifted silver crosses as they passed. Flowers drifted down on their steel-bound heads—there is no winter in Provence. They stopped where vessels filled with dark wine and honey mead were held up to them—there is no haste in the Southland. They smiled at the bright eyes that stared at them from flushed faces.

The joyous company of jongleurs—a little threadbare, and perhaps more than a little drunk—sang, while the bit chains jingled. The led chargers neighed, tossing their caparisoned heads, and the *clang-cling*, of the tower bells echoed the thudding of hoofs. The gay hearts of the Southland made joyful the farewell.

And for Raymond, the count, this was farewell. He had taken oath that he would remain in the Holy Land and never set foot again in Europe. Age had come upon him, and this would be a proper ending for his years.

With him he carried the youthful Elvira and her son, just born to him.

Almost at once Godfrey of Bouillon took the cross. And his pledge was a surety of stanch support for the gathering host. He had the generosity and the fearless spirit of a Roland. Moreover, he was young.

In him ran the blood of Charlemagne, and he had all the pride of the elder Franks who held to the Rhineland castles. He had been well schooled as a boy; he could read and write and speak Latin and Romance as well as German. A captain of war in his teens, he had carried a standard in the host of his liege lord, Henry IV of Germany—had been one of the first to enter the walls at the storming of Rome. His personal courage was beyond question. High-born, mild-mannered, he had a sweetness of temper rare in a leader of war.

Fortune gave much to him, as often happened in this troubled age. Lord of gray-walled Bouillon, the marquisate of Anvers fell to him on the death of an uncle. He was master of wide forests and hunting lands, and he enjoyed life to the full until the day when he rode through the streets of Rome into the Lateran with a bloodied sword and killed Rudolf of Swabia. The dukedom of Lorraine came to him then, from Henry's reluctant hand.

After that he lost interest in the feudal wars, seeming to feel that in some way he had committed sacrilege. A slow fever weakened him, and he took this to be a punishment of his sin. But when the emperor imposed on his vassals, he was quick to take up the sword against his liege lord—and again against the bishop of Verdun.

He was no more than twenty-two, and he held the richest

fiefs of the Rhineland; he had grown weary with war, but could not withdraw from the field. A strange thing in this iron generation, Godfrey interested himself in the affairs of his peasants; he threw himself into the movement for the Truce of God, and he made a vow that he would go upon pilgrimage to Jerusalem, to try to heal the fever that sapped his vitality.

When Urban's summons came he cast his lot at once with the cross-bearers. To raise funds to equip his army, he sold the city of Metz to its commune of citizens for one hundred thousand crowns. He disposed of two principalities to his former antagonist, the bishop of Verdun. The castle of Ramioul he gave outright to the Church, and in the end he pawned Bouillon to the bishop of Liége for three hundred marks of silver and four of gold.

Money had been scarce everywhere, since few coins were in circulation. Trade had been carried on by exchange, and gold and silver hoarded against need. The demand, sudden and almost universal, of the cross-bearers for ready money to carry with them forced prices down. Cattle were being sold for copper coins—as much as seven sheep for a denarius. Real property, cattle and land and goods, was being pressed for sale, while money was eagerly sought. Some men sold everything they possessed for a handful of silver.

Since the monasteries and abbeys held a great part of the supply of coinage in their treasuries, they profited hugely from this excited selling—a circumstance that had its effect in later generations.

Another thing had its immediate effect. The herds of cattle driven to the markets, the foodstuffs hoarded in the granaries until now, when they were sold at any price, relieved the famine that still clung like an omen of disaster in the snow-bound hamlets in that mid-winter.

So the departure of the cross-bearers became something of a feast. Good omens were not wanting. Many eyes had seen a comet crossing the sky, with its tail stretching toward the west in the shape of a sword. One Sigger, a priest of exemplary habits, beheld a greater thing. In mid-afternoon he noticed that among the clouds two horsemen took shape, riding toward each other; and when they met, the one who held a cross in his hand overthrew the other.

Another story was repeated in the villages. A certain priest, who later became a monk, was walking through a wood with two others when he heard a curious sound overhead. He looked up and saw a long, gleaming sword carried upward through the trees in swirling dust by a gust of wind. Instead of falling to earth, it ascended until it was lost to sight in the sky. All this time he heard a sound as of steel weapons clashing.

Before the snow left the ground men were hastening from their homes.

Then husband promised wife that if he lived, he would come back to her. But she, dreading that she would not see him again, could not stand at his side, and fell to the ground weeping for her beloved, whom—although he still lived—she felt that she had lost as if he had been dead already. He moved away, pretending that he did not pity her, and was not moved by her weeping or by the grief of the others around them. He set out, holding firm to his purpose— but still, in his heart, he was troubled. They who remained were sad, and they who went away were glad. What then can we say, more than this?

Among the first to move was Godfrey of Bouillon, with his two brothers, Baldwin and Eustace of Boulogne. Many eyes followed them, on their heavy chargers, pacing behind the blue gonfanon of Lorraine—three gray-eyed youths, laughing for the gladness in them, mighty of bone, and erect in their pride. The red cross was embroidered on their leather tunics, to the right of the heart. Amber rosaries circled their white throats, and their red-gold hair hung upon their shoulders.

Behind them was uplifted the banner of the church of Lorraine, its violet field woven with the images of saints, its silken cords swaying in the wind. And behind this rode thirty thousand men of the Rhinelands.

Next to go out were the gonfanon of France and the standard of Aquitaine. A council had been held by King

Philip in February, and there it was decided that, although he could not go—being outcast from the Church—his brother must. So Hugh the Great, count of Vermandois, took the cross. Baldwin of Hainault followed him, and the wealthy Stephen, count of Blois.

Stephen, it seems, was well enough content at home. Cousin to half the princes of France, a man of fine courtesy and no little eloquence, he had a passion for the hunt, and the means to gratify his passion. His place, however, was with the chivalry. And he had married not long since a daughter of the royal house of England. Adele, his wife, possessed the spirit of a warrior, and even if Stephen had wished to stay at home, she would not have been pleased by that. Stephen was very much in love, and Adele was a determined woman.

And, without discussion or any ado, the quiet Robert, the youthful count of Flanders, joined them, leaving the castle in which he had ruled for only three years.

In early spring, while Urban was preaching near the border of Normandy, came welcome tidings. That other, wayward Robert, duke of Normandy, had taken the cross. And of him a tale was told.

Robert had been the butt of his sire, William the Bastard, who conquered England. Short Breeches, the father called his son, who was indeed short and stocky and strong of limb, with a thatch of sandy red hair and indolent blue eyes. Keen for the hunting, he was—an emptier of cups, a seeker of full-fleshed women. Good-natured, generous, and besotted, gorging himself with venison and boar's meat, and yet a man to be feared when roused to anger. When his father was under the sod—and few were found to mourn him—his brother, William the Red, became master of England, while Short Breeches himself had Normandy.

Only after a fashion was he master of Normandy. His brother baited him as the sire had done, and Robert roused from his cups to fight back without luck or success. It was an easy matter to persuade him to sell an important castle for money in hand, and when he took the field he was readily tricked. Once he might have taken England, but he delayed so long in crossing the Channel that the affair was over before he arrived on the scene. His nobles mocked him and far outstripped him in debauchery. Yet Short Breeches did not lack for friends.

Such was the situation when a certain Gerento, abbot of Saint-Benigne, appeared as legate of the Holy See. Urban had sent him to arrange a truce between the brothers and to urge them to take the cross. William the Red would have none of that part of the matter, but he was willing to profit by the occasion. Gerento crossed back to Normandy and talked with Robert Short Breeches. The sluggish duke of Normandy had been a failure, both as ruler and as warrior. By some strange quirk of chance, the concept of journeying to Jerusalem to fight a holy war stirred the wine-soaked brain, and Robert said he would go.

He was penniless as usual, and Gerento, who had had an opportunity of weighing the characters of the brothers, arranged ways and means. Robert not only made peace with William, but he accepted a loan of ten thousand marks of silver from him. As security for this loan, which was to equip him and his following for the journey, Robert pledged Normandy. All of his heritage, the whole of his country, was in pawn, and forfeit to William unless he redeemed it before the end of three years.

William was hard put to raise the sum. He levied extraordinary dues, and forced the churches of England to melt down much of their silver, but he saw himself master of Normandy, with the obstinate Robert safely removed from the scene for three years.

Robert appeared content. The untamed Normans rallied now to his standard. Philip of the great house of Bellême, who had harried his countryside for years, rode in with his spears. Eude, lord bishop of Bayeux, who had threatened Short Breeches for his sins, came in with his clergy. Robert found himself leader of a host of Normans, with money in his chests. After his customary delay he set out.

The chronicle of Normandy relates that many of the barons, having no understanding of the distance they must travel, started forth with their falcons on their wrists, and packs of hunting dogs trotting beside them, and grooms and servants bringing up the rear.

Instead of one army, six hosts of cross-bearers were forming and marching that spring along the old Roman roads that led to the east. Men stood by the roads and gibed at the dust-covered throngs one day, and the following day sold their goods and joined the marchers. More than a hundred thousand, perhaps a quarter million, had taken the cross already. The six hosts moved slowly, like tranquil rivers, but as they went little streams of human beings trickled into them.

Urban had not expected this. Here was a new power, of men in motion driven by a common resolve. It had not manifested itself before, but now it had started forth at the impetus of his words.

He had called it forth, and he did not try to restrain it, although he did try to guide it. New-married husbands, he decreed, were not to leave their wives for a year; priests should not take the cross without the consent of their superiors. The Truce of God must be kept among the cross-bearers—they must not lift hand against their companions.

The mobilization of the main hosts, unexpectedly swollen to huge numbers, had taken more time than Urban had foreseen. He changed the date of the departure of Adhemar, his vicar, to August 15th, and named Constantinople as the place of assembly. There the first arrivals were to await the others. He wrote, apparently, to the emperor of Byzantium, at Constantinople, saying that Christian princes were on their way to the Holy Land with a host of three hundred thousand men, and that he—the emperor—should help them by his good will, with food and supplies.

Urban did more. He went among the gathering men, blessing the Provençals at Nîmes, and again preaching the voyage of God. He turned back to Italy, praising the people of Lucca and Bologna for taking the cross. His journey home became a triumphal procession. No longer was he the harassed wanderer who had borrowed money to buy back his house at the Lateran.

URBAN II

It was under the inspiration of his speech at Clermont
that the first crusade was undertaken.

ROBERTUS DUX NORMANNORUM PARTUM PROSTERNIT

Robert Curthose in the act of unhorsing a pagan warrior, the oldest graphic representation of the duke now
extant. From an eighteenth century engraving of a medallion in a stained-glass window at Saint-Denis,
which was executed at the order of Abbot Suger. The church was dedicated 11 June 1144, and the window
must date from about that period.

ROBERT, DUKE OF NORMANDY

COURTESY OF ROBERT CURTHOSE, OXFORD UNIVERSITY PRESS

He spoke with a new authority. Legates of the Holy See journeyed to Genoa and to Pisa, where sturdy bourgeois merchants were building ships. They also should take the cross, and aid the army from the sea.

Men besought the golden pope to lead them to the prom:sed land. Whether Urban wished to go, we do not know, because only the guarded answer of his lieutenants has come down to us:

In his thoughts, the Pontifex had set out with them across the sea, but he was restrained by all the clergy, lest in such a crisis of affairs he should leave the kingdom of St. Peter to be torn apart by the teeth of wolves.

Instead, he gave the white and gold banner of St. Peter, his own standard, to Hugh the Great, brother of Philip of France, the first of the leaders to cross Italy.

Guibert and his sympathizers remained aloof from the cross-bearers. What a man could do to check an invasion of multitudes by mockery and brawling, he did. Fulcher bears witness to that—Fulcher, the priest of Chartres who had taken the cross, and had joined the company of Robert of Normandy.

Journeying through Italy, we came to Lucca, a famous city. And beyond it we found Pope Urban. Robert the duke and Stephen the count spoke with him there, and also others who wished to. He blessed us, and we set out joyfully for Rome. But when we entered the church of St. Peter we found there before the altar the adherents of Guibert, that self-styled pope, who drew their swords and seized upon the offerings we laid on the altar. Others climbed out on the rafter-beams over our heads and threw stones down at us when we were prostrated in prayer.

When they encountered anyone faithful to Urban they wished to kill him. One tower of the church was held by followers of Pope Urban, who were guarding it out of loyalty to him, and were fighting with his adversaries. We grieved at beholding this outrage in that place, but we were unable to do anything except to trust that it would be avenged by God. Yet many who had come all this way with us waited for no more, but with shameful cowardice, turned back to their homes.

Stones and swords and gibes, however, could not dam the torrent that was moving across Italy, although many cross-bearers went home disheartened. Two months after this scene Guibert lost his strong fortress on the Po.[1] Rome was abandoned by his sympathizers, and at the end of the year Urban was carried in full procession through the streets to the gray walls of the Lateran. There, triumphantly, he preached for the last time the voyage of God.

He did not need to do more. His work was ended. "In this year," Fulcher explains, "when the westerners passed through Rome on the way to Jerusalem, Urban obtained everywhere his full power as pope."

But the golden pope had called forth an unheard-of power. He had fashioned a sword, and now he wielded it in his own behalf.

No longer was he merely the servant of servants, the counselor; he was also leader of the armed host of Christendom. He was more than king, and before his strength Guibert quailed and Henry withdrew.

And meanwhile the flood of men was moving through the white dust of the ancient roads to the east, crushing through obstacles, moving blindly, as a torrent takes its course toward its destination. It was known now as the *cruciata*, the "cross-signed." The crusade had begun.

---

[1]Some accounts have it that the crusaders fought for Urban in Italy. Fulcher's evidence is that the crusaders kept their swords in their sheaths. But the prestige of the new movement helped turn the balance in Urban's favor. The sentence of excommunication weighed more heavily on Henry after this because, even if he had desired it, he could not have participated in the crusade. He died years later, dishonored, and estranged from his son, and was refused burial in consecrated ground.

X

WHAT PETER DID

𝕬 WARM sun melted the snow in the farm lands early that spring. Rains followed the thaw, flooding the streams and washing away the débris of winter. Men said that it would be a good year for the planting. They brought the wooden ploughs and the yoked oxen out into the brown fields.

In the openings of their sheds leather-workers sat, their hands busied with softened hides, their eyes searching up and down the road. People were moving about early this year, in spite of the mud. In the smithies other men were shoeing oxen, to take to the road. Wheelwrights came along for leather, to shrink on the rims of their wheels. Carts passed through the hamlets, with furniture piled high over the wheels. Sometimes women sat on the driver's seat, holding babies. Barefoot girls tugged at the cords of unwilling cows. Half-grown children, trudging behind the father, ran up to ask in their shrill voices, "Isn't this Jerusalem?"

The cart wheels creaked, the horns of the oxen clashed against the wooden yokes, and rusty trace chains jangled. Horses splashed through the mud, sometimes carrying double. Girdled priests swung past, in stride with hairy shepherds carrying long staves, a bill-hook thrust through their belts. They were going with Peter the hermit, although the roads were little better than the bed of a freshet, and this was not Jerusalem, but the shallow valleys of the Champagne country.

They did not know very much about Peter. Some said he had been born in Amiens and had lived for years as a hermit. He had been going about preaching when the holy Father summoned the faithful to take up arms for the Seigneur Jesus. Then Peter had begun preaching the crusade, riding around on his gray mule with his bare feet hanging in the grass. He wore a gray woolen shirt with a hood pulled over his head and a sleeveless monk's robe flapping around his ankles.

Men who had seen him said that he was sunburned and thin. He ate only fish—no bread or meat—but he drank a little wine. Some claimed that he had made a pilgrimage to the holy places, but this was not certain. He had come up from Orleans, through Epernay, and he was going on to the valley of the Moselle. And then to Constantinople— through Asia to Jerusalem.

Peter spoke to the crowds with a fiery tongue. They thronged in the damp cemeteries carrying lighted candles when he halted near a church in the evening. He spoke as one having authority. Wonderful things were related of such times—how landowners and drapers had thrown money down at his bare feet, and townswomen had pressed upon him strings of pearls and jeweled cloak clasps. All this money he had given away again, to the poorest. He sought out whores and made them live clean—dowered them with his alms so they, who had been creatures, could get husbands.

A knight was his companion, and a Teutonic priest, and a mass of disciples followed them. So greatly did they reverence their leader that they cherished hairs cut from the mule that Peter rode. He became the shepherd of a growing flock all resolved to follow him to Jerusalem.

Whether Peter had intended this in the beginning, we do not know. Before the end of March the monk found himself commander of an army of fifteen thousand. Some of them became impatient when he lingered to preach at Cologne, and went on without him. They followed the knight, his lieutenant, who called himself Gautier-sans-Avoir—Walter-without-Wealth. A few hundred of them disappeared down the highway into the bare forest. They were the advance guard of the crusade. In this month of March the great barons were still mustering their forces, preparing arms, raising money.

Some days later Peter's army began its journey. It has been called the Peasants' Crusade, but it was really an expedition of the people. A few men of gentle blood rode in the throng with their servants, and some scores of men at arms trudged afoot. Beribboned women of the Paris streets sat on the baggage wagons; ragged ribalds trotted beside them—masterless and penniless alley folk. Some, who strode out willingly now, had been *testatori*—made-up cripples of the crew that haunted Notre Dame's steps. In the rabble bands came mock-monks and weepers, halegrins and fit-throwers, hymn-chanters and cut-purses. "All the common folk," a chronicle explains, "the clean as well as the filthy—adulterers, man-killers, perjurers, and thieves. Nay, also women and those who had turned penitent."

Somewhere in the mass was the Tafur, the king of the ribalds. But the bulk of the motley host was made up of bearded Rhinelanders, and stoop-shouldered ploughmen from the north of France. When they had left the upper Rhine, marching through the valleys to the headwaters of the Danube, Peter preached by the way, and contingents of Swabian axmen joined the marching throng, and scythemen from Bavaria.

They spoke a dozen dialects, and they sang the Mass as pleased them best. They were agreed upon two things: their reverence for the hermit-captain and their eagerness to find the way to Jerusalem. Probably not even Peter had a very clear idea where Jerusalem might be. But he could easily follow the road taken by Walter, and come to the Danube. Moreover, he carried with him a curious document, an order from the Jews of France to the Eastern Jews to give

Peter the supplies he needed. From Ratisbon, they aided him along the Danube.

Some of his bands took to boats and drifted down between the forest walls. They found themselves in a land of scattered, open farms, watched over by horsemen in sheepskins and leather who spoke a strange tongue. Here the walled towns were far apart, and the people stared curiously at the wanderers. Yet the spring was fair, the cattle plentiful, and no one need lack for food.

Peter's host went on through this land of the Hungarians in good spirits. The mass of peasants knew how to manage. Some of them pilfered a little, but what of that? They drove cows beside the carts, and bought or stole a sheep here and there; they moved slowly, halting early to put up skin shelters and light the cooking fires. How the women of Paris fared remains a mystery, but for the peasants this march was a long fête after the toil in their stony fields. Peter had taken them out of their misery, and they would see new wonders.

Peter was obeyed without question when he gave an order. His lieutenants herded the mass and kept order. Peter himself had sent to the king of the Hungarians and had made an agreement by which his people were to be supplied with provisions.

They had not any sight or tidings of Jerusalem, but they went on cheerfully, turning more and more toward the south.

Many stories are told as to what happened now. It seems as if in a Hungarian town they came upon arms and coats of mail that had belonged to Walter's men, although the men themselves were not to be found—the penniless knight and his contingent having passed on to the south some ten days before. Peter's followers suspected treachery at the hands of these half-Christian strangers. One of the pilgrims quarreled with a Hungarian trader over some purchase. Swords were drawn and fighting began in the town between the wanderers and the Hungarians. Several hundred were killed, and the townspeople fled to a near-by height or tried to escape across the Danube, pursued by the cross-bearers, now thoroughly roused.

The peace had been broken—not for the first time—and

Peter's men proceeded to loot the empty town. This done, they turned their attention to the farms and made a rich haul of wine, horses, grain, and sheep. For five days they enjoyed themselves, but Peter became anxious. Word had reached him that an army of Hungarians was on the way to attack the cross-bearers, and it was high time that he got his men across the broad river.

A search for boats yielded only a hundred-odd craft of all kinds, and the bands of wanderers rowed themselves across a few at a time. A new enemy appeared on the scene— strange-looking archers with iron breastplates and round shields, in a flotilla of large boats. Undoubtedly these were pagans, and they began shooting arrows at the pilgrims.

These set to work to build rafts out of poles fastened together with twigs. The crowded rafts, being without rudders, were carried downstream by the swift current, while the shafts of the archers added to the confusion. Seeing his men dying in the river, Peter appealed to the bands of Bavarians and Teutons who had not yet crossed, urging them to attack the pagans.[1]

Seven rafts full of the German warriors engaged the flotilla, and some boats were sunk, seven bowmen being taken captive. These were brought before the hermit and he ordered them to be put to death. The rest of the Christians crossed the river safely, and they all moved on, well supplied with provisions and gear. To add to their satisfaction, they found the next town, Belgrade, almost deserted by the Bulgars who inhabited it. Peter's army numbered too many light-fingered vagabonds to pass by such an opportunity. They looted and prowled through Belgrade and found that the highway led across another, smaller, river. They got over without mishap this time, and at the town of Nish they were met by the Byzantine governor, who greeted Peter and came to an understanding with him. Apparently the

---

[1]These archers were detachments of the frontier guard of the Emperor of Byzantium, who had already had a skirmish with Walter's men. They were Betchenaks, a Turkish people from the Eastern steppes, serving the Emperor as mercenaries, and they seem to have had orders to prevent any strangers from crossing the river without authority. Being unable to talk with Peter's men, fighting resulted.

spoils of Belgrade were to be abandoned, and the pilgrims were to refrain from plundering thereafter. In return, they were promised guides and food all the way to Constantinople. So they learned that they had reached one of the outposts of the great Eastern empire of Byzantium. They learned also that Walter's contingent had reached Nish badly cut up by fighting in the forest.

They left Nish seemingly with the best intentions, but some of the rear guard turned back and pillaged an outlying hamlet. Torches were handled recklessly and smoke began to pour up from the dwellings. This proved too much for the patience of the horsemen who served as guards at Nish, and they charged the rear of Peter's column, scattering the bands of ill-armed foot-soldiers.

The skirmish grew into a healthy battle. Peter's men were routed, and worse than that, most of the baggage wagons and all the chests of money were lost. The motley army scattered through the forest, some of the bands in a blind panic, others looting again. Although rallying trumpets sounded for days, several thousand failed to rejoin Peter.

The march began again under different conditions. Bands of the dreaded archer-horsemen herded the cross-bearers from a distance, and they kept perforce to the highway. And they seemed to have lost much of their reverence for the hermit. He was given messages of greeting from the great emperor at Constantinople, and went ahead of the main body to make terms with this lord of the east. Thus shepherded, the wanderers found themselves within sight of the vast wall of Constantinople, and the Golden Gate that led to the east.

They were well fed now, and happy again. We hear of them stealing things from the suburb where they were quartered, and climbing to the roofs of the churches to tear off the lead sheets and sell them in the market. The emperor made haste to ferry them across the strait that separated Europe from Asia. And there, quartered in a strong citadel, they found the survivors of Walter's party, with some bands of Lombards who had come over from Italy. They rejoiced then, the fiddlers playing by the fires at night, and the vagabonds squatting together to talk of the journey. It was the end of the summer, but they were in Asia, and the road to the Holy Land lay before them.

They had been warned not to stray beyond sight of the citadel, and for once they obeyed, because Greek ships brought loads of grain and oil and wine to the shore, and the mob had enough to eat. For two months they sunned themselves on the shore, and then got tired of doing nothing. Peter had told them they must wait for the army of the great lords to come up.

But they saw no harm in wandering a bit. Their camp lay at the end of a long inlet, and on all sides stood blue mountains covered with orchards and scattered farms. Clouds hung around the summits of the mountains, so the pilgrims explored the valleys. They met only stunted Greeks and sunburned shepherds speaking no language that they knew. These, certainly, were not Turks. Some of the cross-bearers drove off the cattle and sold their prizes to the sailors on the ships at the inlet.

The Lombards and Bavarians heard of this, and planned a raid in greater style. They chose one Rainald of Broyes for their leader and marched off. They discovered a reed-bordered lake with the towers of a city rising at its far end. Avoiding this, they continued their exploration, and prowled around a fortified village on a hill summit. No Turks were visible here—in fact, the dwellings lay deserted, and the raiders settled down to pillage luxuriously.

Presently they had their first sight of the Turks. It seems that one of the great sultans, hearing of the mob, had sent a cavalry division to investigate, under command of an officer named Ilkhan. The raiders were not at first alarmed.

Before the gate [a chronicle relates] stood a well. And at the foot of the village was a fountain from which water flowed, and near which Rainald went out to waylay the Turks.

The Turks, coming on, found Rainald and all who were with him, and killed many of them. The others fled, in truth, to the village, which the Turks besieged at once, cutting them off from the water. Our men were so tormented by thirst that they drew blood from the veins of their horses and asses, and drank it. Some urinated into the hands of the others, who drank of it. Many dug into the moist ground and lay down, spreading the earth over them to allay the parching of thirst. This lasted for eight days.

Then the master of the Bavarians agreed with the Turks to surrender all the others. They who would not deny their God underwent death. The Turks placed others at a mark and filled them with arrows, or divided the captives among themselves like animals, buying them and giving them away.

So the first raiders came to their end, and tumult reigned in the camp of the main body when the tidings were known. Peter, in despair at the depredations of his flock, had gone off to Constantinople some time before, but Walter-without-Wealth and the other experienced captains tried to restrain them, urging them to wait for Peter's return before attempting to take vengeance.

A certain Godfrey Burel, leader of the foot-soldiers, gibed at the caution of the knights, until they swore angrily that they would go against the Turks, though they died thereby.

So the mob started off, all of them who had arms, thronging along the road toward the deserted village without order of any kind. Walter and his handful of knights managed to keep five hundred horsemen together. Thousands of them pushed through the thickets and forests, overflowing from the narrow road.

The disciplined Turkish bowmen watched their coming with astonishment and withdrew to an open valley for better maneuvering. The mob poured after. Walter and his companions charged the enemy, and died fighting—Walter with seven arrows through his armor. When they were out of the way, panic seized the rabble.

Burel was one of the first to flee along a mountain path, and the stream of fugitives poured back along the road, the horsemen of Asia riding them down as they ran. In a few hours the last of the stream had disappeared, and the Turks rode into the outlying camps where the Christian sick and the women waited. They cut down all except the young and fair-seeming, and a remnant of the men, who had found a half-ruined fortress overlooking the shore and had barricaded themselves in with their shields.

Tidings of the massacre reached Constantinople, and the grief-stricken hermit begged the Emperor Alexis for aid. Byzantine ships were sent at once to the inlet, and brought off the few hundred survivors who joined Peter under the walls of Constantinople.

The shepherd had lost his flock. The mob lay scattered in heaps in the brush by the roads, down to the shore—bodies in ragged garments soaked by the autumn rains, already shrinking to bones.

Others followed the road Peter had taken, but did not get as far as Constantinople. A certain priest, a burly Teuton, Gottschalk by name, had been one of Peter's lieutenants, and he had remained behind to muster a host of his own. In this he succeeded.

Thousands trooped after Gottschalk, out of Lorraine, and Bavaria. Unruly thousands, it appears. The chronicles give only a glimpse of them:

They were well greeted in Hungary by favor of King Koloman, who gave them permission to buy the things necessary for life. The King ordered that peace must be kept on both sides. . . . But when they delayed, they began to roam around, and to drink beyond measure. Little by little they took from the Hungarians grain and wine and other things; and at length they began to fight with those who resisted them when they laid waste fields, killing sheep and cattle. It is said that they planted a Hungarian boy on a sharpened stake in the marketplace.

Before long Gottschalk's bands were surrounded by the Hungarian fighting forces and massacred. Few escaped, to find their way back toward the Danube. Among these was Gottschalk.

Almost on the same day another army was broken up, and driven out by the now aroused Hungarians. It had as leader one Folkmar, and it had emerged from Bohemia after killing and plundering the Jews of Prague.

Meanwhile a worse thing was taking place in the Rhinelands. Scattered through the towns from the Frisian coast to Ratisbon, communities of Jews clustered in the dark streets around the wooden synagogues. They were in the towns, but not of the towns. They bought and sold, labored in windowless attics, and the richest of them lent gold to impoverished barons. They came and went quietly in their gray shubas and purple robes, with bright-faced children hidden in their carts; they flocked into the narrow alleys, flooded by water from the gutters during the spring rains; they locked their doors and put out the fires at the curfew hour; they appeared with withered grandsires out of Hungary and the east, and they had the news of the world on their tongues.

They had seen the tidal wave of the crusade gathering in the west—almost before Urban had spoken his last word at Clermont, a letter was on the way from their cousins, the Jews of France. Armed men passed along the rivers, and the Jews watched with shrewd, disillusioned eyes. The leader of the Rhine communities, at Mayence, appealed for protection to the Emperor Henry, who in turn wrote to Godfrey, duke of Lower Lorraine, urging him not to persecute the Jews.

"I have never persecuted them," Godfrey answered. But the people of the synagogues sent him a present of five hundred pieces of silver. Godfrey accepted the silver and did nothing thereafter, either to harm or help them—being occupied with his own affairs. Nor were the Jews molested by any of the lawful leaders of the crusade.

Even Peter had passed by, when whispers ran up and down the Rhine, from alley to alley. Bands of cross-bearers had taken oath to avenge the blood of Christ upon the Jews. So the rumor ran, and early in May the first deaths were related, a score at Metz, and a few at Spires. The Jewish quarters were being looted. And loot was the real incentive of the men who came now with the cross on their shoulder, sword in hand, into the alleys as hounds quest through a covert.

Parties of pillagers met and banded together. One crowd, moved by an old peasant superstition, or sheer blasphemy, wandered about with a goose for its only guide. And another followed a black she-goat to still darker deeds.

A name looms up as leader of the bands: Emich, count of Leisingen, a mighty man of the Rhineland, a man with an eye for gain. A miracle, he says, set him upon the road to Palestine. In the hair of his chest a red cross has taken shape upon his skin. Others rally to him, notably one William the Carpenter, vicomte of Melun, who has brought with him a grim and dubious repute from the Spanish borderland. He is called the Carpenter because he strikes blows with his ax as a carpenter drives spikes into wood. And the goose joins Emich.

Emich sets up his tents before Worms and graciously accepts a payment from the Jews within. As soon as he has the silver in his wallet he summons his men to the work, and they break into the town, rush into the alleys, slaying as they go. They throw the manuscripts of the Thora into the mud, and fire the synagogue, and depart after a while with their gleanings, leaving the people of the synagogue dead.

Word of the massacre reaches Mayence, borne by the unseen messengers of the Jews. And the Jews of Mayence put their treasure in the care and trust of Rothard, who is the bishop of the city—sheltering themselves in the hall of Rothard's house, hidden from Emich's sight.

But Emich comes with his followers, and Bishop Rothard flees. The men of the Rhine hold a council, and then attack the house with arrows and spears. They break down the bolted doors, and press in upon the Jews, stabbing and hacking. And a strange sight is to be seen there—for the desperate folk in gray shubas and purple robes, seeing their women pierced with lances and their children cut through, begin to turn their weapons on their own kin. Screaming, they strike at their brothers, sisters stabbing sisters, and mothers cutting the throats of nursing babies. After four days of killing at Mayence, Emich resumes his march down the Rhine—he is going north, away from Palestine.

Apparently he turned about at Cologne and departed for

Hungary. Others carried on the slaughter, down the lower river through Neuss and Zenten. At Altenahr, the Jews did not await them.

The chiefs of the community did penitence before their Creator, and determined to pick out five men who were courageous and God-fearing. These five men were to put to death all their fellows in religion. Among them were three hundred well-known persons, all of whom were put to death by the weapons of the five.

Emich and his army got no farther than the marches where the river Leitha joins the Danube. By now the sight of a cross-bearer was anathema to the Hungarians, who barred the way without ceremony against the count of Leisingen. A strange panic seized his men. They were pursued, cut down without mercy, by the Hungarians in the river and swamps, and no more was heard of them.

But the fugitives, mingling with the survivors of the other bands limping out of Hungary, brought grieving and doubt into the lands through which they passed. Men said that the hand of the Lord had been against the pilgrims, in retribution for the slaughter of the Jews. Doubt seized upon many who had been fired with enthusiasm for the crusade.

Uncertain rumors came out of the east. Peter and Walter and their men had vanished somewhither, out of the known world. It was said that at Constantinople the great emperor of the east had trapped the cross-bearers, like a spider crouching in his web.

Summer waned, and the crops were brought in. The nights became chill, and on the heights of the distant ranges white snowcaps formed.

But no harbingers of the coming winter and no uneasiness in the spirits of the people could check the movement of the quarter million souls who were now on the way to the east. Under the great lords a half-dozen armies marched toward the rising sun. In the valleys the gleaming gonfanons tossed and swelled against the crimson and gold of the forest; in long galleys, driven by heavy oars, throngs in gray armor passed over the sea barrier.

Young Christendom was in arms for the first time, proud of its new strength, caring nothing about obstacles. It had broken the shackles of its long isolation in the feudal hamlets. It had set its eyes on a new land, and its heart was fired by a mighty purpose.

Such a human tide could not be turned aside. No one man could check it—as one man had summoned it forth. It had risen, and it was rushing on, and it would run its course.

PART II

XI

BYZANTIUM

ALEXIS lived among ghosts. Some of them only troubled his memory, but others lurked, wraithlike, in the corners of his many palaces. He was not afraid of them, but he had to live with them, because he was an emperor.

He always sat alone, because he himself was kin to the ghosts, and above other mortals: a man short in stature and broad, and full of dignity. His sun-darkened head, his large brown eyes and curling black beard shining a little with oil, fitted well the rôle that he played hourly. A mask he wore, of quietude, that concealed well his thoughts. Because he was short, he liked to be seen sitting, in a solitary chair or upon the back of a horse.

At such times he wore a purple mantle caught over one shoulder by a rope of pearls, and beneath that a cloth-of-gold tunic. Purple buskins covered his ankles. Tradition a thousand years old fixed every detail of his costume, and he changed it hourly because the rôle he played was a most difficult one, calling for many impersonations.

He was Augustus and Basileus and emperor of the Romans. He was master of Byzantium, high priest and autocrat—

tyrant, if you will—general-in-chief and contriver-extraordinary. He could slay any man with a whispered word or build a walled city by the scrawl of a pen dipped in red ink; but he himself must watch without seeming to do so for the gleam of an assassin's dagger, or listen with other ears than his own for the murmur of the hippodrome mob that meant revolt.

So it pleased him to sit solitary of a late afternoon, the red-robed eunuch with the gold-tipped staff standing well away from him. Then he could lean his head against the gilt diadem on the back of the chair, and rest. He could let his eyes wander beyond the slender white columns of the open gallery out to the dark blue water of Marmora, calm as a garden pool when the wind dies. At this hour the reflection of coming sunset touched the sea with fire. In the clear air the distant hills of Asia stood stark and purple against the cloud line of the horizon. The triangular sails of a fishing fleet drifted in from the sea.

Alexis Comnene wore the mantle of long-vanished Caesars, and the empire of Byzantium[1] that he ruled was very much like a ghost itself, the ghost of Rome. Because a Roman Caesar had once moved east, senate and all, to this city between the seas, which was named after him thenceforth. *Constantinopolis*, the city of Constantine.

For six hundred years it had survived, while Western Rome decayed. Byzantium had kept alive within it the culture of Plato and the philosophy of the Cynics. Christianity softened it, and the close contact with Asia tinged it with mysticism. The Basileus of Byzantium bowed his head beneath a hermit who kept house on the top of a single pillar, but he enriched his court with the splendor of ancient Persia and modern Baghdad.

---

[1] For a while this half of the Roman Empire was known as the Eastern Empire, and is often called the Greek Empire in histories, because Greek became its language instead of Latin. But it was Byzantium in the first place, and it spoke of itself as Byzantium, and the name has been retained in this volume. Constantinople is the city, as distinct from the empire. Alexis, for reasons of state, styled himself Emperor of the Romans, and the popes of the Eleventh Century for similar reasons addressed him as Emperor of Constantinople. The Greek Church had parted already from the Latin, and both laid claim to the prestige of Rome.

At one time the empire had stretched from the Gate, at Gibraltar, to the forests of the Caucasus, including then the great cities of Alexandria and Antioch. The Muhammadan tidal wave had swept these away, but Athens remained, and all the bare hills of Greece.

On the north, too, the barbarians had thronged in, Scythians and Kumanians, crossing the Danube pastures, and wandering around the walls of Adrianople. So Byzantium had shrunk to the skeleton of an empire, extending along the southern coast of the Black Sea and, the Bosphorus Strait, and holding fast to the inner sea of Marmora, and sprawling around the eastern Mediterranean, still keeping within it the rich city of Smyrna, and troubled Thessalonica —modern Salonika—cloud-wrapped Mount Athos where the monks dwelt, and all the fair, mountainous islands.

Of necessity, Byzantium had become a sea power, sending forth fleets of many-oared dromonds with dragon heads arching over the prows—dragons that spewed out streams of Greek fire. By policy, Byzantium had allied itself with that pertinacious young city on the upper Adriatic, whose merchants went everywhere and called themselves Venetians.

But the wandering Normans had driven its governors from southern Italy, and just now the Seljuk Turks had surged over Asia Minor, and occupied Nicea within a day's ride of the Bosphorus.

So Byzantium had become an island, guarding itself behind walls from the influx of the young, barbaric peoples. Isolated, self-sufficing, it remained unchanged for centuries. Its aristocracy had no visiting list, unless a few learned Arabs. It had savored all the arts a thousand years ago, and now it lived ceremoniously, loving luxury, and outwardly most devout. Its best families ruled it, the diadem passing from the hand of a Ducas, to a Paleolog or Comnene as the case might be, after a palace revolution, sometimes friendly and sometimes bloody. The dethroned emperor might be picked to pieces by the fingers of the circus mob, but the new emperor wore his robes no less ceremoniously because of that.

Twelve emperors and two empresses had worn the purple

during the last two generations, and Alexis had known most of them. This same velvet cap, with its covering of flaming diamonds and rubies and the jeweled lappets hanging down, had covered their heads. They were now ghosts, troubling his memory.

A strange succession, these patricians who had hated and destroyed each other with all formality. There was Romanus, shut out and mocked by his people after he led that great army to destruction by the swords of the Seljuks. And Michael, the lover of pleasure. *He* ordered the sun telegraph to be stopped because it flashed bad news from' the Asian border and interfered with his enjoyment of the races.

And Zoe the wanton, who gave at last to the holy images the feverish affection she had once lavished upon men—even being known to roll in convulsions on the floor, while incense burned behind locked doors, with the sacred pictures clasped to her senile breast.

Then there was Monomakh, bulbous with fat and age, so that he had to be propped in the saddle with two stalwart slaves to ride at either knee and support him during procession. Monomakh who made his clown wear the diadem and purple mantle for him, and who vowed that gout was an excellent thing since it kept him from spending the last hours of his life with luxuriant women. And who, in spite of that avowal, emptied the treasury to give new jewels to a dark-browed Alan girl named Mary. He brought her out in public, with gold serpents twining up her bare arms, beside his consort, the empress. Not that Zoe cared.

And then that last specter, now a shaven monk, who had usurped the throne and Mary the Alan as well, until Alexis tricked him out of power. From the monastery he sent Alexis a message of congratulation, adding, "I am quite as comfortable now as formerly, except that I cannot get any meat to eat."

Alexis differed from these shadowy personages who had worn the purple before him. For one thing, he could be merciful when it was politic to be so. Strangely, he lacked vices. He used deception only when necessary. For another thing he loved Byzantium—his empire now.

They had a proverb, these fatalists and aristocrats: "Often will the empire appear like an aged woman, weak and bereft, and then change again into a young maiden, flaming with precious stones."

And Alexis, who cherished Byzantium more than any woman, was devoting his life to bring about such a change after the chaos wrought by the ghost-emperors. For years he had labored in the field, living in a tent with a monk at his elbow, serving his apprenticeship as commander of an army, and fetching in like a faithful retriever the foemen of Byzantium. Until the day when the army, with a little persuasion, hailed him as emperor.

Thereafter, Alexis worked miracles. The Normans crossed the Adriatic and marched against the queen city, and he beguiled them, selling the silver goblets from Zoe's tomb to get money to do so. He had the clear insight of the elder Greeks and the intuition of an Asiatic. He had the will power to force his small body, hampered by gout, through long campaigns in the mountains along the Danube against the Scythians, and he had endless patience. He tricked the Scythians once because he knew an eclipse of the sun would fall upon a certain day, and defeated them by rolling empty wagons down a hill. With the help of the Scythians he drove off the Kumanians.

Once he kept a Turkish sultan from capturing a stronghold of Asia Minor by entertaining him at Constantinople with a varied program of races, fireworks, and feasts until the Moslem lost count of the days. He sold privileges to the Venetians, and hired soldiery from the Viking folk of Scandinavia with the money; he bought a truce with the Red Lion of the Turks, and persuaded the Red Lion to drive the pirates out of Smyrna.

The Byzantine army worshiped him because he was tireless and victorious. Women admired him. To his mother, whose ambition had thrust him upward, he gave the great Sacred Palace, keeping for himself only this waterside palace of the Lion; to his wife, whose family sustained him on the throne, he gave a seat beside himself, and to Mary the Alan, the Maritime Palace by the gardens.

He had worked miracles for sixteen years and he was a little tired.

Even this evening hour of musing was not altogether his. Oars stroked slowly as a guard galley passed the water gate and the broad marble steps that must be touched by no feet except those of the Basileus. A voice chanted in time with the oar beat. The sun had set, and a breath of wind stirred the gray water.

It was the hour of candle lighting. Slippered feet moved toward him, and slaves awaited him at his chambers, to clothe him in robe and girdle. In a moment Alexis the emperor became Alexis the high priest, the incarnation of divine authority, the vicar of Apostles.

So robed, and carrying the scepter, he passed through the corridors where giant Scandinavian axmen stood against the walls, their limbs draped in the scarlet, gold-edged cloaks, and their tawny heads covered by the plumed bronze helmets of the Immortals, the imperial bodyguard.

Torches awaited him in the courtyard—the Basileus must never be seen except surrounded by lights—and he took his place in the chariot before which the cavalry guard of young Greek nobles was drawn up.

They moved at a foot pace outside the gates, climbing the wide avenue that led beneath the white walls of the Sacred Palace, from which trumpets resounded. Beyond the palace, in the open square, throngs stared at the torches. Voices cried salute in cadence.

"Hail to the Basileus, chosen of God!... Hail to the Christ-loving Emperor, always fortunate, always victorious!"

Alexis descended from the chariot at the dark mass of the Sancta Sophia, the domed cathedral that Justinian had built. Bearded priests bowed to him and assembled about him, conducting him through courtyard and arched entrance, around to the nave at the side. He ascended the narrow winding stair that led to his throne seat in the church—the Basileus must never be seen except elevated above the heads of ordinary men.

He seated himself, adjusting his hands and arms to the

pose required of him. At times he bent his head, a glittering effigy in spun gold, poised between the mass of kneeling men and the statues of the saints above the great columns.

Gray incense poured up around him, rising like mist against the purple porphyry and the blue-green marble of the columns, twining about the white figures of the saints, ascending to the gold mosaics of the huge dome.

Against the dome the chanting of the priests echoed.

"*Kyrie eleison . . . eleison.*"

It seemed to the reverent multitude as if the man sitting erect so far above them, his head outlined against a golden circle, was indeed of the fellowship of the blessed saints.

Behind the clouds of incense, in the gallery half hidden by marble fretwork, four women looked down upon him—his mother whose old age had been made glorious by his sublimation, his daughter Anna who worshiped him, Irene his wife who had given him children and power, and Mary the Alan, whose beauty was that of a living statue, who had been the girl-bride of the last emperor, and who was now Alexis's mistress.

XII

THE COMING OF THE IRON MEN

A LITTLE before this there had arrived at the court of Byzantium a letter written upon folded parchment and sealed with a great seal. It said, in effect:

Know, O Emperor, that I am setting forth, and that I am a lord superior to kings. So, do thou prepare to greet me in a manner befitting my nobility.

The signature was that of Hugh of Vermandois. The phrasing of the letter when read aloud by Alexis sent through the palace and all the court circles a stir of amusement. Even the fourteen-year-old daughter of the Basileus could smile at it, when the memory came to her years later, at the time when she was laboring to write the chronicle of her father's reign. The youthful Anna Comnene, born in the purple room, and a scholar in her 'teens—as a patrician Byzantine should be—looked at life through the blind eyes of Homer and at the outer world through the pages of Strabo. She had seen the barbarians often enough—were they not the six-foot savages who wielded axes in the phalanx of her adored father, the Basileus? And it amused her that this

84

barbarian, Hugh of Vermandois, should presume to send such a missive to the Augustus, the heir of all the Caesars.

Anna and the court were a little surprised when Hugh's heralds arrived. Gold gleamed on the breastplates and the greaves of all the twenty-four knights, the heralds. They delivered themselves of the following message:

"Be it known that our lord, Hugh, is about to arrive, and that he is the leader of all the host of the French. He is bringing from Rome the golden standard of St. Peter. Therefore, bid the Duke of Durazzo prepare a proper reception for him and his men, and make ready thyself to meet him."

Upon the heels of the heralds came tidings from the imperial governor of Durazzo, the seaport that faced Italy across the Adriatic. Hugh the Great of Vermandois had arrived. Unfortunately for himself he had made his advent in a manner that injured his dignity.

His ships, few enough in any case, had been caught in a storm and scattered, and he was beached near Durazzo with only three or four attendants. "Spat up by the waves," Anna remarked.

An imperial patrol had come upon him, had given him a horse that he asked for, and had led him in to the governor, who was entertaining him—and what was to be done with him?

Fortune had smiled upon Alexis, who seized at once the opportunity of negotiating with a leader of the crusade before the armed hosts began to arrive. A worldly-wise general, a certain Manuel Butumites, was sent post haste to greet the shipwrecked Hugh and to conduct him with all splendor to Constantinople.

We know this of Hugh, count of Vermandois—he was brother to the king of France, and a man of imposing presence. He had also a gift of oratory. Probably for these reasons he was often chosen to act as ambassador. Besides, he was a man of remarkable hesitations. In taking the cross he had let it be known that he would never return alive from Jerusalem. Even at the beginning, Hugh's words rang braver than his actions. Had a Godfrey of Bouillon or a Raymond of Toulouse been the first to enter Constantinople, matters would have taken a different turn.

Hugh was given more than the usual dose of magnificence at Constantinople. He was surrounded by exquisites in scarlet and purple—courtiers who seemed to have no other duty than to anticipate his wishes and conduct him about. Chambers in the Sacred Palace were given over to him. When he awoke the first day he found a table at his elbow covered with gold-worked caskets holding gifts of jewels from the emperor. When he went out, a white horse with imperial saddle cloth and fringed reins awaited him. Uniformed slaves salaamed to him and then ran to beat a way clear for him through the crowds with their wands. His new entourage of youthful Greeks rode after him.

He was shown the great double walls, thirty feet high, and more than seventeen miles in circuit, that had defied all attack for four hundred years. From the summit of a tower of the Golden Gate he watched the caravans thronging in, the heads of tall camels rising and sinking as they swayed past with their hemp bales from the east, and wagon trains creaking under sweet-smelling wine casks.

Visiting the harbors along the Golden Horn; which was itself the great, crooked harbor of the queen city, gilded by the sunset glow, he gazed at the clustered masts of shipping, and at multitudes of barefoot slaves tramping up and down worn marble stairs, bending double under loads of fruit and bundled furs. Out of the damp decks of the ships came strange odors, of spice and sandal and rotting fruit.

He learned to find his way about, from one forum to another, guided by the gigantic statue of Constantine that faced the east. He discovered that there were cities within the city. Across the Golden Horn the carved wooden façades of the Venetian merchants clustered together; in the dark alleys leading to the jetties, where fresh hides and wet garments hung overhead, lived the Jews. At times he met thin-faced warriors with curved swords and knives thrust through their girdles, with odd cloaks draped about their shoulders. They wore pointed helmets of gray, damascened steel, with a circlet of white cloth around their brows, and Hugh did not know at first that they were Seljuk Turks out of Asia—the Saracens he had come to fight.

He saw others, squatting in the shadows of the bazaar, lean bearded men with hawklike eyes. They were Hagarenes, the Greeks said—Arabs, sellers of brasswork and weapons and silk of Cathay. Their stalls smelled of camphor and oil of sesame seed, and they spoke with all the insolence of a conquering race.

Even in the alleys where the horses floundered in the mud and dogs snarled and beggars screamed, the visitor beheld the domes of the great churches. But above all the city towered the miraculous dome of the Sancta Sophia, and here Hugh was shown breath-taking things. Long-haired priests took him about the nave of the cathedral where candles glimmered in the shadows. They pointed out the gold caskets that contained—so they explained in reverent whispers—the gifts that the three Magi had brought to the feet of the Christ-child.

Hugh beheld the image of the Virgin, from whose eyes tears dripped without ceasing; he gazed upon the cases that held the veritable tablets of the law that had once been grasped by the hands of Moses. He fingered the long bronze trumpets of Jericho, and peered down into the dark recess at the left of the great altar where lived the angel who guarded the Sancta Sophia.

Standing at the rear of the nave, with no one near him, he heard a clear, angelic voice at his ear,[1] "*Kyrie eleison—Christe eleison.*"

From the mystery of the great cathedral Hugh of Vermandois went out into the splendor of the Augusteon plaza, the gathering place of the nobles. Here blazed the white marble

---

[1] The writer of this book noticed this peculiar quality in the echoes of the Aya Sophia—as it is now called. He made a point of going back at the hour of evening prayer, and heard it again, between the rearmost pillar and the wall. It did not sound like an echo, because the voice of the caller-to-prayer seemed to be at the visitor's ear—although the caller must have been in one of the galleries, some hundred feet overhead. Apparently the sound was intensified by one of the upper domes, and caught in a peculiar way between the pillar and the wall. But the call was the familiar Arabic "*Hayyeh alas salat*—Come to prayer," of the muezzin.

of an open court, surrounded by porticos that shielded walls set with mosaics and plates of worked gold and bronze. And before the walls stood the statues of elder Greece. Groups of patricians, in robes heavy with embroidery, turned and saluted the solitary barbarian prince, because the Basileus had ordered it.

Hugh marveled at the *anemodulium*, the wind indicator— twelve bronze figures that moved, as the wind chanced to blow, upon the summit of a square pedestal.

From the balcony in front of the Senate he looked across at Asia and at a tiny eye of light that winked out of blue hills two days' journey distant, the sun telegraph of the frontier.

Even in November, the sun beat down from a clear sky, and if the heat troubled him, he was taken into the wind- ing passages to one of the huge cisterns where he entered a boat and rowed through a maze of stone pillars, coming out into the landing place of a bath house, where he was un- dressed. He swam in pools of hot and cold water, and was rubbed and oiled, and perfumed with attar of rose.

He might have lost his way in the corridors of the Sacred Palace that filled the end of the Augusteon and the side of the Hippodrome, if his slaves had not guided him. Within the mighty circuit of the walls were prisons and hospitals, baths and chapels and audience halls—antechambers where whispering galleries carried the talk of the courtiers to the ears of listening slaves. Hugh was not aware of this, nor could he talk to anyone except his interpreters and the Franks who served in the imperial guard. But he seems to have been intoxicated by the luxury of the place—in his castle of Vermandois he would have sat in the single wooden hall, smoke-filled and swept by wind gusts, with only trod- den rushes over the earth beneath his feet.

Slaves brought him fresh robes, and trays of sugared fruit, and wine cooled by snow from the height of Olympus; he walked through corridors hung with tapestries woven with pictures of mighty wars—fair women, half-veiled, smiled at him, and the echo of distant music soothed his ears. And so he was brought to the dais where sat a figure in gleaming cloth-of-gold whose head flashed with the fire of massed sapphires and emeralds. It was time, the interpreter whispered to him, to take the oath of allegiance to this monarch, favored of God.

Awe-filled and grateful, Hugh of Vermandois knelt and placed his hands between the hands of Alexis and swore to devote his body to the emperor's service.

He had taken the feudal oath of allegiance. He did not know that the sturdy ax-wielders, the Franks of the emperor's guard, had been sworn into service by this same pledge. He found awaiting him in his chambers that evening new and costly presents.

Godfrey of Bouillon came in different fashion. Lances gleamed in the sunlight for miles along the old Roman road; thousands of mailed horsemen drew rein to gaze in admiration at the imperial city; the tents of the knights and the wide pavilions of the great nobles rose along the crests of the ridges opposite the land walls; war horses were led out in droves to graze in the pasture fields, and the men of iron settled down to rest after their long ride across Europe.

For the first time the Byzantines were confronted by the massed chivalry of the West, and Alexis had to deal with Godfrey.

The information that reached the Sacred Palace was not reassuring. Godfrey, duke of Lower Lorraine, had brought his army safely through Hungary, along the road where Peter and Walter had rioted; he had received the envoys of Byzantium cordially, but he was not submissive. When the imperial guards had tried to shepherd him, he had turned on them, and villages had gone up in smoke. Godfrey, it seemed, was a proud baron who thought that he owed allegiance only to God. Not an easy man to intimidate or to buy. Besides, he refused to take the oath of vassalage to Alexis—would not even set foot within Constantinople. Some of the waifs from the shore, Peter's men, had been talking to him.

All in all, it was a problem for the Sacred Palace—for the logothete of Drome who was chancellor, for the Caesar who was a kind of tribune of the empire, for the sebastocrator who was Alexis's brother, for the great domestic, the commander-in-chief of the army, and most especially for Alexis himself.

They knew that this stubborn baron, Godfrey, had come in open peace, with the cross on his shoulder, but the Byzantines had little faith in other men. Godfrey's army was master of the open country. Meanwhile other armies of crusaders were approaching. Bohemund the Mighty was toiling through the mountains north of Greece—and the Byzantines feared nothing so much as Bohemund and his rapacious Normans from Italy.

The Byzantines did not want the forces of the crusaders to unite under the walls of the city. So they sent a gorgeous embassy to Godfrey's barons, to suggest that the Rhinelanders take ship and cross the strait to the Asian shore.

Godfrey refused. It had been agreed that the leaders of the crusade were to meet at Constantinople.

They celebrated Christmas, each in his way—the Byzantines deeply suspicious of the iron men, and the crusaders wary of the Byzantines. Then Alexis suggested, through other envoys, that the season of cold and rain was at hand and he would be grieved if his son, the unconquered duke of Lower Lorraine, should suffer in his thin tents. So he had prepared quarters in the stone castles and wooden dwellings across the Golden Horn, where his guests and all their following could be sheltered.

To this Godfrey assented. He led his army across the bridge, to the scattered towns along the Bosphorus. Here, if not in Asia, he was separated from the city proper and the highroads by the long crook of the Golden Horn—moreover, he could be watched easily. Alexis saw to it that squadrons of Greek cataphracts barred all the roads between Godfrey and the approaching hosts of the cross. He had agreed to send over all necessary food and stores for the Rhinelanders to purchase.

So matters rested throughout the winter of 1096–1097, in a kind of stalemate, until human nature took a hand.

The imperial cavalry around Constantinople was made up

mostly of mercenaries—bearded Slavs, pagan Betchenaks from the steppes, and Turcoples, who were Turks from near-Asia. Alexis always arranged his complex soldiery so that men never had to serve near their homeland; thus, while the Greek cataphracts—splendid mailed lancers modeled after the old Roman cavalry—guarded the frontiers of the barbarians, the barbarians guarded the Greeks in Constantinople. The Heteria, or imperial guard, was recruited from picked Scandinavians, ex-Vikings, and Saxons—the Foreign Legion of its day, and a formidable one. These were fighting men, loyal to their salt. They remembered very clearly all the old feuds of their homeland, and they eyed Godfrey's crusaders as wolves eye a new pack of hunting dogs.

On their side the Rhinelanders fingered their swords when they found Muhammadans posted around them as a kind of military police. The situation was ominous enough, when a patrol of Betchenaks or Turks cut off a party of the duke's men. These were esquires who had been foraging or more probably plundering out in the country. They were killed, and when the crusaders found their bodies, retribution was in the wind.

The crusaders organized an expedition for revenge. They lay in ambush one night and bagged a patrol of Betchenaks sixty strong. A number of these were put to death and the rest distributed around as captives.

Alexis, a soldier at heart, never overlooked an injury to his men. He retaliated by armed attacks on the Rhinelanders, and the truce became a thing forgotten. Godfrey evacuated his winter quarters, which were first thoroughly pillaged and fired. With castles and huts smoking behind him, he moved back toward the bridge and the walls of Constantinople.

His brother Baldwin—who loved nothing better than a good affair of hand-strokes—seized the bridge and held it against the emperor's Turcoples, while the duke crossed back and took possession of his old camp site by the gates.

Thereupon Alexis sent out Hugh of Vermandois as envoy, to remonstrate with the stubborn duke. Godfrey, however, would not be influenced.

"Thou didst leave thine own country," he said to Hugh hotly, "as a king, with wealth and strong following. Now thou hast come down from that dignity, like a slave. Thou comest hither like a man who hath won a great thing, to bid me do the same."

"We ought to have remained at home," Hugh responded, "and not have meddled in matters here. But since we are here, we have sore need of the emperor's friendship. If we do not gain it, matters will go ill with us."

Several days passed, while Alexis continued to harass the crusaders with his cavalry. On their side the Rhinelanders, believing that some of their lords had been made captive by the Byzantines, stormed at one of the gates in force. They had no siege engines, but they built a fire against the gate, and covered the wall with missiles. Near-panic reigned in the palace nearest that portion of the wall, until the emperor arrived in person, and ordered archers into the towers, and a sortie of cavalry from the adjacent gate of St. Romain. The Byzantine bowmen were instructed to kill off the horses of the crusaders.[1]

Godfrey came, saw the slaughter of the chargers, and commanded a retreat at sunset. Angry and irresolute, he set up his tents again in the plain, only to discover that Alexis had forbidden any food to be sold or brought to the crusaders.

His men foraged at once with a will, but it was then near the end of March, the fields bare, the cattle under cover. Confronted by the hunger of his men, Godfrey had only two alternatives—to withdraw into the country and scatter, or to come to terms with the emperor. He deliberated some days and then sent word to Alexis that he would enter Constantinople, if hostages were sent out by the Byz-

---

[1]Contemporary accounts of this fighting vary greatly. Anna Comnene says that her father attacked and defeated Godfrey's forces. But only a small number were engaged on either side, and only seven Byzantines were killed. The crusaders' chronicles say that Godfrey drove the Emperor's men into the city and devastated the country until Alexis came to terms. Both agree, however, that the horses of the crusaders were slaughtered by the Turkish and Byzantine bowmen. Godfrey's knights and men at arms were not prepared for this, and drew off without engaging in force.

antines. This was done, and Godfrey rode into the city with an escort of his barons.

And that same day he signed an agreement with Alexis. Food was to be supplied to his men at a reasonable price, and they were to be ferried over to the Asian shore. On his part he swore by the cross that he wore to serve Alexis faithfully in the coming war and to yield up to the Byzantine officers all the cities he captured in Asia that had at any time been part of the Byzantine Empire.

Godfrey did not know that this empire had 'once stretched as far as Jerusalem. Nor was he aware that the same day a message reached Constantinople—a message from Bohemund to him, urging him to withdraw from the city and await the arrival of the Normans before agreeing to become the vassal of the emperor. This letter Alexis saw fit to keep in his own hands.

Alexis promised a good deal in return—to furnish the cross-bearers with markets, as far as possible along the line of their march, to safeguard the pilgrims who came after them, and to aid them with Byzantine forces by land and sea.

Upon beholding the magnificence of the duke [a chronicler of the Rhineland relates], who was fitly clad, with his honorable men, in rich mantles of purple and gold bordered with ermine white as snow, with marten and other fur, the Emperor admired him. He greeted the duke with the kiss of peace, sitting in majesty upon his throne; and the duke went down upon his knee to kiss so glorious and so great an Emperor. He spoke to the duke in these words: "I have heard thou art a man to be trusted utterly, the most mighty knight and prince of thy land. And so I take thee for my adopted son, and I place my trust in thee, that through thee my empire may be preserved and mv lands restored.

Whereupon Godfrey was escorted out by the Greek nobles, with slaves bearing wands to beat a way for him through the crowds, and other slaves to carry his gifts behind him—across the white marble court of the Augusteon where distant music echoed.

A month later his army was ferried over to the shore of Asia.

XIII

ALEXIS AND BOHEMUND

SPRING had come to the Bosphorus. Judas tree blos-
soms gleamed in the dark foliage of wild vines.
Streams whispered down the banks, under nodding
aspens. The blue-green water lapped, in a gentle, tideless
motion, against the stained granite foundations of Byzantine pleasure palaces. These had been closed during the
brief winter. Now the owners were flocking back in bright-
cushioned caïques, rowed by slaves.

Pennants fluttered from the long hulks of the imperial
galleys moored against the bank. A courier's boat, oars
swinging in unison, dashed by on its way to the guard-castle
of Hieron. Fishermen in blunt barks made haste to get
their nets out of the way.

Late in the afternoon many gilded caïques made their way
toward the palace point of Constantinople. Here, behind the
sea wall in the quiet garden of the plantain trees, the young
women of the aristocracy were gathering for the first out-of-
doors entertainment of the season.

Their slaves spread robes over the rails of the caïques—
which were exactly like the gondolas of the Venetian canals,
without the cabins—and helped them to set foot on the

marble threshold of the St. Barbara Gate. Tall Varangians on duty stared impassively at the thinly veiled faces of the youthful patricians. Robed eunuchs bowed before them to the gate.

It was their nour of freedom, from attendance at court, from husbands and serious talk. They spread through the grove, scattering into little gay-colored groups—saffron silks from Isfahan mingling with rose-and-blue over tunics from Venetian looms. Nearly all of them were wrapped in the purple girdles that marked their kinship to imperial families.

They had come from palaces in all corners of the empire. Lisping Italian accents responded gayly to throatier Armenian laughter—pure Greek voices chimed musically above the soft melody of trained African singers.

Black slaves from the Sacred Palace—this was an evening wherein Majesty played host, invisible—carried about trays of honey cakes and walnuts and chilled cherries and miniature goblets of scented water. (Majesty, being host, could not be guilty of offering heavy wine, even the white wine of Chios.) But the quick clamor of eager voices swelled higher. Gossip was exchanged, the news of the day whispered —it might have been in this fashion:

What were the latest fabrics brought by Venetian merchants? A new lot of splendid Eastern pearls had been seen at the custom house. Was it true that the strategos of the Bithynian Theme had ornamented his wife's palanquin with pearls? Was she really his wife? She had set a fashion when she had walked in the Augusteon with a small ikon of St. Demetrius at her throat, like a brooch.

Had they seen Mary the Alan that evening? She had appeared for a moment at the sea gallery of the Mangana Palace, up there, overlooking the grove. As if she had been one born in the purple chamber!

She had eyes like a leopard. After all, she had only married that aged Nicephorus—was he still alive in his monastery —because she hoped to place her child in line for the diadem. And when he tricked her she began to look at the Basileus, the emperor. He gave her the Mangana.

Had they heard that more crusaders had come? The lord

Bohemund, this time. Red hair and eyes like a hawk . . . Most certainly he would like Constantinople for himself— had not he tried to invade the empire . . . oh, ages ago— twelve years ago. They say he defeated the Emperor in open battle, but got the worst of it in the end. *Par Dex*, he is protected by the crusader's cross. Still, a man does not change in twelve years, much.

Had they seen the women of the Franks? They wore long trains like the Russians and had their hair *braided!* They wore the cross, too. Perhaps they did not want their husbands so long out of sight. . . . Jerusalem. . . . Even in a horse litter, with a canopy, the road was dusty and almost impossible, even to Antioch. They rode horses, like the knights. . . .

The whispers dwindled and ceased, and the youthful patricians trooped off to go to the candle lighting at the Sancta Sophia. Behind the towers of the Golden Gate the sun had set. Lights gleamed from the embrasures of the high monasteries. Armed servitors tramped through the shadows. The sails of the fishing fleet moved in toward the shore.

Dusk hid the Bosphorus. Colored lanterns bobbed in the bows of the caïques. Byzantium was setting out upon the business of the night. Byzantium, with its whispers and fears, was amusing itself as it had done for a thousand years. Pigeons fluttered slowly into the Judas trees, and the warm air became tranquil, redolent of damp grass and cookery.

Only, from the snow peaks of Asia across the water, came a chill breath, sharp and ominous.

The coming of Bohemund caused a stir in the council halls of Constantinople as well as in the garden fêtes. Many of the imperial generals, including the sebastocrator, had spent two winters in the snow-swept mountains north of Greece when the host of Norman swordsmen under Bohemund's command drove into the empire almost to Thessalonica.[1]

---

[1]Modern Salonika. This invasion of 1081–1085 took place just as Alexis seated himself on the throne by his sudden rebellion against Nicephorus. It was then that Alexis sent funds to the German emperor, Henry IV, who was besieging Pope Gregory VII in Rome, and the plight of his holiness, coupled with a revolt of the

And in the pigeon-holes of the grand logothete's office in the Ministry of War the name of Bohemund appeared in many a record. The Byzantine secret service knew his history. Unlike the illustrious Godfrey of Bouillon, Bohemund was not of ducal descent. His father, Robert Guiscard—Robert the Wily—had been a hard-headed adventurer, carving a dominion out of the sun-warmed mountains of Apulia and Calabria, and the Arab strongholds in Sicily. Bohemund was the first-born of a wife speedily divorced. He had served his years as the right-hand man of Guiscard the conqueror, who favored otherwise his sons by a later wife. At Guiscard's death Bohemund had been left heir to no more than one city. And straightway he had drawn the sword against his half-brother Roger, called the Counter by reason of his habit of counting out and back again the coins in his wallet—the careful and prosperous Roger who had become the chief heir of the Norman dominion.

For some ten years Bohemund had vied with the Counter, always victorious in conflict, and usually defeated in peace. Roger, a religious soul, was favored by the popes, who bestowed upon him the title of duke of Apulia. Bohemund, restless, dissatisfied, remained out of joint with his surroundings. He was still at heart a wanderer, a lover of war, he still dreamed of conquest in the east. He held stubbornly to his seaports, Bari, Taranto, from which galleons cruised to the Golden Horn and the unknown cities of Islam. He would not marry or settle himself in any one place. Like his ancestors the Vikings, he had a hunger for distant lands and a moody contempt of home.

And at more than forty years of age he turned his back on all the wrangling of southern Italy with a single gesture. Coming out of his tent before Amalfi—Roger and he were laying siege to Amalfi—he cut his cloak into strips and placed the first cross on his own shoulder. And his men cried out with him, "God wills it."

Norman vassals in southern Italy, induced Robert Guiscard—Bohemund's father—to return to Italy, reluctantly leaving the command of the invading army to Bohemund. When Alexis was able at last to take the field against the Normans, they were forced to withdraw after stubborn fighting. Neither Alexis nor Bohemund ever forgot this struggle for mastery.

And he did not lack for followers. Youthful Tancred, the finest sword of the Normans, took the cross with him, Richard of the Principate and his brother Rainulf, and Girard, bishop of Ariano—more than five hundred belted knights assembled around the crimson banner of Bohemund, leaving Roger the Counter disconsolate and almost unattended at Amalfi. A new road opened before the adventurer. He would go a-Viking. And go he did, to Constantinople, having first assured himself through ambassadors that Alexis would keep the truce with him. Byzantine spies watched his every move, and Byzantine brains mused over his advent. But Bohemund the Mighty could play a part almost as well as they.

And Bohemund rode ahead of his people into the Golden Gate with only ten knights as escort. Anna Comnene, beholding him for the first time, was struck by his aspect. Years later she drew his portrait in the pages of her history:

Such a man had never been seen before in the lands of the Romans, for he was marvellous to the sight. Tall he was, overtopping the tallest by a cubit—slender in the waist and loins, with wide shoulders and a deep chest and powerful arms. It might be said of him that he measured to the standard of Polyclitus. He had strong hands, and a full, muscular throat and he stood firmly poised on his feet, stooping a little.

His hair looked yellow-red and did not hang down upon his shoulders like that of the other barbarians, for the man was not too vain of his hair to cut it short above the ears. His face likewise was smooth-shaven. His clear blue eyes betokened both spirit and dignity, as did his nostrils.

A peculiar charm hung about this man, and yet there was something horrible in him. For in the size of his body and the glance of his eye, methinks, he revealed power and savagery. Even his laughter sounded like snorting. His wit served to show him a way out of every crisis. In talk he was well informed, and the answers he gave were decisive.

Such was the man who knelt before Alexis. If Bohemund could play the ideal guest, the emperor could be a perfect host. He questioned the tall Norman cheerfully about his journey, and even joked with him about that other journey a dozen years ago when they had faced each other on the field of battle.

"I was certainly your enemy at that time," Bohemund answered calmly, "but now I come of my own will as your Majesty's friend."

Alexis sounded him deftly as to whether he would object to taking the oath Godfrey had taken. Bohemund assented at once.

The following day the dreaded guest placed his hands within the hands of Alexis and swore fealty to him. Thereupon Bohemund was led away, through the Sacred Palace. The doors of a chamber were thrown open suddenly before him, and he gazed upon piles of rich garments, and gold and silver vessels. The tall Norman contemplated the treasure with appraising eyes—he was almost penniless and he had a small army to maintain.

"If that wealth were mine," he observed, "I should have conquered broad lands before now."

He was told that the emperor had bestowed these gifts upon him. Thanking the officers who escorted him, he refused them. But Alexis, who knew his guest, had them sent to his apartment, and Bohemund kept them.

Alexis also sent quantities of cooked and uncooked meats, and these Bohemund would not touch until the servitors had eaten of them.

For this man [the Princess Anna wrote of him] was cunning and swift to suspect others. Moody and sad in mind, he had left his country where he possessed no lands to worship, as he said, at the Holy Sepulcher; yet he was in need of everything. He meant, really, to follow in his father's footsteps and to conquer, if he could, an empire in the east.

XIV

THE OATH OF THE BARONS

ALEXIS was quick to avail himself of his opportunity. These crusaders, thronging unbidden out of the West, had caused him anxiety enough. Now he saw that the torrent would not sweep away his city. And he meant to harness the torrent, to do some very useful work for Byzantium.

He had been uncertain when Peter's swarm had infested the frontier. He had given orders to make Hugh of Vermandois captive at once—although in silken bonds. But now, in April, he was able to judge the leaders of the crusade for himself. And the Basileus was a keen judge of men. He discovered that they were gentle men who had sworn an oath before all Europe to march to Jerusalem.

The emperor dealt with his powerful guests in simple but adroit fashion. He kept them separated, received them one at a time, gave them each—after they had pledged loyalty to him—an unexpected and welcome amount of gold. And then he transported each one across the strait to the Asiatic shore before another came on the scene. Once there, they were dependent altogether upon his shipments of food.

The one thing Alexis had dreaded was that they would unite before Constantinople—where quarreling might grow into open war. The emperor's real concern was for his city. He was Byzantine to the very blood, apostolic head of the Greek Church, as the pope was of the Latin. And the crusade could aid hard-pressed Byzantium by recovering the lost provinces of Asia Minor. To this end Alexis now labored without sparing himself.

It was a drain on his resources to feed the multitudes, but he managed it, and the cross-bearers paid for the food. It outraged the fastidious Byzantine patricians when groups of chieftains from the uncultured West loitered about the corridors of the palaces, arguing and asking questions, but Alexis never failed in courtesy. The diplomacy of elder Asia played host to the naïve youths of the new world. Alexis kept Bohemund by him, apart from the others, as a go-between, and because he wanted to weigh the Norman's motives—no easy matter. And Bohemund seconded him admirably.

Above all the emperor wished to have the barons take oath publicly to be faithful to him. If they did so as a body—the newcomers and the lesser lords—the world would know of their pledge. And he felt sure that these men could be relied upon to keep it. So an hour was appointed for the public assembly.

And the emperor prepared for the occasion with some care. First he curtailed the crusaders' supplies, and when Godfrey protested he sent over fresh largesse of gold byzants for the leaders, and doles of copper tartarons for the poor; at the same time imperial heralds summoned all the barons to the audience. They came in groups, Flemings, Lorrainers, French, and Normans—tall men in sweeping, fur-edged mantles. They found the Basileus seated in an outer court, his gilt chair in advance of the gorgeous bevy of Byzantine grandees, with two sword-bearers on either hand. Behind the courtiers stretched the half circle of giant warriors in silvered breast-plates and scarlet cloaks, the Immortals of the Varangian guard.

One by one the barons and knights of the cross advanced and knelt to kiss the emperor's knee, and to acknowledge their assent to the oath taken by Godfrey and Bohemund. "Knights so sturdy and daring," cried a chronicler of the crusade, "why did they take this oath of vassalage? Because they were constrained to it."

The day, however, was not to pass without its comedy. Alexis had instructed his guards to relax the rigid etiquette of the Byzantine court. The distinguished visitors were not to be grasped by the arms when they approached him, and they were to be allowed to move about as they wished. The emperor even rose himself at the end of the ceremony and stood among them in talk. As he did so, one of them, Robert, count of Paris, plumped himself down in the vacated throne chair.

This slight to majesty caused a stir among the Byzantines. But the stalwart crusader remained seated at ease, staring at the muttering throngs. Count Baldwin, Godfrey's brother, went up to him, took him by the hand, and pulled him to his feet.

"That was ill done," Baldwin exclaimed angrily. "'Tis not the custom of these emperors to allow their own nobles to sit near them, and thou art bound to observe the custom of the country."

The offending count glanced at Alexis grimly and muttered: "Why doth a good-for-naught like that keep valiant captains standing?"

Alexis caught the mutter, without understanding the words, and called an interpreter over to him, who repeated what Robert of Paris[1] had said. The emperor did nothing at the time, but when his visitors were making their farewells he summoned the crusader who had sat in the throne.

"Who art thou, and of what lineage?" he asked, through the interpreter.

"I am a Frank of the purest nobility," responded the offender, "and I know this much—in the country from which

---

[1]This incident and character inspired one of Scott's novels—*Count Robert of Paris*. We cannot be certain of the name of the crusader who became tired of standing and sat down in a throne. But the Princess Anna says he was a French count, and adds that he died with forty of his men at Doryleum. Bishop Anselm gives us the names of five nobles slain at Doryleum, of whom Robert of Paris is the first mentioned, and almost the only one who could have been a French count.

I come there is a crossroads, and at this crossroads stands an old shrine. Everyone who wishes to fight in single combat goes to the shrine, accoutered and ready, and prays to God while he waits in expectation of meeting a man who will dare to fight with him. At this crossroads I also have waited long, hoping for a fit antagonist, but never did one appear who dared to draw weapons with me."

"If you did not then find a fight," Alexis responded quietly, "you will have your fill of it now with the Turks. But I advise you not to place yourself in the front or rear ranks when that time comes; remain in the center of the lines. I have had a long experience in meeting the Turks and I know their method of fighting."

And he turned to the listening barons, warning them that warfare in Asia was not the combat they were accustomed to. They would have heavy baggage trains with them, and these must be guarded at all times. And the Turks had a habit of attacking when they were least expected. If defeated, they should not be pursued recklessly, because they liked nothing better than to draw the pursuers into a trap. So the talk drifted away from the defiant Robert.

The crusaders, eager enough to be on the road, agreed to undertake first the capture of the nearest Turkish citadel, the walled town of Nicea, not four days' march from their present camp—the same town that Peter's bands had seen, at the end of a weed-filled lake.

Within a few days they struck the tents and loaded the wagons. Priests lifted high the crucifix, and women knelt in prayer. Horses were led in from pasture, saddled and mounted. Bands of men at arms went on ahead with axes to clear the road through the forest for the multitude. Godfrey's standard was lifted, and Hugh of Vermandois, Robert of Flanders, and Baldwin followed—some embarking in boats to go by way of the lake.

With them went Tancred and Richard of the Principate, who had slipped away from Constantinople with most of Bohemund's men, without taking the oath. Soon the camps along the Bosphorus and the Marmora were occupied only by the sick. The rest—everyone who could walk or find a seat on the wagons—made their way through the deserted hills that marked the frontier. And on the far side of the ravines they came upon heaps of rag-covered bones, the remains of Peter's crusade.

Alexis prepared to follow them up as he had promised. Keeping Bohemund with him as liaison officer, he assembled his army in readiness to cross the strait and watch events. Meanwhile he made certain preparations, which he confided to Manuel Butumites, that sagacious general. Butumites was to approach Nicea and enter into communication with the Turkish garrison. He was authorized to offer the Muhammadans security of life and Alexis's protection if they surrendered to the Byzantine officers. And he was to warn them that they would be plundered and slaughtered if the crusaders entered their walls. Butumites, it seems, was quite adept in negotiations of this delicate nature.

XV

THE MARCH OF THE PROVENÇALS

RAYMOND, lord of Toulouse, had been a long time on the road from the Pyrenees. He was eager to be early in the field, and he rode with Adhemar, the bishop of Le Puy—Adhemar who had been chosen by the pope to lead the crusade, whose stout hand itched to hold a sword instead of his bishop's crook. The size of their host held them back. Moreover, Raymond's Provençals showed an inclination to linger as well as to fight upon the way.

They crossed France safely, and threaded through the mountains of what is now Switzerland. They reached Venice with winter at hand, but Raymond pushed on stubbornly. Either he was misled, or he thought he could get through by following the shore of the Adriatic down. In any case he soon lost his way among the mountain barriers of the Dalmatian coast.

For the rest of the winter he vanished from the map. And what there befell him has been written down by another Raymond, his chaplain, an ardent soul devoted to his lord.

I have taken it upon myself [the chronicler explains] to write not of the others, but of the Count and the bishop of Puy and the army that followed them.

We made our way into Sclavonia, enduring many losses because it was winter by then. Sclavonia is such a barren land, both pathless and mountainous, that we saw neither birds nor beasts for thrice seven days. The people of the country hereabouts were so brutish and stupid that they would neither trade with us nor act as guides. Fleeing from their villages and fortified places they hung around us, setting upon and slaying like cattle the weak and the poor and the sick who followed behind our army owing to their infirmity—as if *they* had done any harm!

Our men of arms could not easily pursue the lightly clad brigands who knew all the ways through the thick woods and into the heights. They could only endure, unable to fight with these people or to pass on without fighting.

A daring act of the Count must be mentioned. He was cut off for some time with several of his men by the Sclavs. He made a charge, and took six of them prisoner. When, on this account, the other Sclavs thronged in on him savagely, forcing him to ride back to the army, he commanded that the eyes of some of the captives be torn out, and the feet of others cut off and the noses and hands of the rest mutilated. So the pursuers were delayed by sight of the captives, and by grieving at their suffering, while the Count was able to escape unharmed with his companions. And in this way, by God's mercy, he was delivered from the agony of death and the hazard of that place.

In truth it is not easy to tell all that the bravery and the craft of the Count did for us. Because we were in Sclavonia almost forty days during which we wandered through low-hanging clouds[1] so dense that we were able to feel them and often to push them away from us as we moved. In this murk the Count was fighting steadily at the rear, protecting his people. He was never first, but always last to take to shelter. Some of the men went into camp at midday, others at vespers, but the Count often came in when the night was half done, or at cock-crow.

At last by God's pity and the exertion of the Count, and the

---

[1]It must be remembered that these men, some thirty thousand of them, were passing through an utterly strange country, without maps or adequate transport. Few roads existed, and the natives were ignorant enough to look upon them as enemies. They had no means of communication with the outside world, and the lot of them owed their lives to the personal exertions of Count Raymond.

advice of the bishop, the army crossed this country without losing a man by starvation or in open fighting. Wherefore, I bear witness, God wanted our army to cross that country. . . .

After many perils of hardships we came to Skudar and to the king of the Sclavs.

With him the Count swore brotherhood, giving him payment of various kind, so that the army could safely seek out and buy the necessities of life. But this was no more than a vain hope. Instead of enjoying peace we endured penance, because at this opportunity the Sclavs, rampaging as usual, killed us and seized what they could from the unarmed. For our part we sought not vengeance, only a way out. That is all about Sclavonia.

We reached Durazzo. We believed now that we were at home, thinking that the emperor Alexis and his henchmen were our brothers and allies. Yet in truth they also rose up like lions and attacked us, peaceful men intent on anything but arms.

They cut us down in hidden places; they pilfered what they could from us in the forests and in villages out of sight of the camp, every night. And while they raged like this, their emperor pledged peace. And under pretense of peace they killed Rainard and mortally wounded his brother Peter—most noble princes, both of them. Although we could have avenged our injuries, we did not, but kept on our journey instead. Along the road we had letters from this emperor, full of peace and brotherhood. This was no more than windy words. For before and behind, to right and to left, there lay in wait for us Turks, Kumanians, Betchenaks, and Bulgars.

One day when we had halted in a valley near the sea, the bishop of Puy[1] who had wandered out a way to find a pleasant resting spot was taken captive by Betchenaks. They pulled him down from his mule, robbed him and struck him a sore blow in the head. Yet, by God's mercy, his life was preserved. For one of the Betchenaks who was trying to get gold out of him protected him from the rest.

Meanwhile the alarm was sounded in the camp, and, thanks to the hesitation of his enemies and the impetuosity of his friends, he was rescued.

When we had passed through treachery of this sort to a certain castle that they called Bucinat, the Count discovered that the Betchenaks wished to attack our army in the heights of the mountains. He hid himself with some men and rode out upon the Betchenaks, and after several were slain, the rest fled. All this time mild

---

[1]Adhemar, the papal legate.

letters came from the emperor to us, while on every side the enemy, his men, caused us grief.

When at last we reached Thessalonica, the bishop fell ill and remained behind there with a few men. After this we came to a certain town called Russa. Here the people were plainly disposed to do us injury and our accustomed forbearance gave way. So, seizing our arms and breaking through the outer wall, we took a great spoil and forced the surrender of the town. Then, having carried our standards in, we shouted "*Toulouse !*" which was the war shout of the Count, and we withdrew. We came to another town, Rodosto by name. When soldiers of the emperor there wished to revenge themselves upon us, we killed a good many of them and took some plunder. Here also our envoys, who had been sent ahead to the emperor, rejoined us. Having accepted gifts from the emperor, they swore that only good awaited us at his hand.

What more? They—and the envoys of the emperor who accompanied them—urged us that the Count should journey swiftly to the emperor alone, with only a few unarmed men, leaving his army behind. For they informed us that Bohemund and the Duke of Lorraine and the Count of Flanders and other princes besought this of him, that he should hurry to consult with the emperor.

Moreover, they reported that a battle was at hand, and with a man of such power as the Count absent, things might go badly. And so the Count should hasten with a few men, in order to have everything arranged and nothing left to delay when the army should come up. At length the Count was convinced of all this. And in this manner, unarmed, he went to Constantinople.

So far all that happened beside me, the writer, was gladsome and prosperous; but now calamity weighed upon us, so that it grieves me to begin the telling. And where shall I begin? With the trickery of the emperor? Or the cowardly flight and unlooked-for desperation of our army? Or the tale of the death of so many princes? Nay, if anyone wishes to know all of this, he must ask of others, not of me![1]

Only of one memorable thing I shall speak. When our men were preparing to fly from the camp, and to desert their comrades and

---

[1]Count Raymond had no sooner left his men than the Byzantine army of observation made what might be called a demonstration in force. A sizable battle was in progress, when numbers of the Provençals fled. The Byzantines regained Rodosto. Whether Alexis ordered this is uncertain. The Byzantines were retaliating for the widespread pillaging of the Provençals. Raymond the chronicler is honest enough in his testimony, but he is making out as strong a case as he can for his countrymen.

all the supplies they had brought hither with such pains, shame and penance led them to return. This should be said.

Most honorably was the Count greeted by the emperor and his princes. The emperor then required of him the homage and oath that the other princes had sworn.

"I have not come hither," the Count responded, "to make another man my master, or to fight for another than Him for whom I left my country and all my possessions. However, if the emperor will go to Jerusalem with his army, I will place myself and my men and goods in his hands."

But the emperor excused himself from taking the road, saying, "The barbarian races would swarm over the empire, if we went on with the pilgrims."

And now, after the audience, the Count heard of the slaying of his men and their flight. He believed himself to have been deceived, and he sent noblemen of our army to accuse the emperor of treachery. But Alexis said:

"It is not known to us that your men were despoiled in our dominion, while on the other hand our men have endured many injuries. The Count hath suffered no wrong. Only, the army of the Count took to flight at sight of the imperial soldiers, while it was pillaging the towns in its accustomed manner. Nevertheless, satisfaction shall be given the Count."

And he gave Bohemund as hostage for this satisfaction. They came to trial about it. . . .

Meanwhile our army arrived at Constantinople, and our bishop who had remained behind followed it. Alexis asked and asked again for homage from the Count, as the other princes had given their pledge. On the other hand the Count was planning eagerly to avenge the injury to his men, and wipe out the disgrace inflicted upon himself. But the Duke of Lorraine and the Count of Flanders and other princes discouraged him from this, saying: "It is folly to fight with Christians, when the Turks are threatening."

Bohemund actually swore that he would aid the emperor if the Count attempted anything against him, or if he delayed longer in taking the oath and doing homage. And so the Count, at the advice of his own men, swore that he would not attempt anything against the life or honor of Alexis—himself, or through any other.

When he was asked for homage, he replied that he would not give it—though he lost his head thereby. Because of this, Alexis gave him little largesse.

And so we crossed the sea and arrived without mishap at Nicea.

Alexis went to some pains to conciliate the old Provençal. Until discouraged by the others, Raymond in a bitter mood had urged that they all unite to besiege Constantinople. At this time the various divisions were making ready to march to Nicea, and the leaders were impatient of delay. Moreover, they had all sworn allegiance to Alexis to help the common cause. Although they sympathized with Raymond's troubles, they were provoked because he refused stubbornly to take the step they had taken. Bohemund especially felt angry.

Noticing this, Alexis kept the count of Toulouse near him as long as possible—until the energetic Norman had departed with a convoy of supplies. The Basileus called the count to his side every day, and confided in him that he—the emperor —distrusted Bohemund. The mighty Norman, he said, was an avaricious soul, at heart an enemy of the Byzantine empire and a breaker of promises. While the noble count of Toulouse was a man of faith, who would not turn his hand against a friend. He advised the count of Toulouse to watch Bohemund's doings closely.

Raymond responded impatiently that he had no reason to trust the Norman, and he would do what was fitting. Whereupon he took leave of the emperor and hastened after his men, rather mixed in his mind.

Within a day or two the last great contingents of the crusade arrived at Constantinople, the forces of the sluggish Robert, duke of Normandy, and the high-born but indolent Stephen, count of Meaux, Brie, Blois, and Chartres. They had lagged through Italy, and Robert Short Breeches had chosen to winter in the pleasant castles of Apulia rather than to cross the windy Adriatic in that season. When he did sail his ill luck pursued him, and a large vessel sank with four hundred souls aboard. Eventually he found himself on the road taken first by Hugh, and then by the Normans of Italy and Raymond—through Thessalonica, the modern Salonika, and the mountain passes to Rodosto.

With the last army came another chronicler, the simple priest, Fulcher of Chartres, who was all amazed at sight of the towered walls and the multitudes going in and out of the great city.

Into this city [Fulcher explains] we were not permitted to go, because it did not please the emperor—for he feared lest, by chance, we should do some harm. He only permitted five or six of the better sort to enter each hour, to pray in the churches.

Oh, what a noble and beautiful city! How many monasteries, how many palaces are in it, all marvelously well built. How many extraordinary things to be seen, even in the streets and squares. It would be tiresome to relate what quantities of gold, silver, varied vestments and sacred relics are there. All things needed by men are brought hither incessantly by boats. I should say that more than twenty thousand eunuchs find habitation there.

Fulcher's lord, the count of Blois, was no less delighted, although for other reasons. These are set forth in the first of his eloquent letters to his wife:

Count Stephen to his most sweet friend, the Countess Adele, his wife: all the affection that her thoughts hold good or joyful.

Know to thy delight that I made my way to Asia in all bodily honor and health. I was careful to send to thee by letter the account of my journey to Constantinople, but in case any misfortune should have befallen that courier, I write thee again these tidings.

We arrived at the city of Constantinople with great joy, by God's will. In truth the Emperor received me most honorably and with all dignity, as if I had been his son, and bestowed upon me most ample and costly gifts; and in all the army of God there is no duke or count or any other person whom he cherishes or favors more than me. In truth, I say to thee, my beloved, there is not such another man as he living under heaven. He gave with his own hand great largesse to our princes, and relieved the soldiers with gifts, and revived the poor with alms. In truth, after ten days in which he kept me by him constantly, I withdrew from him as from a father.

Then, by God's grace, we hastened toward the great city of Nicea. And Nicea, my beloved, hath more than three hundred high towers, and is shut in by marvellous walls. We found that the army had labored for four weeks in a daring struggle with the Turks in Nicea. . . .

XVI

THE KNEELING TOWER

HE first blow fell on a fair morning in mid-May of that year 1097, when Count Raymond was setting up his camp in the long valley surrounded by pine ridges. He had just joined the other crusaders, by the lake, before the yellow walls of Nicea.

Behind the siege lines of the crusaders, out of harm's way, horse herds grazed; boys carried water jars, and women moved about the tables. Black-robed monks gathered in the shade of the cypresses after morning prayer. Some of them sat on the grave stones of the Muhammadan cemetery, under the cypress grove.

Raymond of Toulouse rode in from the court at Constantinople. With his banner, his priest, and his liegemen, he turned off the rutted road into the trampled fields. His pack animals were led in, and his jack-men busied themselves with ropes and stakes, setting up the pavilions. Others started to lead away the horses.

The hot sun and good wine loosened Provençal tongues. Through the clamor penetrated distant cries, half heard. Some of the men at arms turned idly, to shade their eyes and gaze under the sun. They noticed lines of horsemen moving down from the wooded heights toward the road, but they could not make out who the horsemen were. A horn resounded near at hand, and the talk dwindled to silence. Raymond looked at the oncoming riders trotting through dust clouds. "Sire," a voice rang out, "God aid thee!"

The men riding down the hill were Turks—the same cavalry that had butchered the Hermit's followers like sheep. They formed the advance of a strong column that intended to push its way into Nicea, to strengthen the garrison.

They chose Raymond's sector of the crusaders' circle because this had been left unguarded until the Provençal army came up. Or perhaps they headed this way because they had noticed the commotion when the count rode in. Swiftly they came on, hoping to throw the whole Christian host into confusion—they remembered Peter's horde with contempt. And they had galloped halfway to the camp when the first Provençals got to horse.

The Turks were surprised in their turn. Gascons, Catalans, and French reached for their weapons and came out in a swarm, without armor, some without saddles—the men on foot clinging to the stirrups of the riders, stumbling in their haste. They seized the first weapon and the first horse to hand and raced their nearest comrades to the onset. No frantic peasants these, but hardheaded fighters from the frontier of the Pyrenees.

Long swords and battle maces swinging in powerful arms, they crashed into the Muhammadans in the open fields. Their heavier chargers rode down the lighter steeds of the Turks, and the long swords slashed through the thin shields and steel-mesh armor. The Turks broke and raced for the hills, and the Provençals yelled their exultation, and did their best to pursue.

This had been a skirmish. Later in the day the Turkish cavalry came on again in force. Meanwhile, contingents from all the other camps thronged to Raymond's standard when the word went around that the Turks had shown themselves. Normans, Rhinelanders, Flemings, and the rest—they had marched for many a weary month for just this moment, and they volunteered their services eagerly. They had scant discipline, these swordsmen of the cross, but they had stout hearts and they used their spurs when the green standards of Islam emerged from the heights again.

Again the charge of the Turks was met by a countercharge, and the Turks broke. Led by Raymond and the burly bishop, Adhemar, the crusaders pursued until evening. They returned singing, with severed heads ornamenting their lance points. Some of these heads they tossed over the wall of Nicea by way of encouragement to the garrison. The day had begun well, and it ended splendidly.

The Muhammadan army of relief withdrew, after getting word in to Nicea that the garrison must do as it thought best. It could not be aided from without. The encounter had cheered the crusaders mightily, and astonished the Turks, but it did not weaken the walls of the besieged city.

And these walls baffled the crusaders. Hitherto the fighters from the West had had to deal with low earth or wooden ramparts. Sometimes they had faced a single wall of stone. They were accustomed to forcing their way into small gate towers, or the single massive tower of an inner keep. But here——

And Nicea, my beloved, is shut in by marvellous walls [the eloquent Stephen wrote to his wife Adele] so when our good princes saw Nicea so turreted, as I have said, they labored to build towers of wood and other siege engines.

Nicea had been a stronghold of the Romans, and the solid masonry six feet thick had hardened to the consistency of stone. One quarter of the walls fronted the lake, and here—lacking boats—the crusaders could do nothing. From one edge of the lake to the other a moat circled the fortification. Behind the moat rose a narrow wall, about twice the height of a man, with small towers. About fifteen paces behind this stood the main defense, the great wall with more than a hundred towers. Javelin and stone-casters mounted upon these could sweep the outer wall, and the space beyond the

THE LAND WALLS OF CONSTANTINOPLE

Godfrey first pitched his camp opposite this point. The moat, half filled up, is still distinct in the foreground. There was originally a parapet at its inner edge. Notice the double wall, with the great towers of the inner wall built within arrow shot of each other. This wall was attacked by Arabs, Bulgars, and Huns in vain.

THE NARRATIVE OF ALBERTUS AQUENSIS

A Thirteenth Century manuscript of the crusades. This
particular section deals with the battle of Ascalon.

REPRODUCED FROM THE MSS. VAT. LAT. 1999, OF THE APOSTOLIC
LIBRARY, IN THE VATICAN CITY

moat. More than that, the towers were close enough together for the engines and the bowmen to cover the ground between them with a deadly cross-fire.[1]

It was hopeless to think of storming this double line of defense. The men of the cross were willing enough, and they experimented at the cost of a good many lives. Some of them filled in the moat and built *petraria*—stone-casters—to batter down the outer barrier. Little damage was done to the iron-like masonry.

The impetuous Raymond set to work to build a line of mantlets—screens woven out of aspens and willows, to shield his crossbowmen and engineers. Then he put together a tortoise, a squat shed open along the ground. The tortoise was moved up—over the filled-in moat—against the tower at the eastern corner of the city.

This had suffered in a previous siege, and leaned out over its crumbling base. The Byzantines had christened it the Kneeling Tower, and Raymond's tortoise gnawed at it. While his archers on the summit of the tortoise engaged the defenders of the Kneeling Tower, his men in the maw of the tower wielded picks against the masonry—propping up the mass overhead on wooden beams as they penetrated through.

But his effort failed. The tower came down one evening, when no attack could be made, and by daylight the Turks had built up the ruin with fresh stonework.

The worst obstacle was the lake. The Turks were able to bring in supplies at will on their boats, and to come and go over the water. Until this could be stopped nothing would be gained by blockading the city. The leaders of the crusaders met together in council, to discuss the situation, and sent an

---

[1]The greater part of the wall of Nicea is standing to-day. It was built on the same plan and out of much the same materials as the great wall of Constantinople, portions of which are almost intact after twelve centuries of sieges and demolition for building material. The present writer in examining these walls was struck by the placing of the towers. An archer standing on the summit of one tower could easily shoot to the next, or to the space outside the forty-foot moat. The towers project beyond the line of the wall, and have embrasures at the side that command every inch of ground outside the wall. Count Stephen did not exaggerate very much— there were 246 towers at Nicea.

envoy to Alexis to request him to bring ships through from the sea to the lake, and men to work them.

Alexis had been waiting for this request. He was well aware of the strength of the walls of Nicea, and he had seen the inexperience of the crusaders at siege operations. Moreover, his spies kept him informed of all that happened, inside as well as outside the walls.

He wanted Nicea. The city was the link between Asia and Constantinople—only ten years before a most important part of the Byzantine Empire, with its churches hallowed by antiquity, now converted into mosques. But he wanted Nicea unravaged, and he had a pretty clear idea of what would happen if the crusaders got loose inside it. They believed that Nicea was the first citadel of paynimry, the portal of Mahound, the outpost of Anti-Christ.

Besides, Alexis was balancing with the skill of an athlete between the crusaders and the Turks. He saw very clearly that the men of the cross had no idea of the obstacles ahead of them, or of the great powers that lay dormant within Asia. An experienced soldier himself, he had calculated with some nicety just how far they would penetrate into Asia. And the farther they went, the fewer would return. Whereas the Turks would always be there—just outside his frontier.

Above all things, Alexis wished to avoid being drawn into a religious war with Islam. In his cold and wearied spirit there burned no fire of fanaticism, and he dreaded the flare-up of a *jihad*, a holy war, in Asia. So far he had managed to keep on friendly terms with the sultans, while he played the *deus ex machina* to the crusaders. And now he set about gaining Nicea for himself, without antagonizing either the Turks or the men of the cross. Quite a task for an ordinary mind, but a simple enough matter for the Basileus of Byzantium.

He complied with the request of the barons most promptly —he had already got together a fleet of shallow draught vessels at Civitote. In a day or two these were hauled through the roads and marshes to the lake, by workmen and oxen. He withdrew a strong force of Turcoples from Europe and put them in the boats, with plenty of banners, trumpets, and kettledrums. He gave them for stage manager and commander Manuel Butumites, whose agents had been in and out of Nicea urging the leaders of the Turks to surrender.

Butumites reported that the Turks were wavering after the defeat of the relieving army, but a good demonstration would be necessary.

Alexis delved into his bag of tricks—he had a whole arsenal at Constantinople full of military odds and ends, including the dreaded Greek fire that burned upon water and could not be quenched. The emperor selected an officer, a man with his wits about him, born of a Turkish slave—Taticius by name, and grand primicerius by rank. He gave Taticius a small detachment of artillerists and a battery of rapid-fire *ballistae* that shot heavy iron arrows with great force. And he instructed Taticius carefully in what he was to do.

The grand primicerius first reported to Butumites, then went to offer his services to Raymond of Toulouse, opposite the Kneeling Tower. He explained to Raymond what must be done, and the count agreed. The next day Taticius set up palisades and his *ballistae*, and sprayed the Kneeling Tower with iron missiles, while his men and the Provençals attacked in close order. The other barons worked their catapults and crossbows, and the Turks found the parapet of the wall unhealthy. The Kneeling Tower almost fell.

At the same time out on the lake Butumites appeared with his flotilla, banners fluttering and drums beating. This discouraged the Turks, who consented to let the Asiatic-born officer and his Turkish mercenaries in at the water gate to talk things over. Butumites harangued them—promised safe conduct for the wives and family of the great sultan, the Red Lion, who were then in Nicea—showed the commanders a written agreement that they would be allowed to go out with their weapons and property and men, and even be rewarded by the emperor. The document was signed and sealed with a gold seal. The Turks of Nicea agreed that this was much the best thing to do. Butumites scribbled a note to Taticius:

We have the game in our hands. Now you must assault the walls. Do not let the Franks know the situation, but tell them to circle the walls and attack at sunrise.

Princess Anna, who has recorded this letter, adds clearly enough:

This was so that the Franks[1] would believe that Butumites had taken the city by assault, and drama of treachery prepared by the Emperor would be kept secret.

The drama was staged without a hitch. The next morning the crusaders, swarming to the attack, beheld—after a few moments' fighting—the banners and standards of Byzantium displayed along the wall. Nicea had fallen, to the hand of Butumites.

While the men of the cross went back to their tents to rejoice, Butumites did a number of things. He passed most of the Turkish warriors safely out of the city by the lake, and with them the family of the sultan. Some of the Muhammadans elected to join the imperial army, and the others were dismissed with presents and escorted around the crusaders. Butumites took possession of the keys of the gate by the Kneeling Tower—the others had been walled up during the siege. And he kept the crusaders out, except for bands of ten, who were allowed in to worship at the churches.

Butumites was appointed duke of Nicea by Alexis. The emperor's worst moment came when the leaders of the host saw that Nicea would be closed to them. The victory over the Turks was their work; they had been promised the spoiling of the city—at least, the gold and silver and horses—and their anger increased daily. If they had not thought that Butumites won the city by assault from the lake, the grand primicerius and new duke of Nicea would have had a fresh siege on his hands.

Still, Alexis was equal to the occasion. He promised the leaders that the equivalent of the spoil would be paid them, at his own hand. And he added that to receive it, and to bid farewell to him, they should all ride back to his court. And it

---

[1] The crusaders. As most of them spoke northern French, the Asiatics called all the cross-bearers Franks.

would be well if they made good their oath to him, by seeing
to it that their comrades who had not taken the oath did so
on this pleasant occasion.

Raymond would not go. Tancred, the other recalcitrant,
went reluctantly, impressed by the treasure poured out upon
the others. The prim little Princess Anna noticed him:

A youth of haughty spirit. He said he owed fidelity only to
Bohemund. When his companions and the Emperor's kinsmen
urged him to take the oath, he feigned indifference, as it were,
and glanced at the huge pavilion in front of which the Emperor was
sitting. "If you will give me this tent full of money," he said,
"then I also will take the oath."

George Palaeologus could not endure Tancred's conceit, and
turned away from him in contempt. Whereat Tancred, who was
always very hasty with his sword, rushed at him. The Emperor,
observing it, rose from his throne and came between them. Bohemund likewise restrained him, saying, "It is not fitting to act thus
to a kinsman of the Emperor."

Then Tancred, ashamed of bearing himself like a drunken man,
yielded to Bohemund, and took the oath.

When all of them had taken leave of the Emperor, he detailed
Taticius to accompany them, with his detachment, partly to assist
them and partly to secure the towns from them—if God allowed
them to capture any. Then the Franks set out on the road to Antioch, and the Emperor ordered Butumites to hire all who remained
behind, the sick and the well, and keep them to garrison Nicea.

One other man did not go to court that day. Count Stephen
explained the reason to his wife, Adele:

All our princes except me and the Count of St. Gilles [Raymond]
hastened away to the island which is in the sea and where the
Emperor was, to congratulate him on such a great victory. He
received them, almost all, with affection, and when he heard I had
stayed behind at the city, lest the Turks come and beset it, he was
truly delighted, esteeming it more than if I had brought him a
mountain of gold. And this great emperor bestowed on the knights
things like precious stones, gold and silver, mantles and horses....

I tell thee, my beloved, that from Nicea we shall march to
Jerusalem in five times seven days, unless Antioch withstands us.
Farewell.

XVII

DORYLEUM

BOHEMUND THE MIGHTY rode across a little river and cast invisible shackles from his arms. The bridge was a Roman bridge of heavy stone, worn by the floods and trampling of a thousand years. But it might have been the Rubicon—except that Bohemund was riding out of an empire, not into one.

On the far side the tall Norman became another man. For two months he had watched and listened, weighing chances and judging men. Before Alexis he had played the suppliant, to get money for his followers; and he had strained every nerve to keep his turbulent swordsmen from shedding blood in Byzantium. He had seen at once that the crusaders must have Alexis's support—the guidance and the provender of the Byzantines, and Alexis behind them to keep open the road to Constantinople if they were not to be cut off from all aid and communication.

Like Alexis, the shrewd Norman had no illusions, and he knew the warriors of Asia. There the similarity ended, for Bohemund had no other resources than his agile, stubborn brain, his long sword, and the admiration of his followers.

He could keep his own counsel. Godfrey of Bouillon and Raymond of St. Gilles[1] had taken leave of Europe with some ceremony. Bohemund merely turned his back and went away, tight-lipped, alert of eye—not yet quite decided in his mind. Ambition smoldered in him, feeding his hunger for new lands. And when he crossed the river Sangarius a whole continent lay before him, unknown, as rich in its treasure as in its soil. The last Byzantine guard tower was left behind.

Around him stretched red farmland, rolling hills with a gutted palace and a half-deserted village on the skyline, among gray willows and green oaks. Along the narrow road the marching host moved past him, spreading over the fields. Peasants and ribalds, the remnant of Peter's brigade, trudged by with packs on their pikes and a muttered, "Save 'ee, my lord."

Men of arms trotted past with a jangle of rein chains and a clanking of shields—a gust of laughter drowned in the thudding of hoofs. Dust swirled over the bands plodding on foot, the black robes, and jack-men, and sturdy pilgrims. Women clustered together on mules.

Ox carts crawled by, creaking under loads of grain, and men sprawled out, snoring in the midsummer heat. For miles through the veil of dust spear tips flashed in the sunlight, and iron heads rose and sank, like the waves of a dark river rushing on steadily. Brown faces, red faces damp with sweat, moved by. Somewhere bagpipes wailed. A voice intoned a chant:

> "*Lignum crucis,*
> *Signum ducis,*
> *Sequitur exercitus;*
> *Quod non cessit,*
> *Sed praecessit,*
> *In vi Sancti Spiritus.*"

A crude kind of chant, made up on the road. Bohemund had heard it often enough. They made up new verses every day.

---

[1] The chronicles nearly always speak of Raymond—count of Toulouse, and leader of the Provençals—as St. Gilles. Even the Moslems called him *Sendhjil.*

The good Adhemar was off with the other column, with Godfrey and Raymond who had taken a different road. Stephen of Blois was off with his courtiers and barons, in the fields hawking. The green livery of the French falconers flitted through the underbrush, following the bright mantles and the long-striding horses of the lords. Overhead against the blue sky a hawk rose and circled. The few French noblewomen with the crusade were gay, brilliant as pheasants, and each one had gathered her own court about her. Now they were hawking, although they had been warned that bands of Turks had been seen ahead of them.

Bohemund watched the human tide that flowed past him. Then he picked up his rein and turned his horse toward the head of the column. He had to trot for an hour with his knights through the fields before they reached Tancred and Pain Peverel, the standard-bearer of Normandy, who were leading the advance. These said they had seen Moslem cavalry during the day when they crossed a range of low hills, but nothing was visible in the long plain that stretched before them.

The road led down to another, smaller river. The crusaders decided to make camp here for the night, before venturing out into the flat country.

Here they had the hills in a rough semicircle behind them, extending out on either hand. A Roman ruin crowned a rocky pinnacle in the plain, but this proved to be deserted. Already the ribalds and young esquires were fishing in the river.

Armed patrols circled the camp that night, and reported that all was quiet on the plain. Nothing had been heard of the main body, with Godfrey and the Provençals. After daybreak and morning prayer the host began to move leisurely toward the river; horses were saddled, the beasts yoked to the wagons.

Before they had settled down to the march word came back from Tancred that detachments of Turks were advancing toward him out of the mists. The news was passed from mouth to mouth through the multitude. Some of the horsemen began to ride out, eager to catch sight of the infidels; others thronged around their feudal lords. A joyful, excited clamor uprose on all sides. French knights hastened off without their mail, fearing that the Moslems would withdraw before they could reach them.

Women crowded to the tops of hillocks, staring up the valley. Others climbed on the wagons. Nothing at all seemed to be happening. Where was Count Raymond, and where the good Duke Godfrey?

This multitude—perhaps fifty thousand strong—was not an army, although it called itself the army of God. It knew no discipline except the fatherly restraint of the priests and the will of its lords. The commoners grouped themselves by the knight who had been their liege lord, and the knights sought the standard of the baron, to whom they owed military service. The barons joined one of the leaders, and they all forced their way impatiently toward the front. Into this entangled mass rode Bohemund.

"Let the mounted men pass to the front," he commanded, again and again. "Let the men on foot set up the camp, here, at this spot."

His own followers were already obeying, and because he was both calm and imperious others began to obey. Wagons were pulled into place, cattle unyoked, and the heavy tents went up on the poles. The unarmed men and women drifted back to their accustomed places in the camp, and Bohemund made the archers and the jack-men with their pikes and axes go to the tents, to guard the non-combatants. The pack saddles were taken off the animals of the baggage train. Everyone helped at the work. Horns blared, horses neighed as they cantered about.

Bohemund had pitched the camp beside a wide marsh. The shallow river—no more than a stream—offered no obstacle to horsemen, but the marsh would shelter one flank of the encampment and the other must have been near the foothills.

In front of the tents the men of arms were standing by their horses, or forming ranks. They were laughing, trying their saddle girths. Some, kneeling in the grass, prayed quietly, leaning upon their lances, awaiting the moment when the battle would begin.

Across the plain bright bodies of horsemen moved toward them at a trot—stalwart men with dark faces under gleaming, silvered helmets, or white turbans. They rode small, active horses, their saddles covered with gay cloths. Instead of lances they carried bows, ready strung, and round shields. Their curved swords flashed in the sun.

These masses were Seljuk Turks, the army of the Red Lion —Kilidj Arslan, who had been master of Nicea. Green banners fluttered here and there. And suddenly out of the mass of them drums roared and cymbals clanged. Uplifted scimitars swung over wild heads.

As hounds burst from leash, lines of crusaders galloped out to meet them. The long lances came down, and the riders shouted as the heavy chargers swept forward: "God wills it!"

Arrows whipped past the knights, and horses began to plunge and fall. The Turks used their bows with deadly effect and scattered as the heavily armed Christians struck them. They closed in from the sides, and swords clashed. The Normans found themselves beset by shifting and whirling groups. Arrows slew the horses under them, and iron hooks pulled them from the saddle. Heavy axes tore through the links of their hauberks.

Wheeling and striking out with their long swords, they turned back. Bleeding and bewildered, they went to the aid of their dismounted comrades.

And fresh ranks charged into the Turks, to give the first line of crusaders a respite and a chance to trot back to the main line of the Christians. The strident clashing of cymbals mocked them. The clamor of the Moslems swelled louder. At times it sounded like the yelping of dogs, and at times like a roar and a chant:

"*Allah il-allahu! Allah il-allah!*"

Thousands of the strange riders swept across the front of the crusaders, sending flights of arrows into the waiting ranks. The arrows crashed into the loose-link armor and thudded into the horses. Rearing beasts and shouting men added to the tumult.

Bohemund rode among them. "Seigneurs, and knights of Christ—the battle is at hand on every side. Go forward!"

With his Normans he rode out, drove into the roaring masses. Tancred went in, with his great sword swinging about his yellow head; Richard of the Principate charged with his men. Robert, count of Paris—he who had sat upon the throne of the Basileus—galloped forward among the first, and fell dying among the heaped-up bodies of forty of his men. Then Pain Peverel carried forward the standard of Normandy.

The Moslems yielded and closed in about them. The fighting spread over the plain. From the foothills on either flank fresh masses of enemy appeared. When he saw them Bohemund sent a courier galloping from the camp, to find the main body of the crusaders and urge them to hasten to the battle.

"If you wish to take part in this day's battle, ride strongly."

By noon Godfrey and the others had not appeared. The issue was going against the crusaders steadily. A wave of Moslem horsemen crossed the swamps and surged into the camp, riding down archers and servants. When they had cleared a portion of the tents they flung themselves out of the saddles and sabered the wounded and unarmed men. They ran to the groups of clerics and monks and killed them savagely. They pulled the women from the pavilions, flung them down, and violated them, passing their curved knives through their bodies as they drew away.

The screaming of children, the sobbing and hysterical laughter of the struggling women, shrilled above the shouting of the Turks who were snatching plunder from the tents. But nothing of this was heard in the din of the fighting line.

When a throng of knights and men of arms retreated toward the tents, the Turkish raiders rode off from the plundered portion of the camp, fearing that they would be attacked.

The unarmed people of the camp showed their courage then. They had been certain of victory. Had not the men of arms driven away the Turks at Nicea? But they had seen the terrible onset of the Normans broken by the Moslems. Until now nothing had been able to stand against the charge of the iron men on their great horses.

But now the wounded were carried back in growing num-bers to the tents. And presently they were not carried back at all. People gathered in groups, encouraging each other in low voices, "Be firm, all of ye, in the faith of Christ, because to-day, please God, ye shall be victorious."

Priests put on their white vestments and went out toward the fighting line carrying the cross and the Host. They knelt by dying men, performing the last sacrament. And women showed themselves great of heart. They went out with jars of water, and tended the wounded. More than that, they approached the battle line, their clear voices crying encour-agement to the wearied men. In former days these same bright faces and eager eyes had watched the mimic combats of the tournaments. And in this hour of doubt and growing fear they did not hold back from the fighting. Perhaps they already despaired, but they did not let it be seen, even when mounted men began to ride back to the tents and kneel to confess before the priests, or to throw themselves silently on the ground, their arms extended in the form of a cross, to await death.

From the throngs of monks rose a chant: "Weeping, they sang, and singing, they prayed."

Bohemund drew back, as dangerous as a crippled wolf. Tancred and the youths of the chivalry still charged the Turks, on spent horses. By the standard of Normandy a broad massive figure held its ground stubbornly. Like Athelstan, Duke Robert was roused at last to exert himself. "Why run?" he cried to some passing knights. "Their horses are better than ours." With those dour spirits, the mighty Bellêmes and the young veteran of a dozen wars, Pain Peverel, he stood fast. The battle line wavered, divided into struggling groups, and formed again.

And we [the chronicler cries], although we could not drive them back, nor withstand the weight of their numbers—we still faced them and held out together in the common line.

They held out, for two hours or more. In this battle fought the Red Lion himself—off somewhere by the green banners.

The tactics of his Turks amazed the crusaders, who felt for the first time the force and range of the Turkish arrows, and the mad fury of the Moslem onslaught, when the warriors rushed in to die as if going to a feast. All of them were mounted, while less than a third of the Christians had horses.

The Turks came on in spite of dire punishment. The long swords and heavy battle maces of the crusaders struck them down, smashing bones and slashing heads from bodies. After six hours of combat the iron men were still fighting stubbornly. They would neither yield nor run. And the Seljuk Turks had reason to be astonished at this unbroken courage. They had conquered everything in their path, from the steppes beyond the salt inland seas of Asia, and now for the first time they met foemen more steadfast than themselves.

The fighting line of the crusaders held, and in midafternoon the standards of Godfrey and Hugh appeared between the foothills beside them.

Aid had been long in coming. But the main army arrived on the scene in good formation. It swept down through the hills to the attack without a moment's delay—Godfrey, Robert of Flanders, and Hugh the Great riding at the left flank of the Moslems.

That eager spirit, the war-wise Adhemar, in hauberk and helm, led his own followers down, to the rear of the Turks. At the same time the crusaders at the camp formed a new line—Bohemund, Robert of Normandy, Tancred, and Richard of the Principate—and attacked. Only the eloquent Count Stephen was absent. His was the one cowardly spirit among the men of the cross.

Before he could be caught between the two armies, the Red Lion—outnumbered now—ordered his standards to retreat, and the Turks turned back to the plain. The crusaders pressed after them, on wearied horses. They rode in among the Moslems with their spears and the retreat became a flight—to the camp of the Red Lion, where the Moslems scattered in all directions. The Lorrainers and Flemings followed until darkness fell.

By the light of roaring fires the victors ransacked the

Seljuk camp. They took a great booty—silver and gold, brocaded garments, weapons, and strange things they had never seen before. They rounded up masses of saddle horses, asses, sheep, and cattle, and they loaded the pack horses and camels with their spoilings.

The next day they followed the tracks of the Turks, without seeing them. Meanwhile the Provençals, who had elected to guard the non-combatants of the main army, came up and joined the pursuit. But the Red Lion had had enough. He went off somewhither to the east, after warning a fresh army of Arabs that had been on the way to join him. He gave orders to lay waste the country in advance of the crusaders, and he did not put himself in their way again.

Who will be wise enough [exclaims the chronicler known as the Anonymous] to attempt to describe the sagacity, the warlike skill and the valor of the Turks? But, please God, they will never prevail over ours. In truth, they say that they are of the same parentage as the Franks,[1] and that no one has a right to call himself a knight except their men and ours. Now I shall speak the truth and no one will gainsay me—if they had kept to the faith of Christ, the Son of God, born of the Virgin, no people could be found their equal in strength and valor and knowledge of war. Still, by God's grace, they were overcome by us. This battle took place the first day of July.

---

[1] The Seljuk Turks were descended from the nomads of Central Asia. They were at this time a race of warriors, newly converted to Islam, rugged and generous, simple in their habits, and notable for their courage. They had come out of their steppes around the Caspian, and had been first the soldiers and then the conquerors of the rulers of Baghdad. Differing from the Arabs and Persians, they considered themselves superior to the conquered peoples, and they held power through a line of illustrious sultans—Toghrul, Alp Arslan, and Malik Shah. Just before the crusade, Malik Shah died, and the resulting civil war occupied the various Seljuk princes from Jerusalem to the Caspian. Kilidj Arslan was no more than a minor prince of their great empire. The crusaders were not aware of this.

PART III

XVIII

THE ANONYMOUS

IN THE army of the cross-bearers there was an Unknown. We do not know his name or his rank. In his narrative, which has been quoted more than once before now, he says nothing of himself. Yet this narrative, written down from time to time on the road, gives at first hand the inner story of the crusade. The parchment and vellum on which his story was copied down have survived. He was the unknown soldier, the voice of the multitude.

From his narrative it is clear that the Unknown was Norman-born, and that he marched at first with Bohemund's army. He had gentle blood in his veins; he knew how to write, and he rode with the armed chevaliers. He did not sit in the council of the leaders, but he kept track of events. He pondered problems of provisions and water, and the care of the horses—he had at least one horse of his own. Perhaps he had a few followers, but he does not speak of them.

The Anonymous—as the historians have christened him— fought through the battle of Doryleum and helped to bury the dead. He could praise the valor of the Turks, yet he was sure they were pagans—idol-worshipers he supposed—doomed to eternal torment after death. For two days, along the road out of Doryleum, he noticed their bodies lying in the dry grass.

No one can doubt the faith of the Unknown. He was proud of the cross of the Seigneur Christ that he bore upon his shoulder; he admired his lord, Bohemund, "that mighty man," and "the renowned knight, Tancred." A good sword stroke called forth his approval. To his enduring faith victory seemed certain.

What did he look like? He was one of thousands, of the poorer men of arms—hardened by the struggle of life, merciless in battle, and yet pitying the suffering of the weaker ones. A tall fellow, most like, still young in years, and sparing of words. Careful of his arms—long lance and sword or ax— and the great, triangular shield that hung from his shoulder. Yellow hair falling in tresses behind his ears from beneath the conical steel cap with a cross set over his forehead—his powerful body cased in a shirt of ring or scale mail that fell back in a loose coif about his throat and came down to his bare knees. His legs bound with cotton wrappings, his feet covered with soft leather.

At first, after leaving Doryleum in that stifling month of July, 1097, the Unknown thought they were following the retreating Turks. The few villages they passed were plundered and abandoned by the Moslems—cattle driven off and crops burned. A dry and desolate land, that stretched to the Black Mountains.

The Unknown had never seen such country before, and the crusaders were not prepared for it. In Europe there had always been water at hand, or wine. And now they had gone too far to expect supplies from the Byzantines. They numbered more than a hundred thousand souls, perhaps there were two hundred thousand, fighters and pilgrims in the mass of them.[1] And the country yielded them no food or drink.

---

[1] The actual number of the crusaders was never known. Fulcher of Chartres says that seven hundred thousand were at Nicea, but this is undoubtedly exaggerated. Perhaps a quarter million men and women of all sorts reached Constantinople. Many of these were killed in the massacres of Peter's and Walter's crowds, and at Nicea and Doryleum. Many fell sick or turned back. But the host of crusaders at this point was perhaps ten times as great as any army of Europe of that century. The question is discussed in a note at the end of the book.

One day they suffered a great deal from hunger and thirst.
Many women, wearied by the journey, died.

We barely came through [the Unknown remarks]. We had to eat
grain that we pulled off and rubbed between our hands, a miserable
fare. The larger number of our horses died, so most of the chevaliers
walked afoot. For lack of horses we used cattle in place of chargers,
and in this extreme need, goats, sheep, and even dogs were pressed
into service to carry our baggage.

They turned south through the Black Mountains, and
came upon a river. Beyond this they reached a city, with
many Christians among the inhabitants—whose children had
been borne off as slaves by the Turks. They moved slowly,
hindered by cliffs and by the great heat. Raymond of Toulouse fell ill, and Godfrey seems to have been injured while
hunting. But the crusaders had learned how to carry water
along with them, in skins. They took ten days to cover a little
more than a hundred kilometers, and rested before crossing
the next stretch of barren land. They christened the valley of
the cliffs Malabruma.

Again they headed west, across a dry plain, leaving behind
them the city now known as Iconium.

They went on cheerfully enough. Had not the Seigneur
Christ fed a multitude of five thousand from five loaves and
two fishes? Camels and mules began to drop by the way, and
road weariness beset them all. The knights mourned their
hawks that drooped under the heat, and the dogs that fell
down, without strength to go on, even under the master's
hand. They had attempted to rouse up game with the falcons
and hunting dogs.

Sight of the strange beasts of burden moved them to smiles.
The skins of the sheep and hogs were chafed raw by the
weight of the unaccustomed loads. And surely never before
had belted knights been seen mounted on oxen. The loss of
the chargers troubled the leaders, but the poorer people
trusted that they would manage without the horses.

The mutual hardships, and the dismounting of the greater
part of the chivalry, brought them all closer together. They
shared a common fate. They had been more than a year away

from the lords' halls and the peasants' huts. The distinction between the mounted man of arms and the unarmed man afoot no longer existed, as before. Most of the weaker spirits had turned back before now. The long baggage trains that some of the nobles had fetched as far as Constantinople had, perforce, been discarded. And the different nations had jostled together for months. Old antipathies waned, after they fought the Moslems.

Who had ever heard so many languages in one army before? [Fulcher, the simple French priest, observes.] Here were Franks, Flemings, Lotharingians, Bavarians, Normans, Angles, Scots, Italians, Britons, Greeks, and Armenians all together. If a Briton or a Teuton spoke to me, I did not know how to answer. But even if we spoke such varied languages, we were all brothers in God's love, and seemed like close kinsmen. If one of us lost something, the finder would keep it and make inquiries until he discovered the owner. This was the proper spirit!

Early in September the army saw the mountain barrier of the Taurus rising ahead of it—a long barrier that must be crossed. But beyond it lay the rich land of Syria and the great city of Antioch.

The mounted men went ahead and drove off some scattered forces of Turks, and the main army limped in to the walls of Heraclea, within the foothills. It had traversed Asia Minor in the heat of the summer and now it wanted to rest.

But Tancred, eager as an unhooded falcon, had no desire to rest. Either Bohemund sent him, or he took it into his head to turn off to the south, down toward the sea. And Baldwin, Godfrey's brother, kept him company. With the strongholds of Asia almost within sight, these two youngsters itched to go out and conquer for themselves. Freed from the slow-moving masses, they trotted through the valleys of the barrier range, into the gorge of the Cilician Gates, as the ancients called it. Their foray carried them down into the bare hills and the flat coast and the historic city of Tarsus.

Their coming was unexpected. The wall of Tarsus, straddling the little river, might have withstood them, but the Turkish garrison rode out to meet them. Tancred, who was ahead of Baldwin in the race, charged with spears down and pennants streaming, and the Moslems gave way and fled.

All of the Near East had dwellings in Tarsus, and the Greek and Syrian Christians came out joyfully enough to meet the iron men who had appeared from nowhere and who were marked with the sign of the cross. They found the leaders of the newcomers locked in a bitter quarrel.

Baldwin had arrived, angry because he had been forestalled. Tancred wanted Tarsus for his own—himself to be lord of the city. But the stern Baldwin was no man to yield place to another.

"Share the capture with me," Godfrey's brother urged.

"With you," responded the hot-tempered Tancred, "I will share nothing."

The notables of Tarsus intervened. "Stop, lords, stop! We will take for our lord, O invincible Franks, the one who yesterday drove off the Turks."

Baldwin turned to the Norman moodily. "Let us despoil it together; he who is the stronger of us can then guard it—he who is better able to take it."

"I will have none of that!" Tancred retorted. "Nor will I despoil Christians who have accepted me as lord."

The quarrel had flamed up in a moment, but it was long in dying down. Baldwin had the stronger following, and Tancred withdrew in the end, without making peace. While the Rhinelander installed himself in the citadel of Tarsus, the Norman rode east along the coast and gathered in Adana and Mamistra for himself.

Turning back after their brief exploit, leaving details of men to hold their conquests, these two sons of war no longer rode together. Tancred rejoined Bohemund's camp. But the young count of Lorraine arrived to find his wife Godehilde dead of a sickness in his absence.

After he had seen her buried and a cross placed upon the grave, Baldwin would not tarry with the army. Taking a few men with him, among them Fulcher the chronicler, he set out again through the ranges, this time to the east, toward the Euphrates and the unknown land of the Armenians. This time he did not return to the army.

XIX

THE ROAD TO ANTIOCH

THE army made its way through the mountain barrier. It moved slowly, circling far to the northeast to find an open pass. The dark slopes of the forest narrowed about it.

Here the villages were seen up the slopes, on the summits of cliffs, a footpath winding up to the rough walls of loose stone. Goats wandered over the trails—dogs barked at the marching men, and shaggy shepherds ran away among the stunted oak trees at their approach.

The only solid buildings in the villages were small stone churches with brown domes. At times stocky, sallow-faced men clad in clumsy iron breastplates and sheepskins came striding down to greet them, and the Greeks of the emperor's contingent interpreted to the crusaders what these inhabitants of the mountains said.

The strangers pointed to the silver crosses hanging on their bare chests, and smiled. They also were Christians, and their ancestors had worn such crosses for many lifetimes. They smelled of milk and cattle and dung and they were Armenians—refugees from their native hills. They offered wine to the tall warriors of the West, in polished silver goblets, and explained further:

"Three lifetimes ago our homes were yonder, to the north and the east. In the city of Ani we had a thousand churches, larger than these. We were *mthawar*, free nobles, although the Greeks [so they called the Byzantines] taxed us. We drove off the Arabs, but the Seljuk Turks defeated the Greeks at Manzigird in our land, and made the emperor of the Greeks a prisoner. Then we left our homes—some going very far around the Black Sea, others to the Caucasus. We who came hither are nobles.

"Long ago a saintly patriarch, Marses, prophesied that our lands would be redeemed by Christians. And now it has happened according to the prophecy, because we see you, a multitude of Christians, coming with drawn swords to liberate us."

So said the Armenians who thronged to greet the host. They led the advance of the army through the valley; they clamored to be given the isolated Moslem forts that the crusaders stormed. Three generations of exile and oppression had left their mark upon these Armenians, who were both friendly and avaricious. While they offered up prayers of thanksgiving for a miracle, they stole the weapons of the crusaders. Bohemund went off with them, as Baldwin had done before him, to give aid to a valley city that was besieged by Turks, and Raymond of St. Gilles detached a picked force of five hundred Provençals to hasten on to Antioch because the Armenians told him that the Turks were fleeing from Antioch. The information proved misleading in both cases.

When they left the valleys of Little Armenia, the men of the cross found a new barrier before them, the higher Taurus range that had served for centuries as the frontier of the Byzantines and Moslems. As soon as they had watered at the Blue River they pushed into the gorges. Here they found few villages. The forest slopes gave way to cliffs, and the only road seemed to be the dry bed of a stream where the horses floundered cruelly over the worn stones, and the men must needs pick their way afoot.

The light grew dimmer in the gorge. Only in the early afternoon was the sun visible between the heights. The air became cold, and the wind gusts tugged at them when they left the watercourse and ascended a trail that twisted along the face of the cliffs. The Unknown, who had remained with the army, christened this height the Mountain of the Devil.

It was so high and so narrow that along the path on its flank none of us dared go ahead of the others. Horses fell into the ravines, and one pack animal would drag over others. In all quarters, the knights showed their misery, and they struck their bodies with their hands mournfully, asking themselves what they were to do, and how they were to manage their arms. Some of them sold their shields and goodly hauberks with their helms for three to five *dinars*, or for anything they could get. They who could not sell their arms cast them away for nothing at all, and marched on.

They had to camp at night on wind-swept ledges. Lacking wood, they could not light fires. They ate what was at hand and tried to sleep—no easy matter in these higher altitudes.

It was slow work getting the animals over the bad spots in the trail. The number of the sick increased. Nothing could be done for them except to make litters and carry them. In one day five hundred died, and must be buried.

The bodies were carried, covered with cloaks until evening, when the host halted. At the hour after sunset the crusaders always went out of their tents and stood with uncovered heads or knelt for a moment of prayer, while the priests raised the crucifix.

No bells chimed in these waste places, but voices were heard singing. Adhemar had begun it, long before, and now it was done each day. In twilight the throngs listened to the voices that chanted with the strength of enduring hope:
"*Ave Maria!*"
It was the first Angelus.

The road, in the morning, was marked with new crosses over graves. The men said that more had died in these mountains than in the fighting with the Turks.

Before long the road began to descend. The men caught glimpses of wide green valleys below them. They came out

among the foothills, and found a new country here—groves
of dark green olive trees, and sesame plantations. The water
in the wide streams was clear and cold. Water wheels and
windmills stood near the dwellings. A land of rolling hills
and dark, fertile soil baked by a summer's heat. This, they
knew, was Syria. They went on eagerly, toward the orchards
and gray wall of a large city. The Unknown rejoiced.

Coming out of those damnable mountains, we approached a city
called Maarash. The people of that city came out joyfully to meet
us, bringing us a fine stock of things. We had plenty of everything,
while we waited there for Lord Bohemund to join us. And so finally
our knights reached the valley where Antioch, the royal city, is
situated, which is the head of all Syria, which once the Lord Jesus
Christ gave over to the blessed Peter.

XX

LOOT

ONCE Caesar sat in the first row of its theater when the moonlight beat upon its parasol pines; Titus watched its chariot races; Herod paved it with marble, and Diocletian planned its cisterns. Byzantine emperors strengthened its walls and took their pleasure in the hanging gardens among the myrtle trees and the fountains. Old and luxuriant and secure, Antioch ruled the Near East, sister to Constantinople, mistress of the caravan routes, impregnable and very wise. Then came the Arabs of Haroun ar-Raschid, and after them the Turks.

And now the crusaders. In their eyes Antioch was the key of Syria and the gateway to the promised land.

They encamped in the last foothills before it, looking across a wide plain. On the far side of the plain ran a river, and behind the river rose the front wall of Antioch. It was really more like a vast garden than a city. The wall ran two miles along the river Orontes, then it rambled up, in dizzying fashion, over the hills—disappeared and emerged again among the brush and laurel trees.

Three separate hills were enclosed within that rampart of

gray stone, thirty feet high. And on the largest hill, at the back of everything, stood the massive citadel, so distant that it could hardly be seen at all. The crusaders' camp occupied the north side of the plain, the city lay to the south. And the crusaders had never dreamed of a place so strong as this.

Four horses could ride abreast on the summit of the wall. A dry ditch ran around it. At intervals rose massive, square, sixty-foot towers. All the gates were flanked by these towers. The five main gates were all in the nearer half of the city wall—the half below the hills—and the men of the cross had reason to know them well thereafter. The first, St. Paul's, opened to the east and the road that led to Aleppo. The second was called the Gate of the Dogs, and it led down to the river. Where the river nearly touched the wall stood the third, which the crusaders christened the Duke's Gate, in a nest of marshes. Nearly a mile farther on, a solitary bridge crossed the river and they called the gate here the Bridge Gate. The remaining portal opened to the west of the city, upon the road that led down to the port of St. Simeon and the sea, some twenty miles distant. This was known as the Gate of St. George.

The far half of the wall, up among the hills, had only small posterns opening upon narrow paths. It would be difficult for an enemy to quarter himself within these ravines, and almost impossible to make any attack upon this southern side.

Among the people of the countryside there was a saying that Antioch was impregnable to human valor, and that the city could only be taken by surprise, treachery, or starvation.

The crusaders had not enough armed men to surround the great circuit of the wall. Unless they did so, the defenders of the city could come and go along the dozens of hill trails leading to the postern gates. Antioch was like a great garden that could be approached only by the front entrance; the rear of the garden would always be safe, and the rear door open.

And in the front, approach would be no easy matter. If the crusaders crossed the Orontes and pitched their camps on the narrow strip of marshy land, they would be directly beneath the walls, with the river at their backs. If they remained on this side the river, the Turks would be able to pass freely into the eastern plain, toward Aleppo.

It would be idle to think of making a breach in the great wall. The crusaders could not build engines powerful enough to batter that centuries-old stonework. Small wonder that Antioch was said to be impregnable.

There was left the possibility of starving out the defenders. But within the circuit of the wall, green tracts of garden and pasture land were visible—orchards and granaries and ancient baths.

So when they encamped, at the end of October, within sight of Antioch, the army had to decide between three alternatives—to risk everything by attempting to storm the wall at once, to take up a position in front of the city and await events, or to abandon their march and withdraw into the mountains behind them. To reach a decision, they called a great council of all the leading men.

This council was their only government. By now the host of crusaders had wandered off the map. It had left behind the old kingdoms and feudal ties, and had become a kind of warlike democracy in search of a country. Its common council arbitrated quarrels, dispensed justice, and arranged for supplies. Already it had sent envoys back to Alexis, and over to the kalif of Cairo. The council was a board of strategy and a bureau of administration in one. Every leader had a right to bring before it any wrong suffered by one of his vassals. It judged matters of honor by the ethics of knighthood, and questions of property by the old feudal code, and between whiles it tried to shepherd[1] the multitude of pilgrims that still accompanied the fighting men.

It is worth looking at, as it sat in session that day, discuss-

---

[1]It must be remembered that nothing like the march of the crusaders had been attempted by Europeans before now. Campaigning in Europe amounted to little more than marching from one village to the next, and the armies were small. The cross-bearers had a multitude of which no more than half were armed men; they were forced to live off the country as best they could; they were entering a new climate, in the face of hostile armies.

A modern army moves over planned-out routes, with quarters arranged for it in advance—except during action—and with field kitchens and first aid accompanying it. The crusaders lacked all of this.

ing its own fate, under a wide pavilion, the ground covered with captured Moslem prayer carpets. In an armchair at the rear of the pavilion sat Stephen, count of Blois, newly elected head of the council, his long mantle bright with embroidery. They had chosen him because he was courteous and affable, and related by ties of blood or marriage to most of the other lords.

At his right hand sat Adhemar, in full robes—Adhemar whom the crusaders had learned to love, and to heed. Already they called him the friend of every man.

On Stephen's left sat Raymond of St. Gilles, the oldest of the leaders, with his close-clipped gray beard and his sharp black eyes. On the march to Antioch he had proved devout and covetous, irascible and impetuous. He was equally apt to haggle over a shilling or to give away a chest of gold. For long weeks he had been carried in a horse litter—once when his pulse almost stopped they had read over him the office of the dead—and the pallor of illness still clung to his face.

In a wide half circle the others sat upon benches. Godfrey of Bouillon had changed not at all. Always courteous, and always brave, he listened to the talk of the others, seldom making a suggestion himself. In everything he was the splendid duke, lacking only the instinct of leadership.

Hugh the Great had proved less admirable and more hesitant. He had become an eloquent figurehead.

The men of the council looked more to Bohemund. The red-haired Norman was restive as a hunting dog upon the leash, impatient of delay, eager to win things for himself. With fewer men at his command than the other leaders, he was gradually gaining the ascendency, and antagonizing the lord of St. Gilles thereby.

In contrast the two cousins, Robert of Normandy and Robert of Flanders, seldom spoke at the council. Stalwart Short Breeches disliked to exert himself—he ever loved the goblet more than the pen—and the fair count of Flanders was the youngest of the lords, diffident and mild and well content to play his part in battle, leaving decisions to the others.

Near the leaders sat the Byzantine general Taticius, his

dark face intent, his slender figure resplendent in scarlet and gold. He was the eyes and ears of the emperor.

Before the half circle sat or stood the lesser barons, the men of mark, among them that wraith of a lost crusade, Peter the Hermit, in his shabby robe. He had little to say now, because he was leader only of the vagabonds.

Already there were gaps among the rows of faces—Count Baldwin, Godfrey's brother, had made himself master of an Armenian fortress toward the east. Baldwin of Ghent had fallen at Nicea, and Robert of Paris and others in the last battle.

Gravely, they debated the alternatives before them, each chieftain speaking in turn. Taticius favored falling back to the mountains and waiting until Alexis could come up. This drew a protest from the Normans, who remembered Nicea. Alexis was far behind them, occupied in taking possession of the strongholds the Turks had abandoned.

St. Gilles, also, had no love for the Byzantines. Stubbornly he urged that the wall of Antioch be attacked at once.

"Through God's mercy we took Nicea, and after that we were victorious over the Turks. We have had peace and good feeling in the army. So we should not fear another king or another place."

Others spoke against this. Without engines they could not demolish the wall, and to try to scale a height like that would be to tempt providence. The quick-tempered Raymond retorted bitterly.

Ever since the dispute at Constantinople there had been hard feeling between the old Provençal and the Norman nobles. Raymond had lagged behind at Doryleum. And his flying expedition that tried to surprise Antioch had consoled itself with gathering in some of the castles in the vicinity. Such prizes belonged, by feudal custom, to the one who made the captures. If Raymond's banner went up on a tower, the place was his as long as his men could hold it. And Bohemund had not failed to make prizes of his own.

From his first sight of Antioch the mighty Norman longed for it. Here was a fair domain, and a city fit for an emperor.

He saw at once that Antioch held within it the mastery of
Syria. And from Syria other conquests could be made.

But it was another voice that decided the issue of the day
before the council. The knights and lesser leaders spoke
urgently for an immediate siege. Their men, they explained,
were becoming impatient at the delay. The common people
were eager to press on, toward Jerusalem. Already they had
lingered through one winter on the road and at Constantinople; they would not willingly wait out another winter.

The council decided that the host would move forward and
begin the siege, opposite the three north gates. No storm
would be attempted. Raymond, to avoid a quarrel, gave in
to the will of the majority.

So the camps were moved down to the river. Bohemund
took the left flank, to the east, with Robert of Normandy
on his right opposite the Gate of the Dogs, next Raymond
and his Provençals, and on the right Godfrey with the other
divisions of the army, extending as far as the Bridge Gate.

Immediately there began a general exodus from the
crusaders' lines. The army had endured privations in its
march through the barren plains and over the Taurus, and it
devoted itself with enthusiasm to foraging. Small bands
explored the wide valley, rounding up cattle and the few
horses the Turks had left outside Antioch. They found fruit
weighing down the orchards, and swarms of pigeons in the
thatched roofs.

They discovered a reed-bordered lake near by—El Bahr—
and began to fish and swim in it. They stalked waterfowl in
the reeds. In the distant hills they came upon sheep. Meat
grew so plentiful that they only bothered to eat the best
portions from the thighs and the chest; they gorged themselves, after long days of hunger, upon white bread, figs,
quinces, lotus fruit, and wine. Syria seemed to them to be
the beginning of the promised land, where they expected to
find milk and honey flowing. Something interesting always
lay beyond the next hill. They wandered through deserted
gardens, and quartered themselves in the tiny, tiled chambers

where Moslem women had been guarded. Other women smiled and stared at them—round-faced Armenians, and slender Syrians.

Not many women had survived thus far in the army, and they were usually the property of husbands or fathers. Many of the crusaders began to hunt out the Syrian girls, who might or might not be Christians, but who dared not resist these tall warriors.

It was all pleasant enough. The war had ceased for the time being. While their lords occupied themselves by taking castles, the men of arms found diversions of their own. The rabble reverted to old habits, and plundered lustily. Tafur—so the minstrels called the king of the ribalds—wandered with his cutpurses and clapper-claws from the alleys of Paris, dragging after him wagonloads of poultry and garments and weapons that he and his men had conjured up mysteriously at night.

Robert the Pilgrim, who was making up a song that he called "The Song of Antioch," watched their antics and smiled in sympathy. They were stout lads, the ribalds. Death had called many of them—why should not they enjoy themselves?

As the days passed, brawling disturbed this near-paradise. Rival parties of plunderers drew swords over the spoil. Men idling in the tents with a surfeit of meat and wine became annoyed at trifles. They remembered old quarrels. Provençals said that the Saxons made a god of their belly. The Saxons could not think of a retort, but the French improvised a proverb—"The French to the combat, the Provençals to the cook pot."

When the Provençal minstrels made up a song about the drunken Normans, the Northerners called them the Jews of the army. The Flemings, the Dutchmen of that day, did not take part in the brawling, because they could not understand what was said, and no one could understand them.

And then the Turks took a hand. For two weeks Yagi Siyan, in command at Antioch, had watched this encampment sprawled under his walls. By now he had decided that this was a siege and not a halt in the crusaders' march. He had sent gallopers off to the Moslem princes elsewhere, and he began to raid the camp, slashing into the tents and then retiring across the river. At the same time horsemen out Aleppo-way cut off foraging parties.

This roused Bohemund, who led a raiding party toward Aleppo and fell into an ambush on the road. But he fought his way out, and thereafter built a strong tower behind his sector of the camp, to guard this avenue of approach.

Meanwhile the crusaders had pushed a bridge of boats across the Orontes, to enable them to cross the river quickly.

In this way the real siege began, late in November.

XXI

THE SIGN IN THE SKY

AT FIRST Yagi Siyan had all the best of it. He was a Turkoman, a grandson of the mighty Alp Arslan, alert and cruel and thoroughly at home in warfare of this nature. He made the most of his opportunities while he waited for aid to reach him from the east. His cavalry sallied out of the Bridge Gate and raided the cattle herds, guarded by esquires and peasants—driving off all the horses they could find. When the crusaders mounted to repel the attack the Turks withdrew swiftly—their horses were more nimble and in better condition than the half-fed chargers of the besiegers—using their bows with deadly effect. They disappeared across the stone bridge, and the knights who followed them too close were greeted by a heavy fire from a hill where a mosque and cemetery offered cover to the Turkish bowmen, by the Bridge Gate.

At night these archers would go down to the river and drop arrows into the lighted tents across the water.

Meanwhile Yagi Siyan fared well enough within the city. He had driven out all the Armenian and Syrian men who might sympathize with the Christians—but he kept their women as security. He had stocks of food and cattle enough to last out, and he bargained with the Syrians in the hills to bring in more, through the postern gates on the heights.

Heavy rains fell, and the Orontes flooded the marshes. With the rain came wind and cold. Yagi Siyan's Syrians reported that food was dear in the camp of the crusaders. A day's provender—hay or straw—for a horse sold for two dinars. All the Armenian traders this side Aleppo were hastening to reap such prices. A handful of meat sold for a piece of silver. Spies told Yagi Siyan also that one of the princes was very ill, and two more had started with twenty thousand men to comb the eastern hills for supplies. With them had gone the true *sultan* of the Christians, Bohemund.

Yagi Siyan, staring down from his towers at the multitude of wet tents shaking and flapping in the wind, wondered why these men had come hither and why they stayed. Wandering about in their gray woolen rain cloaks in the mud, they lacked all the panoply and magnificence of war. A good many of them seemed to be sick, and their horses were in miserable condition.

But the opportunity was too good to miss. The shrewd Turkoman led his horsemen out of the Bridge Gate and made an attack in force. It struck the Provençals, who were taken by surprise. They stood their ground until a riderless horse threw them into disorder, and the men on foot fled, in spite of the anger of the knights. Panic-stricken men caught at the horses' manes and tails, and the nobles were carried back with the mob, as far as the bridge of boats—nearly a mile.

Adhemar came out with his followers to stem the tide. His standard bearer was killed and his standard captured. Not until Raymond took to his saddle and Godfrey's knights rode up was the attack checked. The Turks retired after despoiling the dead, and left the camp filled with gloom.

They had little cheer in the camp this second Christmas— few candles to burn at the improvised altars.

The rain beat through the sodden fabric of the tents, rusted the link and scale armor, and softened the bowstrings. Mud worked up through the rugs and blankets in which the men slept.

And then one night the earth itself was shaken by a gigantic power. Pavilion poles toppled down, and men who ran out into the open were thrown from their feet. They gathered in groups to wonder at what was happening, when a new phenomenon amazed them. In the northern sky they beheld white flames rising among the stars, and a red glow that changed to purple. The light ascended higher, leaping and falling and brightening, until they could see the mud underfoot and the pallid faces around them. Night had been turned into day—dawn had come before the first cock-crow. It was surely a sign.

After this earthquake and the unusually bright aurora borealis, Adhemar, the only able-bodied prince left in the camp, ordered a three-days' fast and prayer. At the same time he wrote home in a somber mood:

We have fought in three battles; the army has marched from Nicea to Antioch, and has stormed other cities and strong places. We still have a hundred thousand knights and armed men, but what avails it, when the infidels outnumber us? Farewell. Forget not that we labor day and night. Pray for us.

One thing heartened the crusaders. When they explored the coast to the south they found a fertile country still unravaged, and a walled seaport. And, beyond belief, they found English seamen in possession of the town.

Shallow open boats that once had plied along the fishing banks of the North seas were drawn up on the sands of Laodicea. They had the same patched leather sails, square and unwieldy, the same heavy oars. Frisian ships kept them company.

The seafarers also had taken the cross. How they managed to sail and row along the coasts—they could not trust themselves to the open sea—feeling their way from island to island, and putting in to shelter when the wind blew against them, has never been told. The Great Sea held terrors for them, and they lacked both charts and compasses.

They had been fishermen and pirates before they departed on the crusade. Perhaps that is the answer. All we know of them is that they came, and the army found them masters of a Moslem port.

Behind them came other, larger fleets—Genoese galleons, and Byzantine ships of war. These halted at St. Simeon, the port of Antioch, and by sailing to Cyprus and back they were able to bring the crusaders much-needed supplies.

But when the English seafarers heard that Robert Short Breeches was near by they sent for him to come down and enjoy their conquest with them. The Sleepy Duke had grown tired of the siege and the lack of wine, and he rode down to Laodicea with all that were left of his division. And there, in spite of Adhemar's admonitions, he remained, where he could get his fill of eating and drinking.

Bohemund took the young count of Flanders with him on a foraging expedition. But they found their way barred by the Moslem army of Aleppo. The Flemings attacked at once, and were driven back, until Bohemund hastened up. The crusaders won the field, but found little enough in the way of supplies.

Thereafter they separated, Bohemund making a circle through the hills to the north, around the great lake, El Bahr. He came upon throngs of pilgrims and the rabble, who had seized the opportunity to forage on their own account and had stripped the country of everything.

Restraining his anger, Bohemund gathered up the deserters and lectured them. "O most miserable people! Why do you wish to go away in this fashion? Wait—wait, and keep together and do not wander like sheep without a shepherd. For if our enemies find you wandering thus without a leader they will kill you."

He had to return to the camp with less than he had taken out of it. The Armenian and Syrian traders made due note of this, and brought up supplies from isolated villages with which they were familiar. They charged the crusaders eight pieces of gold for an ass load of food—120 silver dinars. "Then died many of our men," the Unknown explains, "who were not able to pay such prices."

The army was paying dear for its heedless waste during the first few weeks. The specter of famine stalked through the sodden tents.

William called the Carpenter, and Peter the Hermit could not endure this misfortune and misery, and went off secretly. Tancred pursued them, caught them and brought them back in their shame. They gave him their faith and their oath that they would return of their own accord to the camp and give satisfaction to the seigneurs. All that night William lay like an evil thing in the tent of Bohemund. The next morning at daybreak he stood with reddened face before Bohemund, who said to him:

"O miserable! Shame and dishonor of the French! Why hast thou fled so vilely? Didst thou, perchance, wish to betray these knights of the army of Christ as thou hast betrayed others in Spain?"·

William remained silent, and not a word came from his lips. A number of the French gathered about them, and requested the lord Bohemund not to inflict any further punishment on him.

Bohemund assented, without emotion, saying:

"Willingly I grant this, for love of you, if this man will take oath on his heart and soul not to turn aside from the road to Jerusalem for good or evil—and if Tancred will agree not to do, or let his men do, anything antagonistic to him."

When he heard this, Tancred consented readily, and Bohemund let him go at once. But before long, in truth, the Carpenter betook himself off furtively, being troubled by a great shame.

The whole camp was suffering from hunger. Godfrey lay ill in his tent. And Taticius, grand primicerius of Byzantium, had had enough.

It is true that he explained his departure very plausibly, saying that he ought to hasten back to Alexis to arrange for supplies to be sent to the camp. He had a conference with Bohemund—agreeing to yield to Norman rule without question the three cities captured last year along the coast, Tarsus, Adana, and Mamistra—pointing out as proof that he would return, that he was leaving his tents and servants. But go he did, and come back he did not. "Foresworn he is," the Unknown says bluntly, "and foresworn he will remain."

Meanwhile Rudwan, amir of Aleppo, had gathered together an army strong enough to attempt the relief of Antioch. He communicated with Yagi Siyan, who agreed to sally out the day that Rudwan should appear.

The crusaders only heard that a strong force of Moslems was approaching by the Aleppo road. A conference was held, the able-bodied leaders meeting in Adhemar's house to discuss the situation.

Bohemund put the issue squarely. "Seigneurs and most wise knights, what shall we do? We are not strong enough to fight at front and rear at the same time. But do you know what we can do? We can separate, the foot soldiers remaining to guard the tents and to stand their ground against the garrison of the city. The horsemen ought to go with us to meet the enemy who are quartered near by at Arak and the Iron Bridge."

The council agreed to this, and all the belted knights volunteered to go with Bohemund. But a search of the camp yielded only about a thousand horses fit to ride. No more than seven hundred of these were in shape to enter a battle. So seven hundred knights were chosen to ride to the east to meet an army of unknown size.

It is strange but true that this small regiment of picked men trotted off without any misgivings and without thinking of appointing a commander. Bohemund, however, had learned several lessons. He saw to it that scouts went out the first night and that the detachment camped on level ground —a stretch of about a mile between the great lake and some marshes. And they watched the horses.

They were roused out of sleep at dawn by the scouts, who rode among them shouting, "Look—look, *they* come! Make ready, for they are near."

The red-haired Norman was already awake and armed. "Seigneurs and knights," he urged, "range yourselves for battle."

While they were climbing into saddles and handing each other—since no esquires or servants were there to arm them —the long lances and great shields, it occurred to the seven hundred that no one was in command. By mutual consent they turned to the big Norman.

"Wise and mighty man," they said, "arbiter of battles, do thou make the arrangements. We put ourselves in thy hands—carry out with us what seemeth best to thee."

Bohemund took command at once, forming the knights in six detachments, each under a noted leader. Five of them he ranged in a single thin line across the plain. El Bahr and the swamps guarded his flanks, so the Turks could not sweep around the line. The sixth detachment, his own men, he kept in the rear. Grimly he watched the Turks advance— thousands of them in two formations.

Since the crusaders did not charge, the Moslems were forced to come on. They approached at a trot, arrows flashing from their bows. Along the line of the Christian knights saddles emptied and horses reared and plunged. To the astonishment of the Moslems, the iron men began to sing under this destructive fire. They had no archers to return the fire, and they dared not charge on their weak horses before they came to close grips with the Turks.

Singing, they waited until the Turks put their horses to a gallop, then the long lances went down and the knights bent over their shields, spurring on their chargers. But the weight of numbers bore them back.

Bohemund groaned and turned to his standard bearer.

"Go in swiftly. Go forward." And he added to himself, "May God go with you!"

The crimson standard moved down into the tumult and pressed into the ranks of the Turks. Bohemund's long sword flashed beside it. And this sight brought the other leaders forward again. They had the Turks at the sword's point now, and heavy steel shore through the Moslem riders, striking through their bodies, crushing in their heads.

In this *mêlée* the swift horses of the Turks availed them not. They drew back before the terrible swords, and the whole mass of them crashed into the second line of battle, which was thrown into confusion and retreated. The line of the iron men moved on as steadily as reapers make their way through a wheat field. Nothing mounted on horses could stand against them.

They cleared the field between the lake and the swamps, and pressed on in pursuit of the Turks, who retired to their own camp and hastily caught up whatever was most valuable, setting fire to the tents and fleeing along the Aleppo road. The crusaders followed grimly, to seize on the last possible horse. And they stormed and took the small citadel of Arak that had been the point of departure for the raiders from Aleppo.

Bohemund and his seven hundred had won a clean victory over as many thousand Moslems.

Going back, they cut off the heads of the enemy dead and piled them on the captured horses. At the encampment they learned that Yagi Siyan had made a sally, but the men of arms on foot had met him and driven him back. The severed heads were placed carefully on pikes and pointed stakes for the garrison to view, and for the edification of the envoys who arrived from the kalif of Cairo about that time. In answer, Yagi Siyan displayed from the wall of Antioch Adhemar's standard of the Virgin Mary, turned upside down.

These Egyptian ambassadors had come to discover what manner of men the invaders might be, and what was happening in Syria—in the general upheaval of Islam, after the death of the great Malik Shah, the Fatimites of Egypt were waging war upon the Turks. They were careful to explain that pilgrims had been well treated in their land, and that they had great admiration for the Christian warriors. Eventually they departed with four horseloads of heads, and some knights of the Christian army, to draw up a treaty of peace.

This was never done. The crusaders had discovered that there were different kinds of Moslems, with vast military power. But they had not yet come to understand the depth of Oriental diplomacy, or the strength of fanaticism in Islam.

The only result of the Egyptian embassy was that the kalif of Cairo in some five months' time sent an army into Palestine that captured Jerusalem from the Turks.

XXII

THE KEY TO THE GATE

RICHARD THE PILGRIM watched the ribalds scurrying about like hungry dogs, and he sang:

> "*They carry never a lance or sword,*
> *Only hammered pikes and long jaw bones;*
> *Their king Tafur hath an ax well-honed.*
> *Sacks at their throats hang by plaited cords,*
> *Over naked ribs and bellies well baste.*
> *Knees all chafed and breeches undone—*
> *Wherever they go the land lies waste!*"

They grubbed up grasses and roots, and chewed on leather to stifle the ache of hunger. They were restless as wolves unfed, these bands of vagabonds from the mud of Paris and the penthouses of taverns. And they hunted in packs, with the puffy-faced drabs who had once been women. The sticky-sweet meat of a too-long-dead camel gorged them for a space —they trapped dogs and mice. Bohemund had them in his charge, but the grim Norman had other matters to attend to than the well-being of the ribalds. Finally they went to beg

Peter the Hermit for food and got no satisfaction from that. Outside Peter's tent Tafur faced the rabble of his companions and grimaced.

"Harken! I begged of him thus: 'Sire, give me counsel for the sake of blessed charity. We die of hunger.' And Peter, quotha, ''tis the reward of your rascality.'"

When the crowd growled, at hearing this, Tafur lifted his head.

"Go," he cried, "and find carcases of dead Turks. They will go down well enough if they are cooked and salted a bit."

"That is true," said they.

The crowd dispersed and hunted out several bodies. These were pounded by flails and skinned, and the entrails drawn out. Caldrons were filled with water and heated over fires, and into the caldrons the ribalds dropped these human limbs.

Word of the ghastly feast spread through the camp and lines of spectators formed. From the summit of the gray wall Moslem sentries gazed in horror. The rabble sat down on the ground and ate, complaining of the lack of bread.

Others grinned. "*Voici mardi gras!*" And they assured the watchers that Turk's flesh was better than bacon or ham fried in oil. Presently four of the great seigneurs appeared in their fur mantles—Robert Short Breeches, Bohemund, Tancred, and Godfrey of Bouillon. They walked through the mob and stopped by King Tafur, and asked him how he felt.

"By my faith," Tafur responded, "I feel revived. If only I had something in the way of wine to go with this!"

The lord of Bouillon laughed. "Sir King, thou shalt have it."

And he ordered a jar of his own good wine to be given to the monarch of the ribalds. After this the rabble often visited the cemeteries, digging up the bodies of the Moslems and picking out the least decomposed to skin and hang up in the wind to dry. So runs the song of Richard the Pilgrim.

Yagi Siyan, in revenge, ordered all the crusaders who were captive in Antioch to be put to death. And now, early in the month of March, the besiegers tightened their lines about Antioch.

From the Genoese and English fleets at the port of St.

Simeon, they brought a detachment of carpenters and masons to the siege. The knoll by the Bridge Gate, with its mosques and dome-covered tombs, had long been a source of trouble to them since it protected the sallies of the garrison. They christened the place the Mahometry. Now they took possession of it and fortified it, the seamen building catapults and mangonels capable of covering the bridge or the road with stones and sheaves of arrows. This put a stop to Yagi Siyan's raids.

The tireless Turkoman, however, struck a blow at the half-finished fort beyond the bridge. And the chronicler of the Provençals tells about it:

In the summer just past, the Count had endured a lasting sickness, and now in the winter he was so worn out that it was said of him that he was quick neither to fight nor to pay, and no one believed he could not have done more than he did.

The Count insisted upon the command of the fort, to redeem himself from such talk. He was surrounded one night, before the first light, by the enemy. With sixty of his men he stood off the attack of the Saracens, being helped marvellously by the heavy storms that had made the dug-up earth a mire, and had filled the moat of our new castle. Some of our men who had been posted at the bridge could not get back to the castle, only a bowshot away.

So these men at arms made a circle among the groups of the enemy and reached the angle of a near-by house. There they stood their ground. Meanwhile the sound of the fighting roused our men in the camp. The enemy gave up the attack, and some of them were cut off at the bridge.

And so the ill talk about the Count was checked, because he alone had stood off the enemy.

Meanwhile Tancred was sent to the hitherto deserted west side of Antioch, to watch the Gate of St. George. The energetic young Norman did more than this—he patrolled the hills in back of the city and cut off most of the supplies brought up to the postern gates by the Syrians.

But before the new fortress was built, and the lines drawn close, Yagi Siyan made an effort to seize Bohemund and Raymond—the two most dangerous spirits of the crusade. They had gone down to St. Simeon in command of the

small column that was to escort back the sailors and workmen. Apparently they approached the camp in the evening,
and a strong division of Turks had gone out over the bridge
without being observed.

These waited by the road while the column with its wagons
and unarmed men drew nearer. The crusaders in the camp
had observed nothing, and Bohemund had no reason to
suspect that death lay in wait in the darkness. Only sixty
mounted men accompanied him.

The Unknown tells the story of what happened at the road:

Seeing Count Bohemund approach at the head of his people,
they started up with a great outcry, and launched a storm of javelins and arrows upon our men. They attacked us so savagely that
we scattered into the rough country, wherever an opening showed.
Whoever could get away quickly saved himself; whoever could
not, found death.

Bohemund for his part did not follow them, but rode swiftly with
some horsemen towards a small group of us who remained together. Angered by the slaughter of our comrades, we who were
thus together followed him in an attack upon the Turks. They
halted in surprise, thinking to wipe us out as they had exterminated
the men with Bohemund and the Count [Raymond]. But God did
not permit them.

Other horsemen of ours came up and charged them valiantly.[1]
They fled swiftly by the bridge to the entrance of the city. Such a
crowd formed at the bridge that many could not cross, and in that
mass of men and horses many went to eternal death with the devil
and his angels. We gained the upper hand, driving them and casting them down into the river. Those who tried to climb out by the
piers of the bridge or to swim were wounded by our men who
covered the bank of the river.

Christian women appeared at the arrow slits of the upper wall,
and, beholding the catastrophe of the Turks, secretly applauded us.
This day more than a thousand of our chevaliers and pilgrims
underwent martyrdom, ascending to heaven where we think they
were clad in the white robes of martyrs. A dozen Turkish amirs
perished in this fight, body and soul, with many of their wise and

---

[1]Apparently Stephen of Blois and others were riding out to meet Bohemund, when
they stumbled into the battle by accident. Bohemund seems to have requisitioned
Stephen's men, while Godfrey came up and took his stand at the bridge.

valiant warriors—fifteen hundred in all. Only the night put an end to the conflict.

Godfrey heard the tumult and galloped up, placing himself in the thick of things where the road entered the bridge leading to Antioch. Some knights of the Rhineland fought their way through the stream of Moslem fugitives to guard his back. The mailed horsemen became a wedge that divided the stream to either side, down into the river. Godfrey, at the point of the wedge, held his ground by dint of sword strokes. He was seen to slash the body of a Turk in two, above the hips, so that the frightened horse galloped on, over the bridge, with only its rider's legs still upon the saddle.

Late as usual, but no less willing, the Sleepy Duke appeared in the gathering darkness, and his sword also wrought havoc. One stroke split the head of a Turk—the half of the head flying off. And Robert cried out, in satisfaction, "Faith, it goeth fast to purgatory!"

The sailors, who had been scattered among the hills, were still dubious about the reality of the victory, but the crusaders rejoiced heartily, seeing some of their poverty-ridden fellows riding among the tents mounted on Arabian horses, while others were seen clad in two or three silken garments or carrying three or four shields.

Tancred hastened up from his post in the west, only to find the fighting ended, and was barely pacified by a purse of 100 pieces of silver, given him by Count Raymond.

So the final struggle began, at the great wall of Antioch. The crusaders had blocked all the five main gates. The hunger within was now as great as in the crusaders' camp. Lean and haggard men drew in their belts and waited grimly for the issue to be decided. The crusaders waited for the first grass and fruit from the orchards, while Yagi Siyan looked for the coming of the combined armies of Aleppo, Mosul, and Damascus, which were already on the march to relieve him.

Reluctantly Robert of Normandy came back from the coast with the remnant of his men when Adhemar threatened him with excommunication. He pitched his tents again in the rain-swept plain, where others not so fortunate slept huddled together by their arms in shelters of brush or in the mud. Stephen of Blois sat down to dictate a long letter to his Adele, at the beginning of spring:

Count Stephen to Adele, most sweet and lovable of wives, and to his dearest sons and all the faithful among his people, great and small—the benefit of all health and his greeting.

Know for certain, dearest one, that this messenger whom I send for thy gratification, leaves me safe and unharmed and in all prosperity by grace of the most mighty God, before Antioch. And now the whole army has maintained the siege courageously for twenty-three successive weeks.

Know for certain, my beloved, that I have now of gold and silver and many other riches twice as much as when I withdrew from your love. For all our princes in the common council of the whole army have appointed me head of the council, and manager and governor of all of them—even though I was unwilling at the time. . . .

Antioch is truly a most great city—I believe the strongest and most impregnable we have come upon. And also more than 5,000 daring Turkish soldiers have assembled in the city, not counting Saracens, Publicans, Arabs, Turcopolitans, Syrians, Armenians, and many other diverse peoples, of whom an infinite multitude convoked there. For this reason we endured many toils and uncounted evils. In truth, throughout all the winter we endured a mighty cold and incessant rains. What some say—that the strength of the sun in Syria can hardly be endured—is false, for the winter here is like ours in the west. . . .

All these matters, my dearest one, are only a few of many. Because I cannot express to you in person, my dearest, all in my heart, I bid thee take care of thyself and of thy lands, and treat the children and vassals with lenience, as becomes thee, for in truth thou wilt behold me as soon as I may come to thee in honor. Farewell.

Bohemund was oppressed by longing, and a dream. Fair indeed was Syria, with its rich valleys and wide, stone-flagged caravan roads. The Norman knew the trade routes. Through here passed endless loads of silk and white ivory, fruit and rugs, and the precious ingredients—camphor, oil-of-sesame, myrrh, perfumes of rose and aloes. In times of peace they would enter the Gate of the Dogs, and be scattered among the bazaars. Ships would bring other loads from Egypt—rice, papyrus, cotton cloth.

Antioch was more to be desired than Rome or the little mountain towns of Norman Italy, where people made wine and quarreled, or slept under olive trees. Antioch was impregnable, in strong hands. He, Bohemund, would know well how to hold it. He knew exactly what Armenian princes he would have for allies, and how the frontiers could be guarded and extended.

Already the taciturn Baldwin, Godfrey's brother, had made himself master of a great citadel—Edessa, out to the east. The Armenians had received him like a veritable King Stork, and had given him a princess for wife. Bohemund dreamed of building an empire around Syria, with Byzantium to the north and the Moslem powers to the south, and the sea here, at his threshold.

And now, as the month of May drew to its end, the mighty Norman had within his grasp a key that would open the wall of Antioch to him.

No one else knew of this, except perhaps Tancred. For the last few weeks the garrison had fared worse than the besiegers. A certain Turkish officer, probably Armenian by birth, Firuz by name, had sent a message to the commander of the Christians to say that he was prepared to let them into the city and to surrender three towers to them.

Firuz, it seemed, had been ill treated by Yagi Siyan. Probably he despaired of holding out. In any case he addressed his message to Bohemund. The Norman had been so active in the siege that the Turks took for granted that he was the leader of the crusaders. Bohemund had responded instantly, encouraging Firuz, promising him reward, safety.

When he assured himself that the Turkish officer could be relied on, Bohemund had called a council of the princes. Without mentioning Firuz or his offer, the Norman had suggested bluntly that they agree among themselves to give all title to Antioch to the one who succeeded in breaking through and capturing it. And they had refused, saying that, since all had endured much in the siege, the city could be given to no single lord.

Moreover, there was the oath to Alexis. All in all, the Byzantine emperor had lived up to his half of the agreement. He had sent supplies and ships whenever possible, and he was now not far behind them.

After the council broke up two alternatives faced Bohemund—to avail himself of Firuz's treachery and enter Antioch, if he could, turning it over to all the crusaders, or to delay, without accomplishing anything. As it happened, he did not need to make a decision.

Within two days alarming news reached the camp. The Moslem army of Mosul, Aleppo, and Damascus was approaching rapidly. It had delayed to besiege Baldwin in Edessa, or it would have been at Antioch before now. Baldwin had held out until the sultans left Edessa. They would be at Antioch within three days. And this mass of cavalry from the east outnumbered the crusaders, who would be caught between it and the wall of Antioch.

Already the barons scattered through the near-by castles were hastening in to the main body, armed for combat. At once the council of the princes assembled. Almost without discussion they yielded to the solitary Norman.

"If Bohemund can win the city, with or without the help of others, we bestow it upon him willingly, on one condition —if the emperor comes to join us, and carries out his agreement with us as he swore to do, the city is his by right. But if the emperor fails to do this, Bohemund may keep it in his power."

Only the stubborn St. Gilles refused to agree to this. Not even calamity, approaching as swiftly as horses could gallop, prevailed upon the old Provençal to yield his claim to Bohemund.

For two days Bohemund tried to get in touch again with Firuz up in the hills. Naturally he had said nothing to anyone of the chance that lay just beyond his grasp. If Firuz's offer became known in the camp, the Turkish spies would hear of it.

The uncertainty became too great for one member of the crusade. The road through the Taurus stood open still; in another few hours it might be closed forever. Stephen, count of Blois, and provisional head of the council, had never fancied himself in the rôle of a dead hero. With all his following he departed to the north, toward the Byzantine army and his beloved Adele.

The next evening Firuz sent out his son to Bohemund as hostage, and urged him to make the attempt on Antioch at once.

XXIII

THE TOWER OF THE TWO SISTERS

IRUZ had planned carefully all that must be done. On the following afternoon the crusaders must sound their trumpets and muster a strong force, riding off into the hills to the south and west as if departing on a foraging expedition. After nightfall this detachment should turn back through the foothills, making no noise, until they reached the ditch below his post—a tower known as the Two Sisters. Firuz urged them to wait until a patrol of the guard with torches had made its round of the wall. Then he would find a way to let them into the tower. But Bohemund must come in with the first men.

There was little time in which to prepare. Bohemund sent his heralds through the camp to warn the leaders. Godfrey and Robert of Flanders joined him and they led out their men in the feint toward the hills, while the Provençals stood to arms at the fort on the Mahometry—now rechristened the Blessed Mary. Not until they were clear of the camp did the Norman explain his project to the duke of Lorraine and the count of Flanders. With a fanfare of trumpets, they passed out of sight.

Evening fell, and the outline of the hills became blurred under the stars. Bohemund turned sharp to the left and began to climb toward the familiar dark mass of the great wall, keeping his distance among the ravines and counting the towers until he thought he was opposite the Two Sisters. Behind him rode the Unknown.

"By God's favor," said the tall Norman, "Antioch will this night be yielded to us."

The word, repeated from man to man, went back through the column and the soldiers pressed forward restlessly. The order came for them to dismount, and they waited for long hours until the flare of torches showed on the summit of the wall. Several Turks passed by with the lights, and when all was quiet Bohemund moved down into the ditch with his men. By then it was near dawn.

Groping along the wall, they came upon a ladder of twisted ropes already in place.

"Go up quietly," Bohemund ordered.

Some sixty of his swordsmen climbed up, one following the other, to the summit of the tower. Then came a pause, and a Lombard descended, asking for Bohemund. "Firuz says," he repeated, "we are too few. He says, 'Where is the invincible Bohemund?' My lord, we already hold three towers."

Without a word the Norman went up the ladder, and his men pressed after him. When he disappeared into the tower shouts were heard, and the clashing of steel. "God wills it!"

And then, under the press of men in armor, the rope ladder broke and a dozen bodies fell among the watchers below. Overhead the tumult increased as the crusaders moved out along the wall and the alarm was given in near-by towers. A hundred men, with Bohemund and probably Count Robert also, were cut off from the waiting column.

The Unknown remained under the wall. Voices clamored around him in the darkness. The first streaks of dawn spread over the ridge of hills, but in the hollow by the wall nothing could be seen. Somebody remembered that a postern gate ought to be near to the left of these towers, and they began to look for it, stumbling along the ditch. Presently there was a shout, and the thudding of axes against wood. The postern had been found, and the soldiers made their way toward the sound of battering.

They broke down the gate and surged into the wall. Some climbed the steps of the towers, others ran down toward the city where everything was still quiet, before the first summons to prayer.

No muezzin called from the minaret balconies that dawn. Antioch had fallen. Moslems clustered on the flat roofs, looking up at the hills, women wailing and children weeping. Bands of mounted Turkomans galloped through the narrow streets. Yagi Siyan with a few followers passed like a gust of wind toward a distant gate. He had been roused out of sleep by the blast of Bohemund's trumpet on the towers, and in the confusion thought that it had come from the citadel. If he had gone up to the citadel instead of fleeing, matters might have taken a different turn.

While some of the Turks hastened up the winding paths to the citadel, others wiped their hands and feet and prayed for the last time, facing the south where Mecca lay. They had seen the crimson standard of the Normans planted on the hill below the citadel, and throngs of the iron men cutting their way down to the Bridge Gate.

This gate was seized and opened, and the Provençals poured in. While Bohemund and his men assailed the walls of the citadel, slaughter and looting began below in the streets.

The crusaders occupied the squares and ransacked the houses, cutting down everyone they found and throwing the bodies from the roofs. They could not walk through the streets without stepping over the bodies. Behind them thronged the rabble, snatching up rugs and silk hangings, smashing chests and cabinets to look for silver and pearls.

They entered the deserted mosques, staring at the carved and gilded *minbars*, kicking over the stands that held the great Korans, dragging white-turbaned *hadjis* from the galleries. They believed that these mosques were the temples of Anti-Christ, built to house some hideous image of the pagan god Mahound. But they encountered only shadow, the dull light from fretted windows of colored glass, and the smell of burnt-out candles and the blood of the newly slain.

In one mosque, the Jami or cathedral, they found a crowd of Moslems huddled, and they struck with ax and club until the bodies covered the great prayer carpets. Knights and men of arms explored the palaces, taking what seized their fancy, breaking into the alabaster and malachite fretwork that guarded the women's sanctuaries, pulling the Turkish slave girls from the sleeping recesses, violating them or putting them to death. Through the long corridors tramped the armed multitude, exulting. They flung themselves down on cushioned divans and made the slaves sing to them.

Pallid Greek girls and slender Armenians knelt before them, making the sign of the cross fearfully to show that they were Christians, hoping to ward off the long swords that slashed the life out of human bodies as wind blows out the flame of candles. In the corners the rabble gathered to strip and torture the Turks, cutting open their stomachs and leading them around by the entrails, or burning them.

The day passed in triumph, but the Normans could not take the citadel. Bohemund was carried down, wounded in the hip.

To him came a party of Armenians from the mountains, who had intercepted Yagi Siyan and his followers. They brought with them the head of the Turkoman governor, and his sword sling and sheath, which they sold for sixty byzants. So says the Unknown.

Antioch fell in the morning of the third of June in the year 1098. On the fourth, the scouts of the Moslem army of relief came into sight beyond the lake at the Iron Bridge of the Aleppo road. Bohemund was wounded, Godfrey and Raymond of St. Gilles were both ill, but never did three men labor harder than these during the next two days.

While revelry roared through Antioch and crusaders feasted on the palace terraces, some of the leaders assembled dependable men and good horses and rode down the Orontes to the port of St. Simeon, requisitioned all the supplies they could lay hand on, and hurried back. The Bridge Gate was strengthened; Count Robert of Flanders volunteered to hold with his men the outwork that had been called the Mahometry and was now known as the Blessed Mary.

Roger of Barneville, a distinguished knight, made a sortie, drove back the Moslem patrols, but was captured and killed. Heavy fighting began along the Orontes, the crusaders being driven back steadily, until on the sixth of June the great army of the amirs, the army of relief, passed the lake and encamped within sight of Antioch's towers.

At this point the men of the cross might still have gone out to meet the Moslems in open battle. A number of reasons restrained them from doing this—Bohemund's wound, the confusion following the seizure of the city, the fact that the citadel at their backs was still in the hands of the Turks. At all events, they did not do so, and the opportunity was lost. They were now the besieged, cut off from the sea and the Taurus, and the Moslems of the Eastern amirs had become the besiegers.

And the newcomers from the east showed themselves to be no sluggish foemen. They pressed the attack at once. Robert of Flanders held out with all his youthful courage in the castle of the Blessed Mary, but was forced to evacuate it when the Moslems brought up powerful engines. He set fire to the castle in the night and withdrew safely with his men into the Bridge Gate.

Meanwhile Moslem cavalry appeared in the hills in back of Antioch. They established communication with Achmed ibn Merwan, the defender of the citadel, and entered the walls through one of the citadel gates. Fresh and full of zeal, mounted on excellent horses, they drove the crusaders out of the near-by heights in several sharp encounters.

The Turks pressed their advantage, descending the slope of the citadel to the ravine beneath it. Between them and the city proper a low ridge intervened, above the ruins of an ancient Roman theater. Here the crusaders made a stand, assailed by stones from the engines of the citadel and by flights of arrows and javelins. At evening, when the fighting ceased, they still held the ridge, apparently without anyone in command.[1]

But the situation of the Christian army was precarious. The enemy occupied the heights within the wall, and the line of the Orontes. Bohemund appeared at the ridge, the menaced point, and ordered a wall to be put up of stones, débris— anything that would serve for a barrier to block up the gorge through which ran the road from the citadel down to the city proper. Either to help in the defense of the ridge or to rout out his men who had grown weary and were sulking in the houses around Yagi Siyan's palace, he set fire to the dwellings behind the ridge.

A strong wind rose, and the flames spread, burning more than two thousand houses and filling all Antioch with smoke and cinders. The crusaders fought the fire and checked it before it reached the Church of the Apostles. It put an end to the confusion and the malingering, because the plunderers and hiders-out hastened to join their various commands at the gates or the palace of Yagi Siyan, fearing that the army was going to abandon the city.

But already the rope-walking had begun. The specter of hunger started it. There had been little food in Antioch, and they were killing horses and donkeys for meat. Discouraged by the hopeless prospect, the weaker spirits were escaping over the walls to the west, at night. They let down ropes and slipped away, some falling into the hands of Turkish patrols and some reaching St. Simeon, where their stories of defeat and approaching famine induced the seamen to man their vessels and set sail from the coast. Before long the Turks appeared in force and burned what was left of the vessels.

In this fashion went the two Grandmesnils, and a certain Vido and Lambert the Pauper, among many others. The crusaders dubbed them rope-walkers.

"All our comrades are dead," the rope-walkers said, "and we only got away with our lives."

---

[1] The citadel height is so steep that the only way to reach the city below is to descend diagonally into the ravine and follow it down. Bohemund's ridge must have formed a barrier across the lower ravine. The present writer camped near this citadel and made a careful examination of the whole circuit of the walls.

Outnumbered and lacking supplies, the crusaders in Antioch had only one hope. They knew that the emperor and the Byzantine army with new contingents of crusaders were moving toward the city, and could not be far from the Taurus. Stephen of Blois and his men must meet with Alexis soon.

Daily the men of the cross in Antioch watched the foothills to the north for a glimpse of the gilded standards of Byzantium, or couriers hastening to the city. The days passed, and Bohemund still fought at the line of his ridge, and they waited in vain.

Food failed steadily. A loaf of bread sold for a byzant, a cock for fifteen shillings, an egg for two shillings, and a single nut for a copper coin. The ones who could not buy food cooked grape vines and thistles.

The head of a horse [Raymond, the chaplain of the Provençals observes] without the tongue sold for two or three silver shillings,[1] and the intestines of a goat, in truth, for five. What shall I say of bread, when five shillings' worth would not ease one man's hunger? Green figs plucked from the trees sold most dear. Very many knights kept themselves alive by the blood of their horses, and awaited God's mercy, being reluctant to kill the horses until now. . . . The Count fell ill, most gravely, and also the Bishop. On the other hand Count Stephen, whom the princes had chosen as leader before the capture of the city, fled on hearing the talk of a coming battle.

Stephen met Alexis beyond the Taurus. He went to the emperor's tent and spoke to him in private. Perhaps he sincerely believed what he said, yet he seems to have thought only of justifying his own flight.

"Know for certain," he said, "that Antioch hath been taken, but the citadel hath not been taken. Our men are sore pressed, and I think by now they have been killed by the Turks."

Urgently he advised Alexis to turn back, with all his forces, and not to advance farther. The emperor summoned the

---

[1]Money in the Eleventh Century was worth probably twenty times what it is to-day.

Grandmesnils to him, and the story of the rope-walkers confirmed Stephen. Only the newcomers upon the crusade who had been on the way to meet their comrades at Antioch objected to turning back. A Norman lord who had hoped to join Bohemund went to Alexis angrily and pointed at Stephen.

"In truth, never have I heard mention of any battle in which he hath had a part. Basely, he turns back, and me-seems that whatever he says thou mayest hold to be false."

Alexis meditated upon what he had heard. Until now his generals had been occupied in mopping up Asia Minor, capturing and garrisoning the citadels in the path of the crusaders. So far the crusaders had been a valuable weapon; they had broken the power of the Red Lion and had restored to him a dozen provinces.

But now, beyond the Taurus in Syria, they were off the map. He no longer had need of them. And he knew from his spies the great strength of the army of the amirs. Here the real power of Islam was gathered for the first time.

At once he gave orders to retreat, taking all the Christians with him, and throwing out detachments to the rear to check the pursuit of the amirs. Retiring, he laid waste the country behind the Taurus.

Alexis's action has been explained and excused. He believed the army of the cross would be annihilated, and to advance would place his own forces in danger. He must think of his empire before the crusade.

This does not alter the fact that Alexis broke his oath to the crusaders and abandoned them at the moment when they had greatest need of his help.

With the ships gone, and the emperor retreating, the crusaders were starving slowly in Antioch, in the stench of dead bodies, while fever and dysentery weakened them daily. They were cut off from the outside world, and it seemed to them that death awaited them there, where the gray walls would be their tomb.

They looked into the skies at night, for a sign from above. They saw a star fall, flaming beyond the lines of the Turks.

XXIV

ADHEMAR AND BARTHOLOMEW

Ⓣ HESE were days of anxiety for Adhemar, bishop of Puy and papal vicar of the army. No longer could the mind of the quiet and courageous prelate dwell on the music of his chants or the singing of the Angelus. To his sensitive spirit the sin and the suffering of the army appeared to be an omen of doom.

The debauchery after the storming of Antioch weighed upon him—not the blood of it, but the fornication with pagan women, and the revelry among the dead bodies. He understood the princes and the belted knights—he had grown up among them, and they were his peers—but the mass of the armed men and the "crowd" seemed to him to have forsaken the bonds of the Church, and to be wandering without hope in darkness. The crowd had raged and destroyed, and now it thronged the churches, praying for a sign from the heavens.

It pleased Adhemar that the princes had taken oath in these last days never to abandon Antioch. Bohemund had been the first to swear, and Tancred had added that so long as he had forty knights to follow him, he would not turn back from the road to Jerusalem. The oath pleased the crowd, that had been saying the princes might forsake it, or go off somewhither to another citadel, as Count Stephen and the rope-walkers had done.

But to the brooding Adhemar the road to Jerusalem seemed to be closed. He did not think he would ever set foot upon the valley of the blessed Jordan, or kneel before the rocks of the Mount.

Daily he performed the offices in the church taken over by the Provençals, near the palace of Yagi Siyan. Into the church thronged the women of his flock with wan faces. Their number had diminished in pitiable fashion, since they were not able to endure hunger as well as the men. The wives of the nobles and the children of the peasants went about together, bearing themselves calmly when the men looked at them, but agonized in their confessions to the priests. There were women who had lost their husbands and had taken, perforce, other protectors. Their sheltered life in the feudal manors was a thing of the past, only half remembered. And they also besought him for a sign. They said that the army had come to fight for the Son of God. It had been victorious until now. But now—would not the Lord of Hosts give aid? He had dried up the waters of a river for another host and had drawn water from rocks to give drink to the thirsty. Would not He offer them a sign?

Men talked in whispers of strange portents, discussed the flaming star. A certain priest, Stephen by name, dreamed that Christ had spoken to him, saying that within five days help would come to the army. Adhemar summoned Stephen and made him take oath that this was true.

After that a bearded and ragged youth approached him, a Provençal peasant who had talked of visions in which St. Andrew had appeared to him. But the youth, Peter Bartholomew, had twice tried to flee from Antioch, and Adhemar's stern integrity questioned the truth of his mutterings. And the people also shook their heads, saying, "How can we believe this?"

Peter Bartholomew came again to the bishop's door, and asked for an audience with him and the count of St. Gilles.

At this audience Raymond, the chaplain of the count, was also present, and he has written down what was said:

When the count and the bishop—so runs the narrative of Raymond—required of him the full story of his revelation and vision, Peter Bartholomew replied:

"During the first earthquake at Antioch, when the army of the Franks was besieging the city, great fear seized upon me, so that I could only pray, 'God help us.'

"It was night then, and I was lying down in a hut without any companion to comfort me. When, as I said, the shaking lasted a long time and my fear kept growing, two men stood before me, clearly, in shining garments. One was old, with red and gray hair on his head, and black eyes and a kind face, his white beard large in size, and his stature middling. The other was younger, taller, and more beautiful than any son of man. The elder said to me, 'What doest thou?'

"And I was more frightened than before, because I knew no one could be there in the hut with me. And I answered, 'Who art thou?'

"And he responded, 'Arise and do not fear and listen to what I say to thee. I am the apostle Andrew. Call together the bishop of Puy and the count of St. Gilles and Peter Raymond of Hautpol and tell them of these things. Why hath the bishop neglected to preach to the people and talk with them, and to sign them with the cross he bears before him? For it would help them much.' And he added, 'Come and I will show to thee the lance of our Lord Jesus Christ, which thou wilt give to the count, since God hath intended it for him since his birth.'

"So I got up and followed him out into the city with nothing on me but a shirt. And he led me by the northern gate, to the church of the blessed Peter that the Saracens had made into a mosque aforetime. In this church, in truth, were two lamps which gave out there as much light as if mid-day illumined it. And he said to me, 'Wait here.' And he commanded me to sit against a column near the steps by which we go up to the altar from the south. Yet his companion stood far off before the altar step. Then going down under the ground, St. Andrew brought out the lance and placed it in my hands and said to me, '*Behold the lance which opened the side of Him from Whom hath come the salvation of all the world.*'

"While I held it in my hands, weeping with joy, I said to him,

'Lord, if it is thy wish, I will carry it and give it to the count.'

"And he said to me, 'Not so—for the city will be taken.[1] And then thou wilt come again with twelve men, and thou wilt look for it here, whence I have taken it out, and where I shall hide it.'

"And he hid it. When these things had taken place in this fashion, he led me back over the wall of the city to my dwelling. Then I bethought myself of my poverty and of your magnificence, and I dreaded to go near you. After that I set out toward a certain castle near Roja, to search for food. On the first day of Lent at cock-crow the blessed Andrew revealed himself to me in the same dress and with the same companion who had been with him before, and a great light filled the house. And the blessed Andrew said, 'Art thou awake?'

"So I was startled, and answered, 'Nay, my Lord—nay, I am not asleep.'

"And he asked me, 'Hast thou said those things which I bade thee say?'

"And I answered, 'Lord, did I not pray you that you would send another? For, fearing my poverty, I dared not go to them.'

"And he said, 'God hath chosen thee from among all men, as a grain of wheat is gathered from chaff, because thou art greater by merit and favor, than all others, as gold excels silver.'

"Comforted in this fashion I went back to the siege. But again, realizing the failing of my poverty, I began to be afraid that if I came to you, you would think I was a serf telling this thing to get food. So I was silent.

"Time passed, and when I was at the port of St. Simeon, sleeping in a tent with my master, William Peter, there came to me the blessed Andrew in the same dress and with the same companion as before, saying to me, 'Why hast thou not told the count and the others what I commanded?'

"And I replied, 'Have I not prayed, Lord, that thou wouldst send another and a wiser one than me? Besides, the Turks are along the road, and they kill people coming and going.'

"And St. Andrew said to me, 'Have no fear—nothing will harm thee.'

"And my master, William Peter, heard these words, although he did not see the apostle.

"Thus comforted, I went back to the army. When I wished to speak with you I was not able to manage it. So I went away to the

---

[1]The crusaders were still outside the walls, at the time of which Bartholomew speaks.

port of Mamistra. And there, in truth, when I wanted to sail to the island of Cyprus for food, the blessed Andrew threatened me much if I did not go back and tell you what had been commanded. I thought and thought how I could return, and I wept because I could not think of a way. Then my master and his companions made me enter the ship. But at sunset a storm came up and we were forced to sail back to the port. There I was very ill. But when the city [Antioch] was taken I came to you. And now, if it please you, put these things I have told you to the test.".

For the strange story of Peter Bartholomew there existed no proof of any kind. It was a rambling story, full of repetitions, and it made much of the count of St. Gilles. The young peasant obviously had tried to flee from the army several times, and he might well have visited the Church of St. Peter after the capture of the city.

Adhemar said frankly that he believed it to be nothing but words. Raymond was thoughtful, half convinced. In the end he turned Bartholomew over to Raymond, the chaplain, for questioning.

And the devout chaplain, who had believed the story from the first, asked the Provençal bishop of Orange to aid him in the questioning. No further test might have been made if it had not been for the restlessness of the multitude. In the next few days the famine became worse, and Adhemar and Bohemund closed the gates of the city to keep the sufferers from giving themselves up to the Turks, to get food.

Feverish and half-starved men related other visions. Priests remembered the star that had fallen near Antioch, and the prophecy of the one named Stephen that within five days aid would come to the Christians. St. Gilles decided to go and dig up the spot where Bartholomew had said the lance would be found—the lance that had been thrust into the side of Christ that day more than a thousand years before.

St. Gilles himself went with eleven men and the peasant, down to the Church of St. Peter, which was cleared of worshipers. A crowd gathered about the doors, increasing as the word of the test spread through the camps. Through the morning hours the crowd waited, at first eager, then despondent and almost desperate. Count Raymond left the church and others followed. But the chaplain Raymond stayed, and he has written down what happened:

For during one night a great star flamed over the city, and a little while after divided into three, and fell down upon the Turks. A little comforted by this, our men waited for the fifth day which the priest had foretold. Then, on that day, after making suitable preparations, with the man who had spoken of the lance, we began to dig, after putting out all others from the church of the Blessed Peter. Moreover, we were twelve men in all, with the Bishop of Orange, and Raymond, chaplain of the Count, who has written these words, and the Count himself, and Pontius of Balazun, and Faraldus of Thuart. And when they had dug from early morning until vespers, some began to lose hope of finding the lance.

BATTLE SCENE IN ASIA

From an Eleventh Century manuscript. Judging by the headdress of the figures in the four scenes, they are all intended to be Orientals. This is an extremely early illumination. It represents probably a European artist's conception of the stories told by travelers. Notice that the swords are of the Western type, and that only one horseman is shown carrying a sword. (The Byzantines and many Persians, however, used the long, straight sword.) The shields are painted in different fashions. The camels are easily recognized. This may be the first attempt in Europe to paint the battle castles borne by elephants in Asia—if they are elephants. (*See illustration opposite*)

Then the Count went away to guard the castle; but in place of him and the others who were weary of digging, we led in other fresh men who began the work again with vigor. Finally the youth who had spoken of the lance, seeing us worn out, ungirdled himself and, taking off his shoes, went down into the pit wearing only his shirt. He implored us solemnly to offer prayers to God, that He would give us His lance, to comfort and bring victory to His people.

At last the Lord was moved to pity us, and revealed to us His lance.

And I who have written these words, when no more than the point had appeared above the ground—I kissed it. But I cannot tell in words what a mighty joy and exultation filled the city.

It can only be said that our men were defeated and dispirited and in agony, when aid came from Heaven.

BATTLE SCENE IN ASIA

REPRODUCED FROM THE MSS. VAT. LAT. 5729 OF THE APOSTOLIC
LIBRARY, IN THE VATICAN CITY

ANTIOCH

West half of city, in Roman days; the Bridge Gate in the foreground.

The tidings spread like wind-blown flames through the multitude. A sign had been granted. God would aid them. The crowd had its token, and it rejoiced. A bishop and a chaplain had witnessed the miracle, and a piece of rusted iron now rested in their hands.

Adhemar said nothing more. The leaders met in council and chose Bohemund to take command for fifteen days. They knew that the feeling of their men had changed utterly in a night. Women and priests now marched through the streets in procession. Hymns were heard in the churches. Even the rabble begged to be led out to battle. And Adhemar commanded three days' fast and prayer.

The exaltation that had seized upon the thousands after the lance-head was found in St. Peter's did not diminish. Heightened by the suffering of the fast, it was shared by every soul in Antioch. They were little better than dead men, but they were no longer afraid. The shadow of destruction lay over them, and they did not care.

> *"Wood of the cross,*
> *Sign of the leader*
> *Follows the army*
> *Never yielding*
> *Always advancing,*
> *Borne on by the Holy Spirit,"*

The song of the crusade rang out clear in those three days. Still the leaders waited and talked among themselves. It would be little better than a final hazard to take out such an army of dying men to meet the princes of Asia. Even Adhemar saw no hope for them; Count Raymond could not rise from his couch; the steadfast Godfrey had nothing to say.

At the last moment Peter the Hermit and a certain Herlwin were sent out to discuss terms with the Moslems. What they offered and what they asked for will never be known. One story is that the crusaders were willing to withdraw from Syria if the Moslems would grant a peace. Another is that the Christian barons offered to meet an equal number of the princes of Asia and decide the issue between them.

But there is no doubt of the answer that the Hermit brought back.

"Return and say to your lords that if they will accept Islam, and become Muhammadans and cease to worship their God, we will give them land in this country. Moreover, they will not be oppressed, but will then be nobles like ourselves, riding on horses. But if they will not do this, tell them that they will die or be kept as slaves to serve us."

Herlwin repeated the words—he seems to have known Arabic. The multitude in Antioch moved toward the churches. Throughout that night they knelt before the robed priests, confessed their sins, and were absolved. They took the communion of the body and blood of Christ, and celebrated Mass.

The following morning they went out to the battle.

XXV

THE LANCE GOES FORTH

FROM a distance the Moslem army watched the crusaders with curiosity. Its commander, Kerbogha, was in no hurry to move from his pavilion. He had heard various tales about these Franks who had appeared from nowhere. They ate, he understood, half a dozen hogs in a day, and human flesh as well. They were poorly armed—an old lance and a broken bow and rusted sword had been shown him by his scouts—they rode mares as well as horses, and were not above mounting donkeys or oxen. In fact, some of them were on the backs of cattle now.

Kerbogha—the Pillar of the State—was prince of Mosul and blood relation of the great sultans. He had with him Rudwan of Aleppo, and Rudwan's brother, Sultan Dokak of Damascus, with the atabeg Tughtakin. Veteran Turks followed them, a force composed entirely of horsemen armed with strong short bows and heavy scimitars and the curved stabbing knives—*yataghans*.

On the flanks beyond them were ranged the armies of Jerusalem, under Sokman-ibn-Ortuk, and the contingents of Arab princes who had led their clans to the mutual quarrel.

Dokak and Kerbogha had fought more or less steadily with these Arabs for several years, but they were all servants of Islam and they made common cause against the invaders. The Arabs of the Kilab had joined the expedition scenting loot.

Kerbogha's army was very numerous and he had some of the finest cavalry of western Asia camped by his standard— regiments of Seljuk Turks in their wide-sleeved *khalats* lined with padded cloth and Persian chain mail, and wearing high damascened helmets.

The army of Jerusalem had thoroughbred horses, with high, peaked saddles and small painted shields and light bows. White turbans and the black burnouses of the desert riders showed among them. Not since the death of Malik Shah had such a host come together in peace, and Kerbogha had no doubt of the issue—although Rudwan warned him that the crusaders were formidable in hand-to-hand fighting.

"They will not save themselves except by the sword," the amir replied carelessly.

He made no effort to advance against the crusaders as they came out of the Bridge Gate and crossed the Orontes. Better to let them emerge into the plain. The Moslems outnumbered them, and were all mounted, whereas only a portion of the unbelievers rode horses—some bestrode camels and asses. Kerbogha reasoned that he should allow them to form in the plain on this side the river, whence they could not retreat again across the solitary bridge. An experienced soldier, he saw his opportunity to put an end to the Christian invasion in one stroke.

Noticing that the Christian line extended itself from the river to the nearest hills in the north—more than a mile and a half—he gave orders to withdraw nearly two miles to a place where the plain widened out. By doing so he forced the crusaders to come forward on foot after his horsemen.

The morning passed, and the glare of the sun increased. Toward midday the lines of Moslems dismounted and knelt on their cloaks or saddle rugs, while the voices of the callers-to-prayer rose in the long cadenced chant:

"Allah is Almighty—Allah is Almighty . . . I witness that

there is no other god but Allah—I witness that Muhammad is his prophet. . . . Come to prayer—come to prayer. . . . Come to the house of praise. . . . Allah is Almighty—Allah is Almighty. . . . There is no god but Allah."

The last low shout died away and the cloaked figures rose, putting on their slippers and soft leather boots. It was time to be in the saddle. A division of Seljuk Turks trotted off to the left, toward the river. Another body rode slowly to the right, into the foothills. They were to go around the flanks of the Christian battle line and attack from the rear, while Kerbogha's main army held its position.

The crusaders had done their best, under Bohemund's urging, to form an orderly battle line. Hugh the Great had emerged first, with the splendor of the royal French arms and caparisoning somewhat the worse for service. But the real strength of his division lay in the knights of Flanders and Normandy who followed him, under the two Roberts. After crossing the bridge they deployed to the right and formed in double ranks near the river.

After them came Godfrey, duke of Lorraine, who took the center of the line with his Rhinelanders. Then from the Bridge Gate rode Adhemar, in full armor. He had assumed command of the Provençals because Count Raymond, weakened by illness, had been left in charge of the garrison in Antioch, to watch the Moslems in the citadel. Adhemar moved to the left of the line, his flank resting on the mountains.

Last of the great lords appeared Bohemund with his crimson standard. He had with him all the Normans of the South, and what might be called the flying column of knights who followed that magnificent fighter, Tancred.

So they formed, and advanced at a foot pace toward the massed horsemen of the Moslem amirs. But there was little order in the advance. Perforce, the few mounted knights had been scattered among the foot soldiers, except for Tancred's small unit. Dismounted knights walked forward without their lances; behind them pressed peasants, bills and pikes over their shoulders. They stumbled through cultivated fields and made their way slowly through orchards, keeping in touch after a fashion with the men nearest them. The line extended as the plain widened. The leaders soon were out of touch with the other commands. Tafur and his ribalds strode along with the rest, cudgels in their fists.

Among the armed ranks marched the women of the crusade, who had come out to share the fate of the men, and who did not expect to survive defeat. That maker of songs, Richard the Pilgrim, noticed them.

> *These women who came to serve Our Lord,*
> *Went out that day from Antioch,*
> *Their hair bound up in long waist cords—*
> *Some in their sleeves have gathered rocks,*
> *But more have water, in bottles poured.*

A strange march, this of dying men eaten by starvation. Husbands carrying broken weapons walked hand in hand with their children in rags. Peter the Hermit in his brown monk's robe strode barefoot at the head of his flock. Bishops and clerics in surplice and cap trudged through the fields, cross in hand. The sun rose higher. Here and there men fell behind, too weak to go on.

Singing was heard toward the left, where Adhemar rode. Before him, a priest carried a new standard, a cross upon which was bound the rusted iron lance-head that had been dug up from the ground.

Fighting began on the right, near the river. The Turks had swept around that flank. Bohemund, however, held his reserve intact behind the main line. A fresh division was hastily formed of Rhinelanders and Robert's Normans, and placed in command of a knight named Reinaud. Reinaud's men went to meet the Turks. But the battle line went on.

The uproar by the river increased, and drew nearer. Fresh Moslem cavalry came up, and the clashing of swords could be heard distinctly. In the shallow valleys on the extreme left, Adhemar's men were engaged, but no one knew what was happening there. Armenians had appeared, thronging from the hills to watch the battle. And a rumor ran from man to man that other unknown horsemen had been seen, mounted on white chargers and carrying white standards. They uttered no battle cry, and their faces and armor were exceedingly bright.

Some of the crusaders thought these unknown horsemen were warrior saints, led by St. George to aid them.

The tumult on the right grew less, but smoke poured up from the river bank and spread over the fields, and the crackling of flames was heard. The Turks, withdrawing at this point, had set fire to the dry grass, and the fire spread before the wind under that burning sun. The crusaders moved around it, beat it out with their cloaks or waited until it had passed. Under the smoke pall the battle line moved on.

A roar went up as the Provençals charged through the foothills:

"God wills it!"

Adhemar charged, and men thronged after the standard of the lance. They shouted, with strained faces and staring eyes. They broke into the line of the Turks, and pulled warriors from the saddles. Here was slain the one who carried the standard of the lance, and Raymond the chaplain took it in his hands and ran on.

In the center nothing of this could be seen. Moslem horsemen galloped toward them through the olive trees, emerging like armed specters out of the drifting smoke. Unarmed crusaders caught at the bridles and went down. Swordsmen grouped together and stood their ground, while arrows ripped through them. Dying men handed their weapons to others and lay quiet, whispering their confession of sins, and with weak fingers plucking grass from the ground to thrust into their mouths as the Host of the last sacrament. Through and over the Moslem attack, the Christian battle line went on.

Men stumbled over the bodies of priests, the white vestments stained with spreading blood. They scattered and shouted joyfully as horsemen in gray mail appeared behind them. With a thudding of hoofs and a rattling of lance shafts against shields Godfrey charged with his knights, and the throng pressed after, staring into the haze, hearing the distant shout, "God wills it!"

The long swords crushed through Moslem shields. Among rearing horses and frantic men who no longer knew what was happening beyond reach of their weapons, the line of the crusaders advanced. They did not shout now, but they wept with joy, dragging forward their companions who lagged or staggered. Reeling, the blood flowing over them, the wounded tried to keep their feet, clutching at pierced intestines or throbbing throats. Panting with the heat, knights flung their helmets ahead of them.

Nothing could stand against this charge of men who had forgotten life and who looked for death. They exulted, and they followed no human leader—only ahead of them, invisible and long expected and now at last at hand, they felt the presence of that other leader, Christ.

They saw the crimson standard of the Normans pass forward, and made way for Bohemund's mailed horsemen. And then Tancred and his riders.

The last reserves of the crusaders had been thrown into the battle. And the battle was won.

So rapidly did the Moslems retreat that their camp was abandoned. For a while Kerbogha and his personal followers made a stand by the tents and tried to gather up the most valuable of their belongings. But the Norman horsemen broke into his ranks again, and he joined the fugitives.

For once the crusaders did not stop to gather up the plunder in the camp. Tancred, as usual, pressed the pursuit, until he reached Harim on the road to Aleppo. And the Armenians thronged out of the mountains to avenge themselves on their late conquerors, the Moslems.

The Unknown, who always was careful to look over spoil for things of practical value, could hardly find words to describe all he saw in the encampment of the Turks. There stood Kerbogha's gilded pavilion, hung with tapestries. The tents of the Seljuk chieftains yielded any amount of rugs; whole trains of camels were roped together near by.

In truth [he exclaims] the foe abandoned their pavilions, and in the pavilions gold, silver, and rich furnishings, and also cattle, sheep, horses, mules, camels, asses, and grain, wine and butter and many other things of which we had sore need.

But the greatest reward was the moral victory. The Moslem host had been overconfident; the onset of the Christians had astonished them, and the Arabs had fled early in the battle. Afterward the Turks blamed Kerbogha for the disaster, and Rudwan of Aleppo as well, who had chafed under the command of the prince of Mosul.

The truce between the contenders for the throne of Malik Shah, always brittle, now broke up. Dokak went back to defend Damascus. Yagi Siyan, whom they had come to aid, was dead, and Rudwan had gone off to Aleppo. Not for years did the Moslem princes in the east unite again to oppose the crusaders. They left the valleys of Syria and the Armenian strongholds to the invaders.

One immediate result of the battle was that the army of the Egyptian sultans—who never had any intention of making an alliance with the crusaders—hastened across the Gaza sands and laid siege to Jerusalem on their own account.

The crusaders, however, knew nothing of this. When they made their way, weary but rejoicing, back to Antioch they found the citadel surrendering to Count Raymond. At first the Provençal banner was raised over it, by mistake, but Bohemund's men saw to it that his crimson banner was hoisted in place of it.

As abruptly as night falls in the depths of a valley, the fighting had ceased. And the survivors of the battle gathered in the churches carrying candles in their hands. Above the deep chant of the men soared the happy voices of the women:

"*Te Deum laudamus!*"

XXVI

THE FIRST FOOTHOLD

THE Battle of the Lance had been won on June 28th. By now the valleys of Palestine to the south would be burned dry by the sun, and the watercourses would be empty. Moreover, the whole situation had changed. The crusaders, too exhausted to take to the road again at once, found themselves masters of quite a territory, stretching all the way from Tarsus to Edessa—enough to supply them with food and garments. And the loot of Kerbogha's pavilions filled the empty treasury a bit.

So they tried to clean up Antioch, and they did consecrate anew the churches that had been turned into mosques and stables. They tore down the Arabic inscriptions, removed the carpets, and set to work to restore the altars. In their zeal they hunted for and found the gentle, bearded old man who had been the patriarch of the Greek Church before their coming, and they paraded him in all splendor to his new office.

They bound up the wounded and prayed over them—for they had no other medicine than that. But bodies had lain in the aqueducts too long, and other things had fallen into the cisterns. Under the blazing sun it was not easy to cleanse away the filth altogether, and they had no means of testing the water. Sickness increased, and grew into an epidemic. A whole regiment of Germans fully equipped with armor landed from Genoese ships, and were wiped out by the pestilence.

On the first of August died a man who could ill be spared, Adhemar, the bishop and captain and counselor. "He was eloquent, and he jested full joyfully," said one crusader, sorrowing, "and he was everybody's friend." They buried Adhemar in the Church of St. Peter where the lance had been found. But his absence was soon felt. He had quieted the quarrels of the lords, and he had been the link between the barons and the common men of arms. There was no one to take his place in the council.

And his death was followed by a strange misgiving. The battle had been a glorious testimonial for the peasant-visionary, Peter Bartholomew, and he had been overwhelmed with attention after it. Whereupon he had related other visions. Adhemar had never expressed belief in his tales, and now Adhemar was dead.

Peter Bartholomew announced that the bishop had appeared before him in company with St. Andrew, and had spoken:

"Gravely did I sin, after the lance was found. And because of this I was led down into hell and most sorely scourged. And my head and face were burned, as thou art able to see. My soul stayed there from the hour in which it went out of my body, until my body was lowered into the dust. If Lord Bohemund doubts this that I say, let him open my sepulcher and my head and face will be seen to be burned. He said that he would carry my body to Jerusalem, but let him not move me, for my body is better here. I commend those who followed me to my lord the Count."

In this way, Bartholomew said, Adhemar spoke to him. Bohemund, of course, did not disturb the bishop's last resting place, but he believed Bartholomew to be lying, and others agreed with him. The prophet had been too voluble, and it seemed to them now as if his visions only served to add prestige to the Provençals, and to disparage the Normans.

No love was lost between the two factions in any case. Raymond refused to agree to Bohemund's claim to Antioch, saying that the city must await the arrival of the emperor, Alexis. The Provençals held and fortified the Bridge Gate and Yagi Siyan's palace, while Bohemund was ensconced in the citadel.

The quarrel was near the breaking point when the epidemic grew worse, and the leaders left the city, going off to the various newly conquered districts, the Normans toward Tarsus and the Rhinelanders toward Edessa, to pay a visit to Baldwin. Hugh of Vermandois and the other Baldwin, of Hainault, were chosen to return to Constantinople to notify Alexis of their victory and to request him to move south to join them—the crusaders had not yet learned how he had left them to shift for themselves when their cause seemed to be lost.

But before the news of the battle reached Alexis, in his palace over the blue water of the Marmora, the careful Basileus had written to Italy—a most curious letter, addressed to the abbot of the monastery of Monte Cassino. At the time Alexis must have believed that the crusaders had been annihilated.

My empire [his missive reads in part] aided them to the utmost, not as a friend might do, but as a father. And had not my empire coöperated with them, who else would have aided them? They are prospering, by God's will, up to now in their service. A multitude of knights and men have passed to the Eternal Sanctuary. But we should not regard them as dead, since they have been borne to life everlasting. As evidence of my faith, and my good will toward your monastery, my empire sends to you an epiloricum beautified by bright gold.

Dispatched in June, during the Sixth Indiction, from the holy city, Constantinople.

Baldwin of Hainault was taken ill and died on the way, but the eloquent Hugh of Vermandois reached Constantinople and delivered his message. He lingered in the palace of the Basileus, reluctant to go back to the crusade. And in the end he went to Paris.

From Antioch, the remaining princes of the crusade sent a letter to the author of it, the venerable Urban II, the pope. It seemed to them to be time to give an account of all that had happened. And now, after losing Adhemar, they felt themselves to be without a leader.

At the end of their missive they urged Urban to join them.

So we, your sons, deprived of the father given to us, ask of you, our spiritual father who sent forth this expedition—who by sermons, induced us to leave our lands and all that we had on those lands, commanding us to assume the cross and to follow Christ, urging us to exalt the Christian name—we ask you to finish the task that you proposed. Come to us, and persuade what others you can to come also.

What in all the world can be more fitting than that? You, standing forth as the head and the father of Christianity, ought to come to the first city of the Christians, and yourself finish the work which is yours.

Again and again we bid you do so, our most loved father, to journey to the city of your fatherhood. As the vicar of St. Peter, take your seat in his church. Thus will you finish the expedition of Jesus Christ which you preached, and we started.

Open to us the gates of both Jerusalems,[1] and free the Sepulcher of our Lord, and raise the Christian name above others. If you will come to us and finish this expedition, all the world will then obey you.

May the living God lead you to come. Amen.

It was an appeal from all the crusaders, and sincere beyond any doubt. They had lost Adhemar whom they had worshiped, and now they urged the apostolic lord to join them.

The army had been absent from home for two years, and it had endured a good deal. Its leaders were still hopeful, but they had sacrificed most of their possessions in Europe to achieve this much. They felt cut off from their people—

---

[1]Antioch, as the seat of St. Peter, was second only to Jerusalem in importance to the Church.

they were beginning to understand that Alexis would no longer aid them—and they hoped that the pope would come to them.

Urban did not come. At the next council, held in the following spring, he appointed a certain Daimbert, archbishop of Pisa, to take Adhemar's place as papal vicar. The crusade had become an established fact; the tidings of victories in Asia brought new throngs in to the churches to take the cross. Already the Germans were arming for the march, and the influence of the German emperor waned as Urban's prestige grew.

At home the tide of the crusade was still rising. And the tide was sweeping Urban into temporal power. He did not go to Antioch.

Meanwhile there was growing up within the ranks of the crusaders a new party. It did not lean toward either the Provençal or Norman factions—rather, it was antagonistic to both of them. It was made up of those who wanted to push the war to an end and to move forward without any more delay to Jerusalem. At first the talk was heard among masterless men and impatient soldiers, who probably did not realize how far Jerusalem was.

When they heard how the Byzantine emperor had withdrawn from them with the count of Blois, they said frankly that the emperor meant them no good. Peter the Hermit was one of the new party, and the poorer knights who had to forage constantly for food. The Unknown sympathized with them. They waited restlessly at Antioch for the return of the lords, who had agreed to assemble there and set out for Jerusalem early in November. They cheered Godfrey when he came in with a small army of Turkish prisoners carrying around their necks the heads of other dead Muhammadans. Bohemund was the last of the great seigneurs to arrive, and immediately the council assembled in one of the Byzantine palaces of Antioch, with many old faces missing and many newcomers on the benches.

The vital question was the disposal of Antioch. Bluntly, Norman spokesmen urged Bohemund's claim. Success had been due to his efforts; he would be able to hold the great citadel safe, and the Moslems were in awe of him; the city had been pledged to him, and Alexis had fled away from the Turks. So said the Normans.

St. Gilles himself spoke against them. He had only one argument—that the princes of the crusade had sworn an oath to yield to Alexis any city that had once been part of the Byzantine Empire. To this argument he clung stubbornly.

For days the discussion went on, becoming at last an open quarrel. Men sprang up, grasping their swords. At this point there intervened not a prelate of the Church, but the spokesmen of the new party, the Jerusalemites, as they might be called. During the last few days they had been discussing the situation, and now they expressed their opinion frankly:

"Since the princes are held back by fear or other reasons, or by this promise to the emperor, from leading us to Jerusalem, we shall choose from among the men of arms someone brave and faithful in service, with whom we will be able to go on. Ho! Doth it not suffice the princes, our lords, that we have lingered here a year, and that two hundred thousand armed men died here? They who want the emperor's gold, let them have it. They who want Antioch, let them have it.

"We shall set out on our road. They who wish to stay here will perish without doing any good, just as the others died here in the past. We have had every day so many disputes about Antioch that we shall tear down its walls to have again that peace which we had before Antioch was taken. Besides, instead of being weakened by hunger and quarreling, we ought to return to our proper road."

The voice of the Jerusalemites could not be ignored. In the end they gained their point. Godfrey and the knights of Lorraine and Flanders tacitly favored Bohemund's claim. A compromise was agreed on.

The Normans were to be left in possession of the citadel, while the Provençals kept the palace and gate. The actual title to Antioch could wait until after Jerusalem was taken.

Raymond said he would begin the advance to the south that month.

The party of the common soldiers rejoiced, and they cheered Tancred when he said that he would go on with them. The Unknown decided to follow the worshiped Tancred. The soldiers believed that the road to the south was now open. But the lords were still brooding over their quarrel. The exaltation of the first two years had not left them, but the unity of the crusade was weakened. The two best soldiers among the princes, Bohemund and Raymond, were enemies. Half of the barons and knights who had started off with all the pageantry of war, two years and more before, were dead or missing. Some of the best of the men of arms had been knighted on the battlefields. Many common soldiers now rode with the chivalry.

Moreover, the status of the barons had altered. Nearly all of them had parted with their money long since, but they still had the obligation to feed, protect, and care for all their vassals. Of course they drew money and supplies from the general treasury of the army—when anything was available. Still, most of them had to forage for their men. Many sturdy vassals and men of arms discovered that they could forage better for themselves as individuals and did so.

Fighters like the Unknown shifted from one command to another. They formed in bands under such gifted adventurers as Raymond Pilet who captured Tell Bashir and sallied thence like a hawk unhooded.

The army moved south. But it marched in separate divisions, wary and uncertain of the future.

XXVII

THE WALLS OF MAARA

ARLY in December the main body of the crusaders was still encamped around a stumbling block. In the corner of Syria, behind the Orontes, they had come upon a stone city with a wall that reminded them of Antioch, and in the center of the wall a hill crowned by a great mosque. They could see the Moslems toiling up the steps of the hill every evening.

The city was Maara-en-N'aman, the key to southern Syria. A rich city with multitudes of slaves. The crusaders camped among the olive trees, covered their huts and tents with dried-up grape vines, and settled down to work in the mud.

They had learned their lesson at Antioch, and they lost no time in shaping timbers and building siege engines until they were ready to make an assault. The Unknown as usual was in the thick of things, and tells about them:

Monday an attack was made so vigorously that the scaling ladders were placed against the walls. But the strength of the pagans was such that nothing much could be gained that day.

195

Our seigneurs, seeing that nothing could be gained in this way, and that all this trouble was in vain—Raymond, count of St. Gilles, built a tower of wood, strong and high. This tower was mounted on four wheels. On the summit of it several knights took their stand with Everard the Hunter, who sounded his horn with a will. Below the flooring were knights protected by full armor who pushed the fortress up to the city wall against one of the towers.

Observing this, the pagan men quickly built a machine that cast large stones on the moving tower, so well that nearly all our knights were killed. They threw out also Greek fire on the fortress, hoping to burn and destroy it. But almighty God did not wish that the tower be burned that time—since it over-reached in height the wall of the city.

Our knights on the summit, among them William de Montpelier, threw great rocks on the defenders of the wall. They struck so heavily upon the shields that shield and man fell mortally hurt within the city. Thus they fought. Others thrust out long lances with pennants, and with these lances and iron hooks tried to pull the foemen toward them. So they fought until evening.

From another side our knights lifted ladders against the walls. Godfrey of Lastour mounted first to the wall from a ladder, but his companions placed too much weight on the ladder and it broke. Yet he was on the wall with a few others. The men below found another ladder and lifted it quickly against the wall. So strongly did the Saracens attack them then, upon the wall and below along the ground, with arrows and spears thrust at them, that many of our men were seized with fear and leaped from the wall.

While these valiant men on the summit of the wall beat off attacks, our men, who were beneath the moving tower, dug under the wall. The Saracens, seeing that our men had sapped their fortification, were seized with fear and fled into the city. All this happened on Saturday at the hour of vespers, about sunset of the eleventh of December.

Afterward our men penetrated into the city, and all that they found of any value in the houses or hiding places, they took. When morning came, wherever they came upon an enemy, man or woman, they slew them. Not a corner of the city was without bodies of Saracens, and we could barely walk through the streets without treading on the bodies.

Bohemund gave command by an interpreter for the Saracen chiefs to take refuge—themselves, their women and children and baggage—in a palace near one of the gates, and agreed to preserve them from death. But later on he seized them, took away all their belongings—gold, silver, and ornaments. Some he killed and others he had taken to Antioch to be sold.

The Franks stayed at that city for a month, or a month and four days, and it was then that the Bishop of Orange died. Many of our men did not find there the things they needed. Owing to the long delay, they found it hard to get food, for there was nothing to seize outside the town. Then they burned the cadavers, because some gold byzants had been found in the bellies of the dead. And some of us cut the flesh of the bodies into pieces, and cooked and ate it.

The Unknown no longer speaks of Bohemund as "that mighty man" or "that illustrious prince." His opinion of the powerful Norman has changed. The Unknown mentions this fresh famine almost indifferently. Men had become hardened to nourishing themselves upon anything that would stay in their stomachs. But he is grieved by the new delay.

It was due to the Norman-Provençal feud. Bohemund wanted Maara because it was part of Syria, and Raymond wanted it as his first conquest. They stationed their men in different parts of the fortifications, when the Norman leader suddenly marched off toward Antioch.

So, in a steady downpour of rain and general discouragement, the year 1098 ended.

The crusaders had reason to be disheartened. During the storms they had to seek shelter in the Syrian villages on the mountainsides. Their tents were about gone, and the number of horses in good condition dwindled daily. Groups of men started off along the muddy roads toward Edessa.

Perhaps Godfrey might have rallied them. All of them respected the splendid duke, who was without fear or reproach. But in that mild and friendly spirit there was no instinct of leadership. Godfrey could lead a charge, with a blast of olifants and a fluttering of banners, but he could not weld together the fragments of the crusade. At present he was off somewhere, diligently settling his men in winter quarters.

Bohemund could have led them on six months ago. Now he had become embittered, and all his thoughts centered on Antioch. Tancred, invincible in battle, might have got through to Jerusalem with a thousand knights, but he would not shepherd a flock fifty thousand strong.

With the crusade at a halt, some of the princes brought the Normans and Provençals together in council, midway between Maara and Antioch. Bohemund came, but would agree to nothing while Raymond held part of Antioch, and Raymond would not yield to the powerful Norman.

A feeling of helplessness seized on the leaders. How could they take up the march again? The army could not travel down through the Holy Land like a host of pilgrims. It must capture and hold all the Moslem citadels on the way. The barons each had thousands of men to provide for, and they expected to keep as fiefs the strongholds they captured. How otherwise were they to exist? Only Raymond and Count Robert of Flanders, among the great seigneurs, still had money. Most of them had burned their bridges behind them. Godfrey had done so, and Bohemund and Raymond. Good-natured Robert Short Breeches did not care. Given a leader, the crusade would go on. But where was the leader?

In the throes of the debate the Jerusalemites came forward again. The bishop of Albara, a Provençal who had taken Adhemar's duties upon himself, headed them with several nobles, and they knelt before Count Raymond.

They said they had waited long for the princes to begin the march, and now nothing was done. The lance of the Lord had been revealed to the count, and by this token would he not lead them on himself?

The appeal touched the chivalrous old Provençal, and he hesitated. He knew that to leave Antioch would be to abandon it to Bohemund. The Jerusalemites then urged that, if he would not go, he would give them the lance, and they would set out with it alone.

Raymond yielded impetuously. The mad project appealed to the old warrior. And he turned to the other seigneurs, offering to divide his money among them, to give them means to accompany him. He would give ten thousand silver shillings to Robert of Normandy, six thousand to Tancred, and so on. He would garrison Maara and resume the march.

Just then news from Maara came in. The multitude left there had taken matters into their own hands. They had heard that the council of the lords had accomplished nothing, and that Count Raymond was thinking of leaving them to garrison Maara.

Raymond the chaplain relates what happened at Maara:

The soldiers and the poor said, one to the other—"Oho! Quarrels on account of Antioch, and now quarrels on account of Maara! Will there be struggles among the princes and a scattering of the army in every place God gives to us? Well, this city will breed no more quarrels. Come and destroy the walls! We will make peace between the princes."

Rising up then from their beds, the sick and the weak armed themselves with clubs and went out to the walls. A serf could easily push from the summit of the wall a heavy stone that had taken three or four yoke of oxen to drag into place. The Bishop of Albara went around the city, arguing, and forbidding all this, and so did other of the Count's people. But when these guardians had passed by, all those who had hidden themselves or run down from the walls at the approach of the bishop and his companions hastened back to the task they had begun. And those who were afraid during the day, or busied with other matters, set to work at night. Hardly any one was too weak or ill to break down the wall.

They stifled their hunger with some bodies of Moslems they found in a near-by swamp, already fetid after lying there for two weeks. Bit by bit the wall of Maara was demolished.

Count Raymond came down upon them from the council, angered at sight of the ruin. When he heard the story of the silent mutiny, and gazed at the haggard scarecrows who thronged around him anxiously—it was an offense punishable by death to injure the property of a seigneur—he said nothing. Instead of punishing them, he made a foray with his knights through the countryside and brought in some supplies of food, and fed the rebels.

"The other leaders would not go on because of me," he said grimly. "'Tis the judgment of God upon me."

And he gave orders to burn Maara, and set out for Jerusalem. Nobles remonstrated with him, pointing out that he had no more than three hundred armed knights and fewer horses, and that the mob would be a terrible handicap in his march. But the old Provençal had made up his mind. These men of his would march in any case, and he meant to go with them.

Everyone would go, he said—the bishop of Albara, and the clergy, and all the poor. While the streets of Maara flamed, and smoke poured from the mosque on the hill and a mist of rain veiled the hills, Count Raymond threw off his boots and walked out barefoot at the head of his flock.

It was sheer madness, and it cheered the spirits of all who saw it. Raymond meant this to be the real march to Jerusalem, because they all had sworn, long ago, that they would approach the holy city on their knees and with their feet bare.

Tancred was not the man to draw back from a desperate quest. He joined the procession with forty knights. The Unknown trudged along. Late as always, drowsy Robert Short Breeches followed a few days after. Through the rain they disappeared up the broad valley of the Orontes.

And the watchers in the hills heard a new song in the moving throng: a chant of the crusade, mournful and yet full of hope:

> *O Mary, Mother of God—God thy Father and Son—*
> *Our Lady, pray Thou for us—and thy Father and glorious Son,*
> *Pray for us, who are thine.*
> *Aid Thou us!*
> *Turn toward us, and behold our tears.*

Weeks later Godfrey and his Rhinelanders and Count Robert with the men of Flanders started after them, but followed the line of the coast. Bohemund turned back again to Antioch. He attacked the Provençals who were guarding the gate and the palace, and drove them out. Antioch was his, and he would hold it with his Normans.

XXVIII

RAYMOND'S PATH

SPRING came early to the valley of the upper Orontes. Thin cattle drifted down through the hillocks to graze on the scum of green that covered the lowlands. Long-haired goats stalked aimlessly about among the children and the dogs. Shepherds in gray *abbas* sat and watched.

Water wheels turned, creaking, in the streams that ran down the rock-strewn streets of the villages. From the galleries in the towers above the white domes of little mosques sounded the *ezam*, the call to prayer.

Hooded horsemen cantered along the river paths, dismounting when they met, to squat against fallen stones and discuss the news of north and south. Among the stones stood stained marble columns, with leaves carved upon their capitals—like forgotten guideposts of a vanished road. Roman gods had rested here before Islam came.

Arabs rode into the river towns with strings of camels, and listened to the tidings of the day. The armed hosts of the Moslems had withdrawn, leaving the country open to the iron men, who were marching along the river, taking cattle and fruit from the villages, but not shedding blood.

The amirs of the towns had opened the gates to them, and had made submission.

What else could be done? These Franks, these iron men, had always prevailed. They had been starved, and they had been slain with weapons, but the survivors did not go away. All-merciful was Allah! It was written, and what was written would come to pass.

At one place the amir had sent all his cattle and horses into a hidden valley out of sight of the main road. Yet when the iron men came, walking on foot like Syrian beggars, the guides given them by the amir had led them through the valley where the herds were hidden. Verily, the guides had not known the animals were there. Now many of the iron men rode good horses. No man may escape his fate.

So said the villagers, and the Arabs listened. When the first mounted scouts of the crusaders appeared down the road the Arabs went off to the hills to watch, and cavalcades of Turks in bright *khalats* went out to surrender and to bargain for their ransom.

Then the multitude of horsemen came into view, with their banners and ox carts following them, and masses of common folk walking among the herds. The keen-eyed Arabs recognized the sheep and horses of Schaizar and Hamah and Hims.

Something quite natural but unexpected had happened here in the south. The local chieftains had listened to many stories of the Battle of the Lance and the taking of Antioch, and they were heartily afraid of the crusaders. They all asked for terms, and Count Raymond, with his mob of pilgrims, did not want any fighting.

So the crusaders left each town richer than they had entered it. They discovered that all Muhammadans were not armed devils serving idols. In fact, the Syrian shepherds and the Arab traders were much like the herdsmen and the Jewish merchants of Provence. "All these people feared us," Raymond the chronicler observes, "but we knew it not."

The expeditionaries began to thrive and to fatten out. It was pleasant along the Orontes in the coming of spring. They heard of wonderful things close at hand—of a city

BOHEMUND'S TOMB
The bronze doors of the tomb at Canossa.

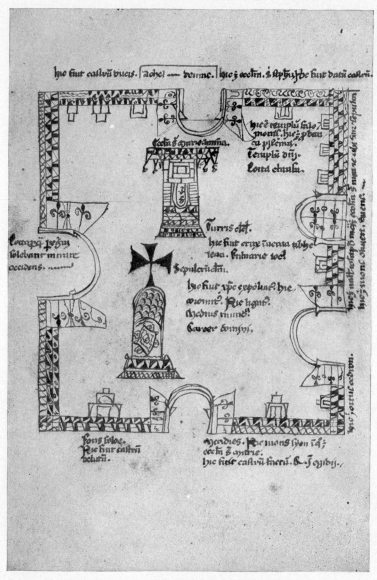

THE SEPULCHER WITHIN JERUSALEM

Map making was still an unknown art in the time of the first crusade.

of tombs and the images of giant beasts that had once been the temple of the great god Baal. But when the mountains rose higher in front of them, their leaders turned away from the river, to the right. Raymond wished to push through to the coast to get in touch with the ships again, if any had ventured this far. So the army climbed into a high valley and entered the silence of a forest.

A good, green land, this. A cool wind passed through the valley, and the crusaders found apple trees in blossom in the clearings where lush grass grew. At first they made their way through groves of cedars, and then under the canopy of heavy pines, where the air smelled of resin and ferns and dark myrtle grew underfoot.

Bare-limbed hermits clad in camel's hair and rough wool lived in the caves of this forest. These anchorites spoke obscure tongues—as some of the priests thought, Syriac or Greek—and they stared at the crusaders in bewilderment and doubt. The crusaders were young and strange and the forests of Lebanon were old.

The hermits pointed out to them a white peak in the haze of the horizon. "The Mountain of Snow," they said.

The robed men among the crusaders—the monks, chaplains, and bishops—looked around eagerly, but fruitlessly. Some of them thought the snow summit was Mount Hermon, and so they must be nearing the threshold of the Holy Land. Pushing on over the damp forest paths, they beheld the clear blue of the sea far below them. The wind grew warmer, and they descended rapidly into a new land. Red rocks rose out of yellow clay. Around the mud walls of little villages stretched bare cotton fields, and dense sugar cane grew in the hollows.

On the heights by the streams the long arms of windmills turned slowly against the sky. Already, in the end of February, the sun beat down on their heads uncomfortably. But the air was sweet and warm, and in the vesper hour the sun sank in a crimson panoply of clouds over a motionless sea.

The crusaders themselves had changed. Many had discarded their dark rags for camelot cloaks and soft white tunics. Some of them wore mantles dyed with the purple of Tyre. The more fastidious had discovered silk that changed color with the hours of the day, to the delight of the few women who still survived. The knights rode in light attire, their heavy mesh mail and great shields carried by the esquires or donkeys. Only the black robes of the clerics remained the same.

It was not easy to tell a noble from an enterprising commoner. Raymond Pilet, the adventurer, had got him a suit made of sheer cloth-of-gold and he wore it. Moreover, he sallied out with his band and took possession of the sea fortress of Tortosa, abandoned by the Moslem fighting men.

The sultan of at-Trabulu—the crusaders christened it Tripoli—sent envoys to arrange the payment of tribute, and Count Raymond, who grew covetous at such times, settled down to haggle with the envoys.

This southern coast pleased the old Provençal. He knew that it was midway between Antioch and Jerusalem, with the ancient and thriving seaports of Sidon and Tyre a little way to the south. And here it seemed to him that he could have his own dominion, out of reach of Bohemund's aggressions. The envoys of Tripoli offered ten thousand pieces of gold and a number of fine horses, and this rather astonished him.

"Why linger here to besiege these cities?" Tancred objected. "We have not ten men, armed and fit and mounted, out of a thousand who set out. If we lose more men, how will we go on? We ought to push on and take Jerusalem. Then, if we do so, others will come from home to aid us. They know Jerusalem, but they do not know these places."

Tancred chafed at the delay, but the lord of Provence was thinking of many things. His host was not fit to meet the Egyptian sultans in battle, and months ago the Moslems of Egypt had taken Jerusalem and its coast from the Seljuk Turks. Tancred was young, and heedless—irresistible in his strength of body; but Raymond was nearing the end of his life, and he longed to possess a strong city where he could shelter his young wife and his vassals. Tripoli reminded him of Arles, in Provence, and ten thousand pieces of gold was a great sum.

Everything that Raymond had attempted for himself, until now, somehow had gone wrong. When he took the cross in the beginning, at Toulouse, he had expected that Urban would appoint him leader of the crusade. He yielded with good grace to the well-loved Adhemar.

But he had been cast out of Antioch, and had lost Maara, and he would never yield to Bohemund. He resolved to make himself undisputed master of the Tripoli district before any others came up. To do so, he ordered the siege of Arkah, a stronghold that lay inland from the seaport. His men obeyed, not too willingly. The wall of Arkah was stone and mortar, stretching back to the foothills.

Christian Syrians told Raymond what lay within. "In the midst of the town is a castle, with a large suburb of its own, on the hill. The place is populous and full of merchandise—with gardens of fruit trees, and mills on the river that runs by it."

A Roman aqueduct ran from the hills into the town itself, and Raymond saw that it was a strong place, and good to hold. He set to work building engines while he negotiated with Tripoli.

Two weeks later nothing was accomplished. Pontius of Balazun, who had worked with Raymond the chaplain on his chronicle, was dead; and the good Anselm of Ribemont, who had foretold his own death the day before a stone from the wall crushed him. The sultan in Tripoli suspended negotiations, to watch events at Arkah.

At their first appearance the crusaders had been looked on as invincible and terrible. But the Moslem princes, watching the siege operations, observed that they were no more than human. The tribute from the neighboring districts—gold and wine and mules and fine cloths had been pouring in—dwindled and finally ceased, and the sultan in Tripoli, which was a citadel almost surrounded by the sea and too strong to capture, did not pay anything at all.

Just then Godfrey and Robert of Flanders arrived on the scene, hastening down the coast. They had been told that Raymond was faced by a great army of Moslems, and when they found him sitting in luxury before Arkah they were taken aback.

The newcomers were impoverished, and the common soldiers, the Rhinelanders and Flemings, were eager to push on. Sight of the herds and swollen storehouses of the Provençals moved them to envy, and Raymond was obliged to pay out nearly half of his new treasure to outfit and feed the Northerners. Tancred, tired of inaction, went over to Godfrey's camp.

A new complication started lively discussion. The envoys of the crusaders returned from Cairo with the proposals of the Egyptian sultans. The crusaders, said the sultans, might keep their cities in the north, and might fulfil their vow by discarding their arms and visiting Jerusalem as pilgrims. The Emperor Alexis, it seemed, had written to Cairo, and the sultans were not inclined to support the crusade.

The men of the cross laughed when they heard these terms, and they raged when a letter reached them from Alexis urging them to delay their march until he could join them. They had done with waiting for Alexis. Only Count Raymond, with his instinct for putting himself in the wrong, argued that they should wait for the support of the Byzantines.

The argument spread to the ranks and occupied the attention of the idle men of arms. At this point there intervened on behalf of Count Raymond no less a person than Peter Bartholomew, the visionary.

Since leaving Antioch the young peasant had not ceased to repeat his stories of marvelous apparitions. Raymond the chaplain had kept Bartholomew in his tent to observe him, and more than once the worthy chaplain had been wakened out of sleep to hear Bartholomew talking brokenly with no one else in the tent. Raymond had gone out and looked around, and—being suddenly roused out of sleep—had felt moved by spiritual grace as he peered into the darkness. Bartholomew did not lack for champions, but his stories had become incredible.

Arnulf, chaplain of the duke of Normandy, headed the opposition, which had reached definite conclusions by now. Bohemund had mocked at the vision. The lance, said Arnulf, was an Arab spear point, and hence different from the weapons of the crusaders.

"Why was it found by Bartholomew himself, alone in the pit, in near darkness, instead of being revealed in open light to a multitude? Why did the vision come to Bartholomew, a frequenter of taverns and a deserter from the army? When did Pontius Pilate and his soldiers ever visit Antioch? Why has no one except this Bartholomew shared in the visions?"

So they argued, and it seemed to them that the discovery of the lance was no more than a bit of trickery. The victory in the battle at Antioch had come from God, but Bartholomew's supporters claimed that it was due to a piece of iron that they cherished.

The duke of Normandy and Tancred agreed with Bohemund, but took no part in the debate. Arnulf, however, was insistent, and one day in the council Peter Bartholomew rose to defend himself.

"Let a great fire be built, and I will take the lance in my hands and pass safely through it. Then, if the lance be of the Lord's sending, I shall be unhurt, but if not I shall be burned."

The trial by fire seemed to everybody the only solution. The Provençal clergy bade Peter fast, and preparations were begun.

On the fourth day a level stretch of ground was selected. Brush had been piled loosely in the center of it for a distance of some five paces. Soldiers crowded the slopes all around the place of the ordeal—the army had turned out *en masse* to watch. In the center of the cleared space were grouped priests who were to bear witness to what happened before their eyes. They stood in their bare feet, clad in their vestments.

Early in the afternoon Peter Bartholomew was led out and stripped of his heavier garments. Raymond the chaplain advanced to meet him, and what then occurred has been written down by Raymond himself:

Fire was set to the dried olive tree branches. The pile stretched for fourteen feet, and was divided into two heaps, each four feet high. Between these two heaps a space of about one foot had been left.

When the fire blazed hot, I, Raymond, spoke to the multitude. "If almighty God spoke to this man, face to face, and the blessed Andrew revealed the lance to him when he sought it, let him pass without harm through the fire. But if it is otherwise, and he is a liar, let him burn with the lance that he carries in his hands."

And all of them knelt and responded, "*Amen.*"

The fire burned high, and heat filled the air for sixty feet; no one could approach nearer than that. Then Peter Bartholomew, clad only in his tunic, knelt before the bishop of Albara, and called upon God to witness that he had not made up anything, and that if he had lied, he would perish in the fire. And he urged all the people to pray for him.

The bishop placed the lance in his hands, while he knelt and made the sign of the cross. Then, holding the lance, he went into the fire manfully and without fear.

A bird, flying over the fire, fluttered down and plunged into it. In the midst of it Bartholomew delayed an instant. And then he passed through safely.

When he emerged from the fire, his shirt was not burned, nor did the very delicate stuff in which the lance of the Lord was wound show any injury. He ran toward the people and signed them with the lance of the Lord and shouted with a loud voice. All the people hastened toward him, eager to touch him or to tear off something from his shirt, and they struggled to get near him. In this way they injured his legs in three or four places, and in crushing him they broke his backbone.

He would have died then, meseems, had not Raymond Pilet, a distinguished soldier and a brave man, broke into the turbulent mob with some companions and freed him by fighting to the death.

Then, although the fire was still hot, the people ran to gather up coals and ashes, so eagerly that in a little while nothing was left of the fire.

When, in truth, Raymond Pilet carried Peter to my house, I bound up his wounds and asked of him why he had delayed in the fire. He replied, "The Lord came to meet me in the midst of the fire, and taking me by the hand, said to me, '*Because thou didst not believe the lance would be found when the blessed Andrew revealed it to thee, thou shalt not pass on without hurt, but thou shalt not see hell.'* Look, and see if I am not burned."

There was something of a burn on his legs, but in truth not much. Yet his wounds were great. After this we called in those who had not believed in the lance, so that they might see his head and face and other limbs, so they would know that what he said of the lance was true. Many looked, and glorified God, saying that they had not thought an arrow could pass through that fire as this man had done.

After this Peter left this life in peace and at the hour ordained for him. And he was buried at the spot where he had carried the lance through the fire.

Such is the testimony of Raymond, his champion. The evidence of a Norman chronicler is brief, and contradictory:

Branches were set in a double row and kindled. Peter, wearing breeches and tunic, ran through it, and fell, burned at the other end. The next day, he died. . . . People confessed they had been deceived, and that Peter was kin to Simon the magician.

The ordeal by fire had not decided the question. And Peter Bartholomew, trickster or dreamer, was dead. Most of the army seemed to think he had failed in the ordeal, and as time went on they lost their belief in the lance. Count Raymond, however, still carried it with him.

Meanwhile the Moslems sallied out from Tripoli, and the crusaders smashed them back again, but Arkah did not fall, and the common soldiers talked daily of taking to the Jerusalem road. They knew how it could be done.

Even now, early in May, they could get beans from the gardens here, and grain from the fields. Soon the heat would dry up the fields. If they were going to take up the march, now was the time.

The men discussed it among themselves and the feeling grew stronger, until one evening thousands of them started out along the coast road to the south. They went on foot, spears and packs on their shoulders, without baggage or carts, and they marched through the night. They did not stop until they came to Beirut.

This ended the uncertainty of the leaders, who broke up the camps around Arkah. Camels and ox carts were loaded again, and the main army followed after the night marchers. Raymond had to turn his back upon the fertile coast of Tripoli and his dream of a province of his own.

XXIX

TANCRED RIDES TO BETHLEHEM

O N THE nineteenth of May the army passed through the long pine forest south of Beirut. It filed into the narrow coast road that runs down the shore of the Holy Land. But it was no more than a remnant of the great host that had gathered at Nicea two years before.

During the siege of Nicea the cross-bearers had numbered more than one hundred and fifty thousand, men and women of all sorts. The survivors, hastening down Palestine between the mountains and the sea, were some thirty thousand, all told. Less than half were fighting men.

Yet the thirty thousand felt that they were near the end of their road. Even now they were entering the threshold of the Holy Land. They pressed forward without thought of anything else. And they marched five leagues or more between sunrise and sunset under a glaring sky. They carried water skins on their shoulders, and paid no heed to the swarms of gnats and stinging flies that rose out of the sand. Every league brought them nearer to a sight of Jerusalem.

Although the sea lay below them, they did not see any Christian ships. In fact, they did not expect to find any vessels accompanying them, because hundreds of sailors were trudging along the road beside the camels—stocky, red-faced men in dark wool or leather jacks, who walked somehow as if one leg were shorter than the other. These were the survivors of that first fleet: English, Frisians, and silent Danes—sea rovers, pirates, and fishermen. They had plied between the island of Cyprus and the mainland for some time, bringing in much-needed supplies in spite of the danger from the fleets of Moslem galleys out of Egypt. Some dozen of the English boats, unfit for further service, had been beached and abandoned at Beirut, and the seamen had joined the army.

Raymond the chaplain noticed them:

We should not forget those who did not hesitate to sail, for love of the holy expedition, through the unknown and vast waters of the Ocean and the Mediterranean. For the Angles, hearing mention of the vengeance of the Lord against those who unworthily held possession of the birthplace of the Lord Christ, set forth into the Anglican sea. Circling Spain, and laboring through the Mediterranean, they captured the port of Antioch and the state of Laodicea before our army arrived there. These ships and the Genoese aided us at that time. For we had, at the siege, trade with Cyprus and the other islands, owing to these ships and their safeguard. Ay, every day these ships plied over the sea, and the Greek vessels followed them. And so the Saracens dreaded to attack them.

Then when these Angles saw the army setting out for Jerusalem, and knew that their ships were damaged by long service—they had only nine or ten left out of thirty—some beached their vessels and abandoned them, while others burned theirs, but all hastened to join us on the road.

The men of the good ship *Argo* saw no stranger sights than these pirate crusaders. They tramped through the marble blocks that had been Herod's bath, and under a Roman granite arch that they thought was the entrance to the gardens of Pharaoh. Staring at lines of solitary columns, they tramped on toward the speck in the sea that grew into marble walls and square towers, out in the water.

Only a marble bridge joined this citadel to the land, and the Arabs called it Saida, the priests Sidon.

Here they cut quantities of honey-sweet reeds, known as

zucra, and carried them along. It tasted good to cut the canes and suck them. The natives told them that *zucra* was pounded and the juice strained off and set in jars until it hardened. After that it looked like salt or snow, and could be spread on bread or dissolved in water. Most of the crusaders had never encountered sugar, and they liked it.

They crossed a rocky plain, and saw the walls of Tyre outlined against the sea. Some of the curious went close to the city, and came back with a tale to tell. Beside the walls they had seen, far down in the clear water, the massive foundations of the other, older city—ruins of towers and huge blocks of stone lying like the fallen bones of a skeleton among the rocks.

The army hastened on, to the south. From the blue heights of Lebanon barefoot and bearded men flocked down, to gaze at the cross-bearers and to greet them shyly. They also were Christians—Maronites they called themselves—and centuries before they had been forced to leave the towns and to live in the mountains, beyond the persecution of the Muhammadans.

"In our towns," they said, "we could not keep any holy images if we did not pay a monthly tax to the Muhammadan collectors. If we did not keep on paying the money, they threw the images of our saints in the dirt, and broke out the eyes. Then, too, the Muhammadans took away the fairest of our boys to put in brothels, and our girls also were carried off, to be sold for wine. And our wives dared not weep at such times."

The Maronites advised the crusaders to turn aside to the broader road that ran south through the mountains, where good water could be found. Here on the shore little water would be found, and at narrow places like the Twisted Mouth the highway could be held against them by a small force of the enemy.

But the crusaders kept to their road. Within a week they might see Jerusalem, and they did not trouble their heads about military strategy. They straggled for miles along the shore road, where a flank attack would have driven them into the sea. Their retreat was cut off, and their supporting fleet

scattered behind them; every day took them farther from
Bohemund's army at Antioch, and they had no idea what
hostile forces might be gathered in the unknown country
ahead of them.

No one, however, appeared to oppose them. The Moslems
in Damascus had not yet recovered from the Battle of the
Lance, and the kalif at Cairo believed them to be still north
of Tripoli. The commanders of the maritime citadels prudently kept aloof.

After leaving Acre behind them the crusaders were surprised by a kind of miracle. A hawk was seen to attack a
pigeon in the air above them, and to wound it. The pigeon
fell where it could be found, and they discovered that a
small silver cylinder was attached to its claw. Within the
cylinder lay a scroll of paper covered with the curlicues of
Arabic writing. Someone deciphered it:

The Amir of Akka to the lord of Caesaria, greeting. A race of
dogs, stupid and quarrelsome, hath passed by me, marching without order. As thou lovest the Faith, do what thou mayest, and
have others do, all that may hurt them. Send this word to other
citadels and fortresses.

The race of dogs, for the most part, had never seen paper
nor heard of messenger pigeons, and the incident heartened
them mightily. Even the birds of the air were aiding them,
they said. For two days they lingered on the sun-baked plain
to celebrate Pentecost, and hastened on. The mountains fell
away to their left, and they found the watercourses dry.

Moslem horsemen appeared behind them, cutting down
stragglers and raiding the camel trains. This roused Count
Raymond, who was holding the rear of the army with his
Provençals. He knew by past experience how to deal with
such a situation. Taking a picked force of mounted men,
he drew off to one side and lay in hiding within sight of the
road. When the raiders galloped past him he sallied out
and drove them down to the rocky shore and scattered them.

After this skirmish he became more cheerful. When his
scouts told him that they could find no water, the old Provençal answered simply, "God will provide."

The next day they came upon a river. It was little more than shallow pools along the rocky bed of a ravine, but they could drink the water and the leaders decided to follow the river inland. There lay Jerusalem, only ten leagues away. So said the Syrian Christians who were serving as guides. Some of the barons wanted to keep on along the coast, to attack Cairo before attempting to besiege Jerusalem.

This proposal was voted down at once. "None of that! We have too few armed men. Let us hold to our way."

So they followed the river, up toward a line of bare foothills. And they came upon food, as well as water, in the plain of Ramlah—fields of fig trees and date palms crackling in the dust-laden air when the hot wind blew. Here the Moslems had evacuated the white-walled towns and the city of Ramlah where the highroads met.

Nothing green was to be seen. The sun glared on baked clay and wind-furrowed sand. Through the deep shadows of deserted alleys the crusaders went forward, sword in hand. They found the great *khans*, the hostelries of this desert country, empty of human beings—the arched recesses with their flea-infested carpets littered with the belongings of the departed merchants.

In the market place bearded and smiling Samaritans dressed in clean garments bowed to them, and ran up to press the crusaders' hands against their foreheads. The Samaritans led them to cool water in the ancient underground cisterns and abandoned bath houses. They wandered across the marble flagging of the court of the White Mosque near the town, and pushed through the high cedar gates. The mosque was empty, its great beams still black and smoking from the fire that the Moslems had lighted, to destroy the timbers that might be used in siege engines.

In this way the first city of Israel fell into the hands of the crusaders. Legend said that the tomb of St. George lay beneath the colored marble flooring of the mosque, so they stripped the White Mosque and cleansed it and consecrated it anew, and made it a church again. They gave it to a bishop, and gave to him servants, horses and mules and money. It was fitting, they said, that this, the first of the holy places, should be made into a bishopric to the glory of God. And then the thirty thousand thronged toward Jerusalem.

One man did not wait for the others. Tancred had seen the damage done by the fire above the tomb of St. George, and he resolved that nothing of the kind should happen to the church of Bethlehem. Before midnight he rose from his couch and woke the knights and esquires at arms in his pavilion. They lighted a lanthorn and slipped on their chain mail quietly, tightening their girdles and trying the long swords in the sheaths. Then for a moment they knelt around the light, crossed themselves, and whispered a prayer. Donning the conical steel helmets, and throwing over head and shoulders the loose white Arab *khoufies*, to protect the metal from the sun's glare, they left the pavilion and joined other similar groups of mailed figures under the starlight. Low-voiced greetings passed from man to man.

Here were Tancred's brothers in arms, the youth of the chivalry—and a boy newly knighted, Baldwin of the Mount, cousin to Godfrey the duke and once esquire to Bohemund. Out of the darkness powerful chargers were led to them, and they swung themselves into the high saddles, taking up shields and spears from the armor-bearers. Tancred settled himself in the stirrups, spoke to Baldwin of the Mount:

"Forward, messires, with God."

A hundred of the youthful riders paced through the sleeping camp, passed the outer pickets, and trotted into the gloom of the hills.

Four years before, Tancred d'Hauteville had been a youth of overbearing conceit, occupied with endless quarrels and the tumults of Sicily. They called him the Sicilian then. He was one of the few who knew Arabic and the customs of the Moslems. He adapted himself easily to this new warfare of the swift horsemen of Asia, and his sword had been one of Bohemund's mainstays. He had the craft of his Norman sires, and he dared rein his horse where the elder men hesitated. The Moslems called Bohemund the little god of the Christians, but they said that Tancred was a *djinn*, an unearthly spirit.

In the gray half light before sunrise Tancred trotted into the silent shadows of Bethlehem, with his standard lifted and his hundred trooping behind him. Through the murk they saw only crumbling stone huts and blind walls of masonry. The chill of the night still hung in the alleys where dogs barked unheeded, except by the echoes of the hills.

The Syrian Christians scattered in the huts, and the small colony of monks who tended the basilica of the Virgin Mary —the only whole edifice in the village—heard the tramp of heavy horses and the clank of steel and took the newcomers for Turkish cavalry. They peered from the roof-tops and wondered what was in store for them, until the day brightened overhead and they saw the red crosses on the mantles of the knights.

Unbelieving, they opened their doors and approached the mailed riders. Not until Tancred and his companions spoke to them were they convinced that these were actually Christians with weapons in their hands. Then tumult reigned in Bethlehem. Patriarchs hastened to get out hidden robes and to snatch up crosses and rosaries. Women and children thronged out to see the miracle. They put on their holiday dresses and ran before the horsemen, singing. This was a joyful dawning—truly a day of days for the people of Bethlehem. They were free to do as they liked, and their church also was free.

But, so strong is habit, they could not rid themselves of fear. They saw the hundred cross-bearers, the great gray figures with the long golden hair falling to their shoulders; they heard the laughter and careless talk of the armed men. Yet they were afraid because it seemed to them that the hundred would be observed by the Moslems and hunted down.

The knights thronged into the narrow door of the long church to kneel in prayer to the Virgin. And when they mounted again to go on, Tancred's banner stood at the door of the church, with a guard of his swordsmen.

Tancred, however, was not content. Instead of turning back to the army he asked the Syrians to show him the road that led to Jerusalem. This was a mad kind of whim, but no man drew back when Tancred led the way through a ravine in the bare foothills. Two leagues they galloped, and then he left them in a village by a stone bridge hidden by rock ridges.

Alone he went on, climbing past olive groves and dry grain fields. He did not dismount until he had come out on the height that the Syrians had pointed out to him. And the morning sun behind his back revealed every stone of the hillside in front of him. It fell away beneath his feet to a small church and a shrine near the dry bed of a brook, a little to his right. Beyond the church lay a deep and desolate gorge.

On the far side of the gorge uprose a steep slope, crowned by a mass of gray stones larger than any he had seen before. The stonework seemed to grow out of the hill, and above its outer wall he noticed a small dome, beautiful in shape, and farther to the left the summit of a square white building. Outside the wall, far to the left, was another treeless hill and a low edifice upon it.

Tancred could see no gate in the wall on his side, only a quarter of a mile away. There was a portal that seemed to be filled up with stones. But to the right and left tiny figures and horses were moving in and out of the city on the hill. Dust rose around them, under the sheer blue sky.

He was standing, probably unknowing, upon the Mount of Olives. The little church below him, in the garden of Gethsemane, was that of the Blessed Mary, and the great blind wall on the hill across the gorge had been built by Solomon ages before. And the city within the wall was Jerusalem.

Here it lay, gray stones upon a hill among many heights; aged stones having about them something sorrowful and half ruined. The hatred and the enmity of men had darkened its gates with blood for many ages. It had been torn down and rebuilt, and not always in the same limits, for the foundations of the Jews extended in places beyond the walls of the Romans and the Arabs.

But it was not like other cities, because it held within its walls the hope of multitudes of men. The stones had fallen from their places, and aged Jews wailed the dead kings of Israel; but the memories of Jerusalem had been kept unchanged by faith.

The churches of Constantine had crumbled with the prae-torium of Pilate. Moslem mosques rose over the caverns of Solomon's stables and cisterns. But the grotto of the Sep-ulcher was there, and Calvary. And even the Moslems called the city *Al Kuds*, The Holy.

So Tancred beheld it, that morning with the sun behind him. Out of a cavern beside him came a bent brown figure, a hermit in a robe of hair. And for a moment the faded eyes of the anchorite looked into the clear eyes of the youth in armor. No armed Christian had stood there, a free man, for four hundred and sixty years.

Then the knight rode away to join his men, and the hermit remained to meditate. This day was not like others, because throngs of Moslems hastened into the gates of the city and Christian Syrians were driven out. The governor's men were at work in the outlying villages, filling up the wells. Within the walls of Jerusalem could be heard a steady murmur, like the ebbing and flowing of surf.

In the afternoon Moslems were seen crowding the parapet of the walls. They watched the multitude that came slowly up the road from the sea. Thousands of strange men walked afoot, some leading horses. Among them appeared the black robes of monks and even the figures of women.

They came forward slowly, carrying crosses and, from time to time, groups of them knelt together. Some hid their faces in their hands, weeping.

O Mary, Mother of God—God thy Father and Son—
Our Lady, pray Thou for us, and thy Father and glorious Son.
Pray for us, who are thine.
Aid Thou us!
Turn toward us, and behold our tears.

The crusaders had reached their goal, and their long road ended here. For that day they could think of nothing else. Grown men went around singing like children, doing noth-ing. They had come to Jerusalem.

XXX

THE VALLEY OF THE DAMNED

THE army reached Jerusalem the seventh of June, and for three days it was occupied in settling down to the siege. Tancred and Raymond Pilet sallied out to search the hills from Nablous to Ramlah, while the leaders reconnoitered the city.

Their numbers were not sufficient to surround it altogether, so Godfrey and Robert of Normandy and Robert of Flanders agreed to make their attack on the north side, from the Damascus road to the Tower of David that loomed beside the gate on the west. The Provençals were to encamp on the west, but Count Raymond had explored the hill of Sion, to the south, with its church where legend said that the tombs of the Israelite kings lay. And this seemed to him a better place, although his own followers murmured at the change that separated them from the other camps. Raymond insisted, and took up his quarters on Sion with his personal followers, leaving the mass of the Provençals down in the valley.

This done, the leaders assembled to discuss the situation. They had no siege engines with them, and no supply of wood was at hand from which to make new machines. Without them the massive walls could not be breached, and they had learned from experience that such a citadel could not be carried by storm. They went around to the Mount of Olives, to look at things there.

Between the Mount and the city wall lay the barren valley that the Moslems called the Valley of the Damned, above which Tancred had stood on the first day. And the wall opposite them had for its foundation the massive blocks of Solomon's day. They studied it with grave faces and talked in low voices, until a hermit from the caverns of the Mount joined them. The gaunt recluse spoke with authority.

"Attack the city on the morrow," he assured them, "from the first light until the ninth hour. If you do this, the Lord will deliver the city to you."

The great seigneurs meditated. "Nay," one of them made response, "we have not the machines we need for storming the walls."

"All powerful is God," the hermit said. "If He wills, ye will storm the walls with no more than one ladder."

The words of the hermit stirred them. It seemed to them that he had said only what was true. In the will of the Lord lay victory or defeat, and they had been wanting in courage to hang back from the test. Among the mass of the soldiers the words were repeated as a prophecy. They had only to go forward bravely and before the ninth hour Jerusalem would fall.

But there were some who doubted. Experienced warriors stared up at the mighty parapets and shook their heads. Ten men on the summit of such a citadel could hold off five hundred. Gaston of Béarn, the skilled engineer, urged them to wait until *petraria* and towers could be assembled. But where was the wood?

"No more than one ladder is needed," they answered him. And during that night carpenters worked by candlelight, piecing together ladders out of palm stems and soft poplar and the twisted olive trees. Rams were improvised out of pavilion poles and boulders and ropes.

Before the first light, men rose and armed themselves and

sought their leaders. With the makeshift ladders and rams they moved toward the hill. With the glare of sunrise in their eyes they advanced to the ditch and assailed the outer wall, sword and ax in hand.

They were eager to attack—the doubters went forward with the rest, and the standards of Normandy and Lorraine were planted close to the ditch.

The outer wall was low, and in poor repair. In several places the cross-bearers broke through, or climbed over it, driving the Moslems back to the great city wall. All that courage could do was done. Men tried to climb, sword in hand, under the lash of arrows and the fall of rocks from mangonels. The ladders broke under them, and the rams availed them not at all.

For three hours the attack surged forward. Once the crusaders got a footing on the great wall, and a shout went up. But they were thrown back. At the end of the third hour the assault was abandoned, and they carried the wounded back in silence.

If scaling ladders had been at hand [the Unknown wrote] the city would have fallen to us, for we pulled down the outer wall. Many of our men were killed in this attack.

For two days inaction lay upon the crusaders' camps like a blight. They had been too hopeful at that first attack. Failure made them moody. They had time, too, to feel the hardships of their situation. Bread was not to be bought at any price, and good wine was no more than a memory.

The condition of the animals troubled them. The Moslems had cut off the water supply for miles around the city. Springs had been filled up, cisterns emptied or broken, and streams flowing from distant hills had been dammed up. The bed of the Kedron was dry.

Some water could be gleaned, here and there, but not enough for the animals. Oxen, suffering from thirst, lowed and surged restlessly through the camps. The horses and sheep weakened steadily, and herded together on the hillsides.

One source of water remained, the Pool of Siloam, outside

the southern gate. This was stagnant, except when it filled intermittently from underground springs and overflowed. The crusaders had not known about this, and the first time the overflow came, the animals were aware of it as soon as the men.

A general rush for the pool followed. Mules and horses and human beings ran down to it before the leaders could restrain them. Others pressed after them, carrying along the sick people. They pushed the first comers into the water, stirring up the mud. Throngs hastened after them, beating aside the half-maddened cattle, and in a few moments the pool became the center of an ever-increasing mob. Men struggled to get near the water, heedless of the screams of those who were trodden down and forced under the surface. The banks caved in, and under the trampling the water became a mire. The strongest men forced their way to the clearer water, by the rocks at the end of the pool, and the sick were only able to drink the mud at the edges.

When order was restored the seigneurs met in council. They felt the lack of Bohemund's impetuous guidance, but the common danger roused them to action.

Water must be found, at once. They agreed to drive the herds to the northern hills, where wells and springs were unharmed. For the men, water must be carried from sources six miles away. Buffalo and goat skins could be sewn up to hold it.

The siege could not be carried on without the necessary engines, so timbers must be brought in. Syrians informed them that no suitable wood existed nearer than thirty miles. Parties of workmen were detailed to go to the forest and begin cutting and shaping the tree trunks.

No one thought of giving up the siege. They had reached Jerusalem, and here they would abide, and the final issue lay in the hand of God. Nothing could be more certain than that. And one bit of cheering news came in to the camps. The blessed ships had joined them again—a score of Genoese galleys had put in at the port of ruined Jaffa and begged the army for a detachment to hold the tower and castle of Jaffa, to protect their landing.

The good tidings spread through the tents. Here was a supply of timber—fine, dry wood—and skilled craftsmen and fresh food. No more fetid water and barley bread! Perhaps there would be wine, for who had ever seen a sailor of Genoa without his cask and jug?

Two companies of knights and bowmen hastened down to the coast with Raymond Pilet in command, and fought their way through the Moslem cavalry that barred their road. The Arabs and Turks numbered more than six hundred, but the knights charged them, and reached the ruined walls of Jaffa with Moslem shields and cloaks hung upon their saddles.

The sailors greeted them joyfully—they had been cruising for days along the coast without a trace of Christian occupation. When they heard how ill the army had fared in the last week they set to work to make ready a feast of good bread and wine and cooked fish, and Provençal knights and Genoese seamen sat down together in the roofless hall of the castle, around bright fires. Platters were emptied and goblets passed from hand to hand, and the watch on the ships came ashore to have their share. Was not all danger ended, now that they had found the army?

They feasted too well. An Egyptian fleet sighted the lights in Jaffa from far out at sea and stole in on them, surrounding the galleys.

When dawn lighted the scene, the Genoese hastened to their vessels again, but found it useless to give battle. They were able to carry ashore a good part of their weapons, gear, and supplies before abandoning their galleys. One of the galleys managed to put to sea and escape the Moslems, and it sailed back up the coast, to Laodicea, to tell the others there how the army of Jerusalem was faring. Later on, two other Genoese vessels put in at Jaffa and stayed there without harm.

But by then Pilet and his knights and the stranded seamen had traveled into the foothills to Jerusalem. "Thus," says Raymond the chronicler, "they came home, after winning a battle and losing a battle."

They found matters going badly at the siege. The heat

increased each day when the sun rose over the hills and struck the tents, rousing the sleepers who were still damp with sweat after an uneasy night. Wind swirled through the ravines, drawing clouds of dust from the hollows. When the wind ceased sweat broke out again on the bodies of the men. Water was still scarce. Skins of foul water brought in on camels sold for high prices, and a flagon full of clear water could be had only for five or six coins. In fact, money did not have much value here.

The dust stung the eyes and parched throats, but the stench from the dead cattle filled the tents. Reports from the parties who had taken the herds to the hills were not reassuring. Moslems had attacked them repeatedly, holding them off from the wells and raiding the animals.

Some of the weaker spirits had stolen off to the deep valley behind the Mount of Olives, where they found the river Jordan. They bathed in it and hastened to gather some reeds from Jericho, intending to end their pilgrimage and go down to the coast to gain the ships that might carry them back to Laodicea or even Constantinople. But they learned that the ships were lost.

Meanwhile the leaders held the steadier men to work without respite. At the end of June the first timbers came down from the hills, dragged on wheels by mules and camels, or carried on the backs of men. Godfrey called on the Genoese to help in cutting the timbers and plaiting ropes for the torsion machines—they had saved mallets, spikes, and axes from the ships. Gaston of Béarn, the master engineer, was placed in command of the workmen, and drew the plans for the machines.

He ordered the unskilled men to weave mantlets out of the softer wood around the city. Each knight was to furnish two mantlets and one ladder. The carpenters and engineers set up stone casters, powered by the twisted ropes. These could be moved around from point to point. But the master placed his chief trust in two great towers. St. Gilles agreed to be responsible for one, and Duke Godfrey for the other.

These were to be greater towers than the one built at Maara, since they would have three stories—the lowest for the men who pushed the wooden tower forward, the mid-story as high as the level of the ramparts for the armored knights to cross to the wall, and the upper level for the archers who would cover the rush of the knights. Gaston also built some "sows," or strong sheds open at each end, that could be pushed up to the wall and shield men who tried to break through the lower courses of the stonework. But he had little hope of undermining the wall of Jerusalem.

Godfrey wisely left all this work in his hands. The Rhineland and Norman princes occupied themselves in guarding the workers who were laboring with the timbers along the road of thirty miles to the hills. Daily the number of mantlets grew, and the skeleton of the giant towers rose higher. Men worked with a will, going with little food in order to check the uneasiness of thirst. And the native Christians brought into the camp their own stores of food to aid the cross-bearers.

At the same time other forces were at work. Some of the bishops and princes found cause in the general uncertainty for dispute. They blamed Tancred for placing his banner over the Church of the Nativity as if it had been a captured castle, and they called a great council to discuss the siege. For a long time the military leaders had been convinced that the army would be defeated unless someone held the supreme command. And the only single authority they knew was that of a king. It was time, they said, that the great seigneurs and barons should assemble and select one of their number and render fealty to him. He alone should give orders and be obeyed.

The clergy opposed this. They had entered the Kingdom of Jerusalem, but the Holy Land was to remain without human authority. They had come thus far by a united effort, and what had been gained by all should not be given into the hands of one.

"It is not yet gained," the barons answered. "And if it should be, who is to care for it?"

"You may not choose a king to rule, where Christ suffered and wore the crown of thorns," the clergy responded. "If a second David, unworthy, should reign here, holding this kingdom, he would say in his heart, 'I sit upon the throne of David.' Has not the prophet proclaimed, *'When the Holy of Holies shall come, unction shall cease, because it will be manifest to all people that He has come'?"*

So they debated, and in the end they agreed to wait. No one was placed in supreme command.

The towers were roofed over, and the last of the mantlets finished. Still the great council sat, and the men at arms thronged the camp about it, to hear what the decision would be. They knew by now that the Moslem garrison within the city was better supplied with food and water than they, and that the siege could not go on like this. Would there be an assault and who would lead them? The towers had been dragged close to the ditch, and the Provençals were at work carrying up stones and throwing them into the ditch to make it level with the base of the tower.

Then a new word was heard in the camps. The beloved Adhemar had not deserted them. For he had been seen in a vision, and had spoken, saying that it was time they made peace, one with the other: time for them to confess the evil they had done, and to seek the forgiveness of the Lord, and to humble themselves—who had sinned by too great pride— by marching barefoot in procession around the city where One had died for them.

The soldiers and common people cried assent, and the princes agreed gladly. The general council was disbanded, without anyone willing it, but simply because a holy man had repeated in words the vision that had entered his mind during the night. Adhemar, dead, brought peace once more to his restless flock.

Tancred even rode in and asked forgiveness of old St. Gilles.

The crusaders fasted and unburdened their consciences, until the morning appointed for the procession. Then they assembled in ranks, the lords walking among the men at arms. Without any blast of trumpets they began the march around the city, raising the crucifixes and singing hymns.

A strange processional, that thronged the ravines and climbed slowly over rocks. The Moslems came out to watch, suspecting a trick. And their curiosity changed to amazement. Surely this mournful march of the iron men was a wailing and a lament!

Down into the Valley of the Damned moved the throng, and along the walls followed thousands of Moslems, carrying wooden crosses in mockery. Arab women cast dirt and refuse down at the marchers, and screamed shrill taunts.

The deep-throated chant of the crusaders did not falter. The procession went on, and the rocks of Jehoshaphat echoed the chant.

The Moslems had not been idle. They were experienced soldiers—regiments of African bowmen and infantry led by marabouts, with the Syrian Arabs who had come in from the countryside, all under the command of the Fatimite governor, who was called the Guardian of the Two Holy Places. A year ago this army out of Egypt had wrested Jerusalem from the garrison of the Turkish lords of Damascus, but it had been a bloodless capitulation, and now the two factions made common cause against the Christians.

For the last few days they had been at work raising the level of the wall at the two points opposite the crusaders' siege towers. So well had they done their work that Duke Godfrey and Sir Gaston decided that the wall in front of their tower was impregnable.

Godfrey knew that he could not risk a second failure. If the tower failed, his last recourse was gone. And somewhere in the west the Egyptian kalif was mustering an army to relieve Jerusalem.

That night he gave orders to dismantle the tower, timber by timber. These parts must all be carried a half mile along the wall, to a spot where the wall was lower and the ground level—near the northeast corner of the city. And with the tower must go the lines of mantlets and the *petraria*.

The crusaders heard the tidings in silence, and set to work grimly after nightfall. Gaston and his artisans stripped the great siege tower, passing down the beams to the waiting soldiers, who shouldered them and disappeared into the night.

They dared not light the way with torches, or make use of the ox sledges, lest the garrison take alarm and sally out. Progress was painfully slow; the short hours of darkness passed before the last timbers had been carried to the new position.

Daylight brought amazement to the Moslems, who found the siege engines vanished from the menaced quarter. But it brought bitter disappointment to the Normans and Lorrainers who gathered at the new site and beheld a welter of beams, planks, chains and ropes, mallets and pegs and tents and poles. It was easier to take down such engines than to set them up again. Their attempt at surprise had failed, but the crusaders were not discouraged.

It took them three days to rebuild the engines, and in that time the Moslems raised the level of the wall around the northeast corner, but they built it up with wood, not with stone.

At sunrise on the fourteenth of July the olifants sounded in the crusaders' camps and they advanced to the attack.

XXXI

THE BRIDGE OF FIRE

TORTURED wood creaked and crashed. Ropes whined and hissed, and the long arms of the stone-casters shot toward the sky. Heavy stones soared and fell, splintering against the wall. Crossbows snapped, and the short black bolts whirred up toward the ramparts. Beneath the tumult echoed the steady *thud-thud* of the rams pounding against the foundations.

At times a shout of warning could be heard, followed by the roar of falling masonry. Dust and lime hung in the air, and drifted slowly over the siege engines. Mailed figures, clustering behind the rows of woven shields, peered up. Other men rolled boulders toward the machines or carried bundles of arrows on their shoulders. Swordsmen walked impatiently through the lines, long shields on their arms.

Around the banners of the lords, behind the engines, throngs sat and watched, with ladders on the ground by them. Men brushed sweat from their eyelids to stare into the dust and sun glare. They listened to the crash and thud of the front line with accustomed ears, judging the progress made by the laboring engines. A distant horn clamored—

a Provençal horn, and no doubt Count Raymond was leading another assault over yonder.

Here near the northeast corner they were still gnawing
at the barbican—the outer wall. Gaps had been opened in
it, and through the gaps they could see at times the dark
figures of Moslems. Other tiny figures came and went in the
crenels of the mighty gray wall that loomed against the
sky, forty feet overhead. From this rampart arrows flashed
down, into the earth or into the men who were struggling
with picks and ropes to clear away the débris of the outer
wall in front of the wooden tower, that waited like an
inanimate giant for the moment when it would be pushed
forward through the breach, until it stood fair against the
inner wall. Then, the waiting men knew, the real onset and
onfray would come.

With a creaking of timbers, the tower moved. Orders were
shouted from within it, and soldiers gathered behind it, to
heave and thrust with their shoulders. The tower was nearly
fifty feet high, and its top was much smaller than its base,
because it sloped inward on three sides. On the fourth side,
toward the Moslems, it rose sheer from the ground, and near
the summit poised the drawbridge.

This drawbridge was drawn up—held so by the ropes attached to the end—covering the opening through which
armed men would run out upon it the moment it was lowered
against the rampart. But the tower was still feeling its way
through the breach in the outer wall.

Women drew nearer the battle line, shading their eyes
and seeking out certain steel-clad figures among the moving
throngs. They covered their heads and waited, their lips
moving. Girls carried water jars in their arms, and the men
jested with them.

The heat grew worse as the sun passed overhead, but it
would not do to think of that—or of the unconscious figures
carried back from the vicinity of the tower. There, among
the engines, men labored on the ground that was baked by
the sun as hard as the stones of the gray wall. At times,
maddened by the hot blood rushing through his veins, a
crusader would throw off his helmet. The waiting men

jested, but their eyes were somber. Hours passed, and the tower advanced only a little way.

Duke Robert of Normandy—Robert Short Breeches, his men called him—went down to the engines and walked among them, stopping to talk with the engineers. They laughed when he came up to them, for it was his way to gibe and joke at such a time. Tancred paced along the line, without his shield. A strange banner was carried behind him, a white banner with a single red cross. The men liked to see Tancred. Things went well where he led.

Duke Godfrey watched from a knoll, with Sir Gaston and Count Eustace his brother, and the youthful paladin, Baldwin of the Mount. The tower was Godfrey's and his the responsibility. If he could gain a footing on the walls Jerusalem would fall. He *must* do this.

But he had done his utmost. In his patient spirit there was no wolflike craftiness. He could only fight with his hands. And he did this—going forward to the tower and taking an archer's bow in his hand.

Smoke swirled from the gray wall. The Moslems were using fire against the tower. They bound faggots of wood and straw together with iron chains and cast them flaming from the mangonels. Smoldering beams soaked in oil and pitch followed, twisting in the air, and crashing into the solid planks of the tower.

With axes and wet hides the crusaders fought the fire. Stones flew after the faggots, and the shrill ululation of triumph rose from the Moslems on the wall:

"*Allah il allahu!*"

The sun was setting, and surely the holy men on Sion had prayed in vain.

Tancred went up with the scaling ladders and crossbowmen under the drifting smoke to cover his assault. But the ladders failed, and the smoke cleared, and the sun went down. Godfrey gave the order to cease fighting. The tower remained where it was.

It had been shattered on the side facing the wall, and the beams were charred where fire had caught. But it stood, and its base was undamaged.

From the west of the city came the same story. The Provençals had broken through to the great bastion called the Tower of David. Otherwise their assault had failed.

Night fell over Jerusalem, but the crusaders did not sleep. Godfrey remained at his engines, and the artisans labored over repairs, while the men at arms watched in the ruins of the barbican. No one wanted to go away, because the Moslems might sally out and destroy the machines that were less than a bowshot from the wall.

It was a night of fear for both sides [Raymond the chronicler explains]. The Saracens dreaded that we might storm the city during the darkness, since their outer wall had been broken down, and the ditch filled up. And we on our part feared greatly that they would set fire to the machines that were now so close to the wall. So it was a night of watching and work, and unsleeping care.

Within the city muffled sounds told the crusaders that the garrison was afoot. Behind the veil of darkness the Moslem artisans were mounting new mangonels on the broad summit of the wall, and covering the wooden superstructure with sacks of straw.

Dawn flamed along the Mount of Olives, revealing to each side what the other had accomplished. The horns resounded in the camps, and the crusaders manned the engines again, drawing them nearer the wall. Tancred and Robert of Normandy were no longer among them, because they had gone off to assault a new point, the gate of St. Stephen.

Their new battery gave the Moslems the advantage at once. Stones and beams crushed one machine after another beneath the wall, and a foretaste of defeat brought weariness to the men of the cross, who had labored for twenty-four hours without sleep.

The lords who attended Godfrey spoke of abandoning the engines and withdrawing, but the duke would not. Instead, the great tower creaked forward, rolling over the débris, and settling down within a spear's length of the wall. Godfrey was at the end of his resources, but withdraw he would

not. Perhaps he felt that this was the last effort of the crusade. He would not yield while he could stand his ground.

When the waiting thousands saw the tower against the
wall they ran forward with scaling ladders, and climbed over
the outer ruins.

"God wills it!" The cry went up from straining lungs, as
men fought for a place on the ladders and fell back wounded.
"God wills it!"

The Moslems roared their exultation, and smoke covered
the fighters again. Someone had ordered the Christian archers
to use fire arrows, and shafts wrapped in flaming cotton
flew into the wooden scaffolding and the straw sacks of the
platform above the wall. The fire caught and spread along
the wall, and defenders and besiegers drew away from it.
The Moslems hastened toward the clashing of steel where
a knight, Lethold of Touraine, and his brother had gained a
footing on the wall at the head of a scaling ladder.

And at this moment Godfrey ordered his men to let go the
ropes that held the drawbridge.

The ropes were cut through and freed, and the bridge fell
against the flaming rampart. It was caught by two beams
the Moslems had thrust against the tower. Godfrey, his
sword in his hand, ran across it and leaped into the smoke.

Eustace was at his shoulder and Baldwin of the Mount
behind him. They jumped clear of the fire and ran along
the wall. After them came their knights and weapon men.
Their long swords hissed and crashed, and they fought their
way like maniacs through the smoke. This was Godfrey's
moment, and no foeman could stand against the power of
his arm. They held the wall, these few, while the flaming
scaffolding was cut down and tossed away and hundreds of
armed men poured through the door of the tower across the
drawbridge.

Their coming freed the men who had climbed the scaling
ladders, and more surged up from the ground, driving the
Moslems down the inner stairs of the wall, driving them
back into the streets of the city.

Seeing this, the garrison at the St. Stephen's Gate faltered,
and Tancred and Duke Robert broke in the gate. The

mounted crusaders galloped in, and a roar went up that was answered by the throngs on the Mount of Olives. The white standard with the red cross stood on the wall. Jerusalem had fallen.

At nine o'clock in the morning of the fifteenth of July the gate of St. Stephen and the postern of Magdalen were thrown open, and ten thousand crusaders with weapons in their hands went mad.

They were mad with joy. An hour before they had been struggling almost without hope. Wild rumors inflamed them —some saying that an unknown knight in full armor had taken his stand on the Mount of Olives and had waved his shield, signing them to go forward. Who could this be but St. George? Others cried that Adhemar had appeared among them in the flesh, to lead that last attack. God had yielded them their desire.

Fever burned their veins, bred of the pitiless heat, the weariness, and the strain of the fighting. Down the streets before them fled a mob of figures in cloaks and turbans, and to the crusaders these seemed to be the vanquished soldiery of Anti-Christ, profaners of the holy places, enemies of Christ. Sword in hand they followed, past the empty stalls of the dark bazaar, past the open doorways. Their swords hacked and thrust, scattering blood on the panting men.

Godfrey and the great lords ran with them. Thin faces gleamed with exultation, and meaningless cries came from parched throats. Into the street of the Sepulcher they turned, without knowing whither they went.

When groups of Arabs, penned in the alleys, faced them without hope, they leaped forward, struck furiously into the bodies of snarling men, and passed on, stumbling and shouting. Here and there Moslems defended the roofs with arrows, and the crusaders ran into the houses, cutting down the wailing women who shrank back from them. Behind them lay the broken bodies of children and young girls lying with sightless eyes. Blood dripped from the stairs and stained the white walls.

Down toward the heart of the city they fought their

way. Along the *Via Dolorosa* armed knights passed, like a black storm cloud. The hour of retribution had come, and death for the unbelievers. In the narrow courts of the mosques throngs moaned at their coming, and the horsemen slashed with ax and sword blade until the fountains turned red and the frantic horses slipped upon the hot, wet stones and the fragments of human flesh.

In the half darkness of the mosques families gathered to await the end of life. Resistance ceased here—their fate was revealed to them, and this was the hour and the spot appointed. Old men stood, with the calm of fatalists, and saw the heads of their sons roll to the musty carpets. They in turn were struck down, their skulls shattered by axes or their bowels cut open by a sword's edge. Women clung to their bending knees, screaming and panting until steel wrenched open their soft bodies and they cried out no longer.

Within the courtyard of the Sepulcher other families gathered, maddened by fear. Women for the most part, Syrians and Christians. This was the hour of their deliverance, but they heard the tumult of the slaying drawing nearer, and knew not how to save themselves from the swords. Dark eyes were fixed on the courtyard entrance, and they prayed. Because they could not make the iron men understand that they also served the Lord of the crossbearers. No priest was here to raise a crucifix over them.

They began to sing, with quivering throats. The crusaders dismounted at the courtyard and came forward, sword in hand. The Syrians sang:

"*Kyrie eleison—Christe eleison.*"

And the iron men understood. They sheathed their swords and walked among these Christians of the Holy Land, stroking the heads of the children and smiling at the patriarchs.

"*Kyrie eleison—Christe eleison!*" Joyous was the song. Other Syrians, hearing that the steps of the Sepulcher had become a sanctuary, hastened toward the singing.

But in that other sanctuary, up in the great enclosure of the Temple of Solomon, the Moslems gathered to find only death. There the crusaders rode through human blood above the fetlocks of their horses. Blood splashed the knees of the horses and the reins. Only late in the day did Tancred grant safety of life to some three hundred Moslems clustered on the flat roof of the Aksa Mosque. With Gaston of Béarn, he took them under his protection and gave them a standard as token. They remained on the roof, afraid to come down.

At the same time the amir who held command in the citadel of the Tower of David surrendered to Count Raymond and opened his gate to the Provençals.

By then Godfrey and the mass of the crusaders had ceased the slaughter. Utterly weary, they put away their weapons and washed their hands and arms. Taking off their armor, they put on clean mantles and walked through the littered streets to the narrow entrance of the little Church of the Sepulcher.

The anger had left them, and they were filled with happiness. They stared at the small white churches and smiled. They walked with clasped hands, saying little. The sun was setting and glowing in the sky over David's Gate, and they had redeemed Jerusalem. Surely God had willed it.

But the next day new throngs of crusaders entered the city and the slaughter began again. The streets were obstructed by the piles of bodies that had lost all human semblance. Horses trampled on severed hands and heads in the gutters, and smoke from the burning synagogues of the Jews hung in the air like a pall. On the Temple, the miserable captives were slain by the newcomers in spite of the safeguard of Tancred's standard.

Not until the second night did the massacre end and quiet settle down on the streets.

The city was indeed ours [says Raymond the chaplain] and we had then the reward of all our labor when we beheld the devotion of the pilgrims at the Sepulcher of the Lord—how they applauded and exulted, singing a new song to the Lord. Out of their soul they offered a thanksgiving of praise that cannot be expressed. It was a new day and a new joyousness! And it drew new words and new songs from everyone.

And this day, I say, shall be renowned through the ages. It

changed all our sorrow into joy. "*This is the day the Lord hath made, let us rejoice and be glad in it.*"

Two weeks after the taking of Jerusalem, and before he could have heard the tidings of it in his city of Rome, died Urban II, who conceived the crusade and sent it forth. But in his last hours he had the satisfaction of seeing German lords who had served his enemy, the emperor, take the cross. The crusade, beyond his sight, had won his life's battle for him. Upon his tomb they placed these words:

Urbanus Secundus
Auctor Expeditionis in Infideles

PART IV

XXXII

GODFREY

A WEEK after the capture of Jerusalem the cross-bearers
met in council and chose Godfrey of Bouillon to be
their leader—Baron of Jerusalem and Defender of
the Sepulcher. It was like Godfrey to refuse the title of king.

The quiet lord of Bouillon was still in the prime of his
life, but the lurking fever had taken its toll of his strength.
He had exerted himself to the utmost during the siege, and
to accept the responsibility of leadership now meant that
he would have no rest. Knowing this, he accepted. And in
so doing he took into his hands the fate of the crusade.

It was clear to him that the capture of Jerusalem had not
ended matters. The victory had saved his army, which was
now safe within the walls. Nothing else had altered.

The cross-bearers were scattered all over the map. Their
conquests resembled, in shape, a battle-ax—an ax standing
upright upon the ball of its hilt, Jerusalem. The head of the
ax lay far in the north, the blade with a curving edge turned
toward the east. That was Edessa, where Godfrey's brother
and the Armenians held broad lands. The center of the ax-

head was the land of Antioch, where Bohemund ruled. And the rear of the ax-head, tapering to a point in the west, was Little Armenia, ending in the city of Tarsus. The shaft of the ax was the narrow strip of seacoast, some three hundred miles in length, between Jerusalem and Antioch.

The crusaders had not conquered this strip of coast. They had only passed over it. So the battle-ax really lacked a shaft and the head was separated from the pommel. Godfrey could only communicate with Bohemund by ship. He heard that new fleets were coming, but he could not tell when or where they would arrive.

Neither Godfrey nor Bohemund held a fortified point on the coast. Antioch had the port of St. Simeon, of course, but that was merely a village at the mouth of the Orontes. The Byzantine fleet had taken possession of the valuable Laodicea, in the north. As a matter of fact, Bohemund was occupied just at this time in trying to oust them.

Down in the south Godfrey had access to the sea at Jaffa, which consisted of a tolerable beach, a broken wall, and a ruined castle. Between Jaffa and Laodicea—the crusaders began to call it La Liche—lay the three almost impregnable citadels of Tripoli, Sidon, and Tyre, with half a dozen other towns, all in Moslem hands. Naturally they were not inclined to let the crusaders pass along the coast highway. And behind the mountains lay mighty Damascus.

Moreover, both in north and south the Moslems held strongholds that the crusaders could not venture to attack —Aleppo and Ascalon. Ascalon, where the sands of the Jifar begin, was within two days' ride of Jerusalem. Godfrey had heard rumors that Moslems were coming over the sea from Egypt and gathering there.

In the north, some twenty thousand cross-bearers had lingered. Here, in the south, Godfrey had about the same number, because one man in three had left, after the capture of Jerusalem and the fulfilment of their vows. They had marched or sailed toward the north in large companies, and what happened to them no one knows.

At this moment the crusaders needed a leader who could organize and fortify and work miracles by negotiating with

THE UNKNOWN'S NARRATIVE

The first page of a Twelfth Century manuscript of the unknown soldier's narrative.

A PRINCE OF BYZANTIUM

And his cavalry escort, visiting a Moslem city

the invisible Muhammadan powers. Where Bohemund would have played politics, Godfrey dreamed. He took up his quarters in the lofty eastern enclosure, in the Aksa Mosque. From the flat roof he could look across the valley to the shade trees of Gethsemane. In the porch of the Aksa sat the sergeants-at-arms of the Rhineland. Godfrey's chamberlain and seneschal waited in the carpeted anteroom that had been the sitting place of *hadjis*. They slept in tiny blue-tiled chambers hung with brocades, the divans covered with white linen. Even the lattice-work was fragrant—olive and sandalwood, old and sweet. Their horses were stabled in the arched corridors beneath the mosque.

Godfrey's chaplain had set up an altar in the eastern alcove, and men were at work casting a bell to be hung in the silent minaret. Other artisans were gilding an iron cross to be raised over the tower of the Sepulcher of Christ. And Godfrey dreamed.

Almost within arrow shot of his new palace stood the beautiful Dome of the Rock, the white cupola rising on slender pillars. Here Godfrey liked to go at sunset, when the light softened in the small windows of scarlet and purple glass. Men said that here David had walked, and Abraham had offered sacrifice, and surely the Ark of the Covenant had rested here. The crusaders called it the *Templum Domini*, unaware that the Moslems, too, held it to be a holy of holies. Godfrey lingered there through the evenings while the glow of sunset faded along the red hills and his household waited impatiently about the tables in the palace refectory.

He ruled a city nearly deserted. Only the Moslem captives were seen in the streets, where the stench of dead bodies still hung in the air. All the Jews had vanished, as if at the command of some invisible power, leaving their dye vats and their stalls in the alleys near the wailing place. The companies of crusaders clustered together in a few streets, on the heights by the Sepulcher.

They set up strange households. They had no furniture and few garments of their own. So they sat on ebony taborets and slept on low, cushioned divans; they drank sherbet and wine out of glass vessels, and they feasted upon mutton and dried raisins, olives, and white, wheaten bread. The women made hoods out of long, soft turban cloths and bright silk kerchiefs. They fingered the pearl-sewn veils of the Moslem women, and wondered at the jeweled slippers and enameled bracelets. At night they lighted their rooms with oil lanterns of worked brass, or colored glass—much better than the smoking cressets or guttering candles of their own homes.

What would come to pass now, Godfrey did not know. He explained his dreams to the priests who followed him around. Soon the great fleets would arrive from Europe, bringing new hosts of crusaders. With their aid, the coast citadels could be captured, and Jerusalem extended to Antioch. Then the new domain needed a code of laws. No king would ever sit upon a throne here, so the laws must be drawn up anew for the land—to provide for a high court of the lords, laymen and churchmen, and a lower court of the bourgeoisie and merchants. The conquests must be rearranged as fiefs, and title given to the vassals who would hold them.

Likewise the half-ruined basilicas of the holy places would be given gradually into the keeping of the servants of the Church—some to the order of St. Augustine, some to the Benedictines. Then the work of rebuilding could begin. He visioned a new Jerusalem, with cathedral churches and hospitals soaring skyward—cloisters hemming in tranquil gardens, filled with monks and belted warriors. Evening bells chiming the Angelus, while the light softened in high windows of colored glass. A city of rest and devotion.

Half ascetic, half warrior, Godfrey dreamed, as many men before and after him have dreamed, of a new Jerusalem. And then tidings arrived from the coast. No fleet had been sighted, but a Moslem host had come out of Egypt and was mustering at Ascalon.

Godfrey summoned Tancred, who was absent then at Naplous. He led out his own knights toward Ramlah, and sent back a message to Count Raymond in Jerusalem: "In truth, there will be a battle. Prepare, and come without delay."

There was need of haste. When Godfrey dismounted at the Ramlah villages and gave the order to set up the tents, Tancred came to him full of news. The impetuous Norman had made a wide circuit down by the sea and had gathered up several Arab warriors, who had talked after some persuasion. Tancred repeated their tale bluntly.

The kalif at Cairo had proclaimed a holy war, and the armed host of Egypt had been on the march across the white sands of the Jifar, when Jerusalem fell. They heard the news of the city's capture at Ascalon, where the Egyptian fleet had put in, to assist them.

Whereupon, the wazir in command of the host—Malik al-Afdhal he was called—waited to gather more men. He had the Arab clansmen of Syria with him, and some Turks. His host increased in number daily, and he planned to march on Jerusalem, shut the Franks within its walls, and rouse all the coast against them. He had vowed to make an end of them, and to tear down the Sepulcher stone by stone. He was still at Ascalon.

So said the captives. That evening Tancred and Godfrey, and the duke's brother Eustace, sat down to discuss the situation—after Godfrey had sent the messenger to the other crusaders lingering in Jerusalem. They decided to advance toward Ascalon instead of retiring to Jerusalem. To stay in the plain of Ramlah, with the hills on three sides of them, was impossible. Ramlah was a trap, in the center of the triangle, with Jaffa, Jerusalem, and Ascalon at its three points.

Hundreds of keen, hostile eyes watched their fires that night, and swift horses carried word of their actions to the malik at Ascalon.

The next day the standards of Toulouse and Normandy moved down through the hills. The Sleepy Duke and the wayward Provençal joined the defender of the Sepulcher. And Godfrey lost not a moment in setting out. He left all the tents and heavy baggage at Ramlah and marched south, toward Ascalon. Moreover, he marched in a new formation— in three lines, each in three separate bodies. This made a rough square, and by simply wheeling into line the separate bodies could face to right or left. The knights and mounted men at arms were grouped in solid companies throughout the nine detachments,

The crusaders had learned their lesson, and had abandoned the single battle line of their fathers. The moving square could meet an attack of the swift Moslem horsemen on any side and the center squadron would form the reserve, under Godfrey's command. And the knights themselves, for the most part, bestrode rangy Turkoman horses, fleeter of foot and more enduring than the heavier chargers of Europe.

Tancred's scouts, flung out on the flanks, took possession of the clay watch towers that crowned the ridges along their line of march. They moved on steadily, through a broad valley covered by a scum of sedge, until they reached a river bed with some stagnant pools of water.

Here they found something entirely unexpected. The shallow valley and the plain beyond were filled with tawny herds —camels, cattle, sheep, and goats—and frantic Arab herders. In the sun glare and dust, it seemed to the crusaders that this must be part of the malik's host. Two hundred knights rode out to investigate, and the Arabs fled, abandoning their animals. Some were taken captive by the hard-riding Christians and brought in to be questioned—not too gently.

"The host of the malik is not here," they said. "Nay, it is distant five leagues from this river, waiting in its tents. We do not know its numbers, for we were driving the cattle thither, to sell to the malik's officers. But the host is a great host."

Tancred's scouts confirmed what the Arabs said, adding that the Moslems knew of the movement of the Christian army, but thought it only a sally to drive in cattle before the siege—because the crusaders had no more than twelve hundred horsemen, and some nine thousand foot soldiers. Al-Afdhal had some twenty thousand warriors with his standard. Moreover, the soothsayers in the Moslem tents had warned the men of Islam not to advance until the seventh day of the week—any day before then would be unfortunate.

Godfrey and his companions discussed the situation and decided to go forward. This was a Wednesday, the third day of their week but the fifth of the Moslem week. If they meant to attack the malik, it would be better to do so on the morrow. The day after that the Moslems might be on the move themselves—might avoid Godfrey's small army and strike at Jerusalem.

So they crossed the river and pushed on through a beautiful valley, where the level light of late afternoon beat against the red ridges of limestone, and the cool breath of the sea refreshed the marching men.

The stars were out when they halted and laid aside their weapons to gather around the fires, while mounted patrols paced along the ridges.

It was told throughout the army [says Raymond the chaplain] that every man should make ready for battle on the morrow at dawn, and everyone should keep close to his leader. In the battle, no one must delay to plunder—if he did so, he would be excommunicated. We passed that night in poor fashion, because we had no tents, or wine. Some of us had bread, and a few had grain and salt. But meat was plentiful as the sand itself. We ate beef and eked it out with fat mutton for bread.

They had brought the herds along with them, and they slept among the masses of restless animals, until the horns of the duke roused them. They armed themselves and were formed in three divisions, Godfrey taking the left and Raymond the right near the shore—the bowmen and pikemen moving forward in advance of the thin lines of horsemen.

Then something unforeseen happened .The cattle came, too. Riderless horses and cattle followed the mounts of the knights, and camels moved after them. When the soldiers halted, the animals did likewise. The sun rose in a clear sky and revealed to the startled Moslems in the malik's camp a confusion of dust and moving figures advancing along the edge of the sea.

Many stories are told of what happened next. The Moslems rode out like bees swarming from the hives, and formed in dense masses a little way in front of their camp. In the center of them rose the silver and gilt standard of the malik, surrounded by the fine cavalry of Cairo. Each horseman had a small water bag hanging from his neck or saddle horn.

They realized by then that the Christians intended to give battle. But the men of Islam did not charge as usual. They peered through the heat haze at the Christian bowmen advancing on foot. And behind the bowmen they beheld dark lines of animals that seemed to them to be horsemen—for the horns of the cattle gleamed in the sun like steel, and the dust hung over the herds like a veil.

The Arab clans took their position, as always, on the flanks of the malik's array. They trotted out to either side, swinging around the crusaders, intending to charge in upon the rear.

So Godfrey's army went forward against the center of the Moslem arc that extended and curved inward as he came on —as Hannibal's wild horsemen had closed around the advancing legions of the Romans at Cannae. The duke saw the danger, and hung back with his knights and men at arms, to keep from being surrounded. The sun rose higher, and the hot breath of the plain became a torment to the armored men.

Still the Christian bowmen advanced, until they were within stone's throw of the motionless array of the Egyptians. Then they loosed their arrows. A roar went up from the Moslems.

In another moment the Arabs might have cut off Godfrey and his men, and the drums of Malik al-Afdhal would have sounded a charge. But at this instant Robert Short Breeches took matters into his own hands.

For once in his life the drowsy Norman was on the field, armed and ready for action. With Tancred and Gaston of Béarn, he had paced forward behind the archers—they had rid themselves of the cattle herds by now. The archers stopped, but the Norman duke went on alone.

He saw before him the dark ranks of the Moslems, and the green banners uplifted. He saw the silver pole and the gilt ball that was the standard of the malik, and he headed his horse straight toward this.

With lowered lance, his steel-capped head bent over the edge of his shield, he smashed into the first horsemen, and disappeared. His lance broke and he dropped it, pulling out his long sword. Spurring on his horse, he lashed a way forward, his great shoulders twisting and straining.

He reached the standard of the malik and cut down the standard-bearer. And the standard fell.

His knights had charged after him, and while they fought to reach him, his comrade in arms, the youthful count of Flanders, rode out at the head of the Flemings. Tancred saw, and charged through the archers.

A thousand chevaliers rode into the cavalry of the kalif, and the men of Islam gave way before them. The flailing swords smashed through shields and armor and bones. Saddles were empty where the swords struck, and the center of the malik's array became a mass of frantic horses and maddened men. Tancred did not stop until he had reached the heart of the Moslem camp.

And by then the Arab clans, seeing the flight of the malik, had turned and galloped from the field. The Moslems fled through their tents and raced toward Ascalon. Behind them rode the crusaders, mounted for once on horses as swift as their own. So the battle swept from the plain, as dust whirls before the wind. In an hour the Christian bowmen were left to stare at the dead and the deserted tents.

They found spoils that amounted to treasures in the rich pavilions of the Egyptians—silver chests, carpets and gold inlaid weapons, rosaries and Koran boxes—splendid *khalats* scattered over the ground, jeweled girdle clasps and armlets set with topazes and amethysts. There were rare vases in the quarters of the chieftains, and gleaming chalcedony, and soft jade, suits of steel mesh, gold-washed, that could be rolled within the fingers of a man's two hands. Some of the riderless horses had saddles ornamented with precious stones, and gold stirrups.

More than that, they found supplies that they needed badly.

All the hills were full of the enemy's herds [the Unknown relates]. We found piles of arms, and when we had chosen what we wanted, we burned the rest. Our men rejoiced in the camels, and the grain and cereal, and butter and bread and oil and all kinds of goods. They carried them back to Jerusalem.

All the ships of the infidels had come to the battle, but when the seamen beheld the Amir and his army in flight, they raised their sails and hastened out to deep water. Our men found the standard of the Amir, which the Duke of Normandy bought back for twenty marks of silver and bestowed it on the patriarch for the honor of God, to be placed in the Holy Sepulcher. Someone else bought the Amir's sword for sixty byzants.

And so, by God's will, our enemy was overcome. This battle was fought the day before the Ides of August, our Seigneur Jesus Christ granting it to us. May the honor and glory be to him for the ages of the ages. Let all souls say, Amen!

These are the last words of the Unknown. His narrative ends here, on the plain of Ascalon, after the victory that secured the Holy Land to its defender, Godfrey—while he was marching back to Jerusalem beside the animals laden with the spoils that he had counted over so carefully. How did the Unknown fare afterward? We can only guess that he remained among the exiles of Jerusalem, because the western chroniclers never knew his name, and the copies of his manuscript were found two years later in Jerusalem itself. He was the Unknown, and he told the truth. That must suffice.

XXXIII

THE CITY

THE battle of Ascalon proved that the chivalry of Asia could not withstand the charge of the knights of the cross—though the odds be five to one. And it showed that the knights had adapted themselves to the warfare of the East. Not for five years did al-Afdhal make another great effort to retake Jerusalem, and a good deal happened in that time.

The crusaders might have taken the city of Ascalon if St. Gilles had not been too eager to gain it for himself. "Ascalon on the sea," an Arab told them, "is a great city and well garrisoned. Fruit is plentiful there, and the sycamore trees. The Jami mosque stands in the *suk* of the clothes merchants and is all paved with marble. The silkworms of the place are famous, and indeed life is pleasant there, and the markets crowded. Only the water is bad, and the sand-fly called *dalam* is harmful."

The old Provençal in his disappointment felt that now he could not serve beside the new baron of Jerusalem. When the other leaders mustered their men to begin the march back to Europe, he went with them.

Hardly had the dust settled down again upon the plain

of Ascalon when the last main army of the crusaders disbanded. Most of the survivors were homesick. They had marched and fought for three years, and had endured hardships almost beyond belief. They had fulfilled their vows, and they knew that fresh armies were on the way to reinforce Godfrey.

They gathered together at the duke's camp to take leave of him. For the last time they feasted together, while the laden camel trains moved away and laughing esquires hastened to saddle and lead up the horses. Godfrey gripped them in his arms and kissed them, and one by one they rode off, turning to salute his standard and wave farewell. Raymond went, with the remnant of the Provençals, and the young Robert, count of Flanders, with his boon companion, Robert of Normandy—now the hero of Ascalon—and Eustace of Boulogne, Godfrey's brother.

After their departure Godfrey found himself indeed baron of Jerusalem. Only two hundred knights remained with him —they called themselves the exiles. But Tancred stayed, with sixty or seventy knights, up by the lake of Galilee. Word came back from him at intervals: he had reached Nazareth and found the house of Mary with the crypt beneath it—he had captured Tiberias, sweltering within its brick walls, in its chasm far below the level of the sea.

Godfrey went to work patiently. His spirit was not that of the empire builder, and the fever lingered in his veins, but he had his dream and the tranquil faith that sometimes makes reality out of dreams.

Since he could not have Ascalon, he sent his marshal to besiege Arsuf, the little citadel on the far side of Jaffa. Sailors were quartered in broken-down Jaffa, to rebuild the walls. The great Venetian fleet was drawing nearer, and Godfrey must have a port ready for it, where it could lie secure.

He divided his time between the camp at Arsuf and the made-over mosque at Jerusalem that was his palace. And where he labored the law of chivalry and of property began to take shape. Lands were divided among Norman lords and Rhinelanders, who in return vowed to serve Jerusalem.

Thanks to Tancred's zeal, all conflict around the city

itself had ceased. Some of the Moslem peasants went off, but most of them remained, when they discovered that their lives and certain rights would be left them. After the terrible massacre of August fifteenth and sixteenth the crusaders had sheathed their swords. They ruled the land by feudal law, which was very much the law of the Turks. The native Christians acted as interpreters and agents for the new lords.

A few at first, caravans began to appear on the narrow roads leading through the hills to Jerusalem. Armenians and Syrians had olives, dried figs, silk and cotton, and glassware to sell, and the crusaders had wealth in their coffers, after the gleanings of the field of Ascalon.

The fields around Jerusalem yielded cotton and raisins. From the Galilee hill towns came carpets and bundles of paper made in Damascus out of cotton.

After a while the governors of the still untaken coast citadels sent in envoys to negotiate. They were secure behind their walls, but the crusaders were equally at home in Jerusalem, and the Moslems, being traders at heart, wanted communication with the interior. Acre and Ascalon agreed to pay tribute to Jerusalem, for a yearly truce and the privilege to trade. They had stores of the glassware and the purple cast up by the sea at Tyre, camelot, and sugar. From the valley of the Jordan, on the backs of donkeys, came loads of indigo and saffron.

Godfrey was content to have truce in his new barony—he had no more than the skeleton of an army to defend it. At any time the Moslems might have swept in and overpowered him. But in that year the men of Islam were looking toward the east, where the two brothers who claimed the throne of Baghdad were struggling for mastery in the steppes of Khorasan. Besides, Tancred was riding beyond Galilee, and the Moslems had learned to dread the unconquered *Darkat*, as they called him.

And that autumn another indomitable cross-bearer rode into Jerusalem. Bohemund of Antioch fought his way south, through the rains and the Arab tribes, in company with Baldwin of Edessa. The two princes came to fulfil their vows—that they would journey to the Sepulcher—and for another purpose. They stayed only a few days, to pray at the holy places, to go over to the Jordan, and to attend the first Christmas service.

They were really, in the new scheme of things, Godfrey's vassals, and he should have required them to take the oath of allegiance, and do homage to him. But he did not insist, and Bohemund managed to do something quite different. He rendered homage, instead, to Daimbert, the papal legate who had arrived to take Adhemar's place and who was now installed as patriarch of Jerusalem.[1]

In return, Daimbert acknowledged Bohemund's title to Antioch. The shrewd Norman was now, by sanction of the Church, prince of Antioch, and Baldwin likewise became prince of Edessa. So they turned their backs on Jerusalem and rode north, masters of two independent states. By this simple act Bohemund had accomplished two things—he had gained the right to defend Antioch against the Byzantine emperor, who had a claim of his own to it. Since Daimbert had also required Godfrey to render homage to him, Bohemund could say that he was Godfrey's peer, not his vassal. It was a pretty bit of statesmanship. But fate upset all Bohemund's calculations in the coming summer.

So ended the year 1099. The sun rose upon the first day of the Twelfth Century.

Godfrey passed the days untroubled by misgivings. Daimbert was spiritual head of the new domain, and he was its defender. That was right and fitting. He desired nothing different.

True, the land was barren, a great portion of it. Here he

---

[1]After the capture of Jerusalem, Arnulf, the chaplain of the duke of Normandy, had been elected patriarch by the clerical council—the Provençal clergy dissenting. Many tales are told about Arnulf—that he was priest-born, a wine drinker and buyer and seller of privileges. Some called him "the first-born of Satan." However that may be, he seems to have been a faithful worker, and he aided Godfrey. When Daimbert—an archbishop and legate of the Holy See—appeared in the autumn, Arnulf resigned his office. Daimbert was ambitious. He brought with him Urban's plan of government, which aimed at ecclesiastical supremacy in the Holy Land. Urban and Paschal after him insisted that the Church should rule Jerusalem as it ruled Rome, and that the baron of Jerusalem should be inferior in authority to the patriarch. Godfrey yielded to Daimbert's insistence.

had found no grassy hills and sleek cattle—little of the milk
and honey and the treasures that Urban of blessed memory
had foretold. The Syrian peasants shook their heads and said
that the crops had failed that spring. Little rain had fallen,
and the wheat was drying in the fields.

As the heat increased the mountain streams failed, and
the headmen of the villages complained that they could not
collect the taxes because the peasants were leaving the land.
They came in to Godfrey's officers and told the same tale
in many languages.

When Easter drew near strange men thronged into Jerusalem, from the slopes of Lebanon and from unknown shrines
—Greek priests, with their long hair braided behind their
ears and their black skirts gray with the dust of travel.
Bearded Armenians appeared in their pointed hats upon the
Via Dolorosa, and blessed the rabble of dirty children who
ran out at sight of them.

Jews in long gray shubas slipped furtively through the alleys, uncertain of their fate, but bound toward the common
goal. Maronites came down from Syria, and dark-skinned
Kopts rode in with the camel trains from Egypt. Candles
gleamed at night in the squat churches within the enclosure
of the Sepulcher. The murmur of prayers in Syriac and Armenian echoed the chanting of the Latin priests.

For more than a thousand years these visitors had thronged
in at Easter, in spite of wars and plagues. They had their
shrines, where the statues of the saints were covered by
embroidered garments and clusters of precious stones. Even
in the Church of the Resurrection itself hung grotesque Byzantine brocades, and behind glass the haggard figures of
mosaic saints.

The strange priests knew every inch of the great enclosure,
from the cracks in the Rock of Calvary to the marble recess
of the Sepulcher, and they knew every particle of their
ancient rights. On the day of the miracle they came in
crowds, with the first light of dawn, to the courtyard, hug-
ging their candles. While the crusaders watched, the great
throng prayed and waited, and the Greek patriarch stood
in his full robes at the entrance to the Sepulcher.

For a thousand years the lamps that hung within, unlighted, had been seen to give forth light on this day, although no man entered the sepulcher, where they hung. This was the miracle of the sacred fire that the thousands came to behold.

This year they waited through the morning, and heard only the tidings of the Greek patriarch: "It is still dark."

The crowd in the courtyard moved uneasily, waiting with its candles. Godfrey and the crusaders were troubled, for Jerusalem was in their keeping, and if the miracle should fail . . . Some of them withdrew to discuss the meaning of the portent.

Early in the afternoon the bell in the tower chimed, and the patriarch held up his hands. The pilgrims rushed forward, struggling to be the first to enter with their candles. The word was cried through the streets:

"God hath sent the fire."

The candles were lighted from the lamps and the throng scattered, to carry the flame back to their homes.

And Godfrey understood, what others before him had known—that Jerusalem is a city shared among many men, hallowed by old customs that no new master may alter. It fitted into his dream of a city unlike others, freed by the crusaders and defended by them.

In the month of June brown sails dotted the sea and moved in slowly toward Jaffa, two hundred of them. With long oars creaking, and red pennants flapping from the mastheads, the great fleet of Venice floated in to the sands where a small throng of crusaders had gathered to greet it. Here was power from the sea.

The Venetians had been drawn to the Holy Land by the magnet of trade. They were thrifty and far-looking. They knew the blind paths of the sea, and the value of strange monies, and the worth of a king's bond. Furthermore, they were allies of Byzantium, and of the Emperor Alexis.

They knew how to make a harbor out of a shelving beach. The largest vessels of the fleet, the double-decked dromonds and the long galleys, were roped together, thwart bound to thwart with chains, the armored prows facing the open sea. Then this solid line of ships was anchored, to provide shelter and protection for the smaller craft run up on the beach.

Not until then did the seamen of the lagoons throng ashore, the nobles, in their short cloaks and soft velvet boots, greeting the leaders of the crusaders before riding off to the half-built Jaffa. Here Godfrey sat down with the admiral of the fleet to make plans.

The Venetians were willing to aid the new dominion of Jerusalem. The conquest of the Holy Land had opened up a door of trade.[1] Not until now had the sea merchants of Europe been able to deal directly with the land merchants of Asia. Of course the Venetians had had the run of the Byzantine ports, but for years they had looked longingly toward the heart of Asia from which ran the arteries of the caravan routes. Cathay, off in the limbo of the sea of darkness—the kingdom of Prester John—the treasury of the Indies—these were no more than names. Silk, musk, cinnamon, and spice came out of this shadow world. Off in the shadows, somewhere, grew the spreading Tree of Life, and from the legendary lands had come the three Magi with their gifts. It was all unknown, vague, and a little monstrous, buried in the heart of Asia with the dog-headed men and the flaming dragon of Cathay.

Nevertheless the Venetians had felt the pulse of this invisible heart. They knew that two arteries led from it toward them—one running up through the mountains of the Armenians to Trebizond on the Black Sea, from which the Byzantine ships brought strange goods to Constantinople.

The other main artery led west, through Baghdad. There

---

[1] The Genoese and Pisans were the natural allies of their neighbors, the Provençals. A fleet of 120 vessels had escorted Archbishop Daimbert down from Pisa and had been attacked at sea by the Byzantine flotilla under command of Taticius. Some of the Pisan ships had been burned by Greek fire and the fleet retaliated by raiding the Byzantine island citadels and by aiding Bohemund, who was now at open war with the emperor, in besieging the emperor's garrison in Laodicea. Until now the Moslem galleys had kept the Genoese and Pisan ships from the eastern trade. The Venetians, on the other hand, had sided years ago with Alexis against Bohemund, and they were bound by treaty to Byzantium.

it branched into two veins—two caravan routes—one going
to Damascus, and thence to the sea at Acre, almost within
sight of their anchored ships. It reached Egypt by water,
to Alexandria, or by caravan across the sands of the Jifar
to Cairo. Godfrey and his crusaders had blocked this channel of trade.

The other route from Baghdad to the west ran up the
river Euphrates to Aleppo, and across the short highway to
Antioch. At Antioch Bohemund was master. Just now, in
June, 1100, he was setting out to invade Aleppo.

If the Venetians could gain footing in the ports, they
could tap these channels of trade under the protection of the
crusaders. More than that, they could bargain at first hand
with the merchants bringing incense and dried dates and
carpets from Damascus and the Arabian cities. They wanted
the steel of Damascus, and glass and embroidered stuffs.
And they wanted to venture themselves into the shadow
world of the Far East.

They did not see fit to explain all this to Godfrey, but
they found out readily enough what he needed—the aid
of a fleet to capture the Moslem strongholds on the coast.
So they named their terms: they would lend their fleet for
seven weeks, to coöperate with Godfrey's army, and they
required in return the privilege of trading without dues or
taxation at all points held now or hereafter by the crusaders
of Jerusalem; and in every place captured by the assistance
of Venetians, a church, a warehouse and market, and one
third of the streets must be awarded them.

The Venetians were looking into the future. Godfrey
found the terms hard, but had no recourse except to agree.
They decided to make the first attack against Acre, which
had one of the best harbors along the coast, and the greatest wealth within it. The Venetians began to overhaul their
ships and to build floating towers.

Godfrey summoned Tancred down from Galilee, and rode
back himself into the lifeless heat of the valleys, to muster
his men at Ramlah. It was not easy to travel, even in the
cooler hours of the evening, because the water was low in
the cisterns and pestilence lay like miasma in the lowlands,

especially where half-buried bodies sprawled, as if forcing themselves upward out of the sand. To Godfrey, lying on his couch beneath the great pavilion, two priests came. Kneeling, they presented to him a roll of parchment bearing the signature of the new pope, Paschal. The letter, addressed to "All the people of the triumphant armed host of Christendom in Asia," said in part:

Our tongue cannot relate our joy, for we behold Christian peoples oppressed until now taking refuge everywhere, every day in the regions redeemed by your hands. After long ages of captivity, we see the eastern Church with a great part of its former glory restored. Now in our hearts and with our tongues we should say *"Glory in the highest, O Lord, and upon earth peace and good will to men."*

Now there is need of prayer and watchfulness, that what is begun may be fulfilled, and your hands, which are purified by the blood of the enemy, must be kept sanctified even to the end—and firm in piety.

Godfrey read the message but made no response. Paschal, sitting in Rome, could not see the stagnant wells or the rotting bodies creeping out of the sand. Godfrey's head was heavy with fever, and he did not rise from his couch. Truly the work was near its end and achievement in sight—when he should take Acre and Bohemund should ride into Aleppo. A month more and Paschal would have the welcome tidings.

The fever did not leave him. Instead of going to the hospital of Jerusalem, he ordered his couch carried into Jaffa, where the workmen were pounding the stone for the new walls. He did go back to Jerusalem, however, suddenly, in the night, carried upon a horse litter.

In the hall of the hospital where the knights in black mantles stood guard, he summoned the patriarch Daimbert and Arnulf to him.

"I have called you to counsel, while I live, to select the one who will reign in Jerusalem after me."

Daimbert made response: "We say that this is for thee to decide."

"If it is indeed to be settled by me," Godfrey answered, "I

deem Baldwin, my brother, fitted to carry on the achievement."

In mid-July died Godfrey, count of Bouillon and baron of Jerusalem. And after his death the pestilence increased. Tancred tried to take the reins of command, while a messenger rode to Edessa to summon Baldwin. The Venetians had to abandon Acre and content themselves with the storming of Haifa, a weaker point near by.

Then, true to their terms, the Venetians sailed off in mid-August, having accomplished little enough. And word came down from Antioch that Bohemund, riding with his men, unarmed in a moment's thoughtlessness, to the aid of a friendly Armenian, had been set upon by the Moslem cavalry and taken captive.

Godfrey's body was carried through the streets in procession and placed within a sarcophagus at the foot of Calvary, and this was a day of sorrow for the chivalry and the common folk of Jerusalem. Lacking in leadership he had been, and perhaps weak where strength would have gained much, but his enduring faith and invincible courage could ill be spared. Men have made of him a legendary hero, but we will remember him as a man who kept faith with a dream.

XXXIV

WHAT FULCHER SAW

For a few weeks, at the end of this summer of the year 1100, Daimbert, once archbishop of Pisa and now patriarch of Jerusalem, was the master of the Holy City. And Daimbert was ambitious. He had come out to the East with a full knowledge of Urban's plan for restoring the churches, and for asserting the spiritual authority of the pope here in the birthplace of Christianity. None of the great leaders of the crusade could interfere with him—St. Gilles being in Constantinople, Bohemund a captive, and Baldwin, the baron-elect, far in the north at Edessa.

Daimbert had all the political sagacity of the robed men of Rome, and he had a mission to fulfil. Jerusalem must be linked to Rome and made a papal state.

Already the powerful Benedictines of Cluny had received from the dead Godfrey the grant of the grotto of Christ's agony and the Garden of Gethsemane. Mount Sion, where Daimbert was repairing a palace for his own use, was in the hands of the Augustines. And Daimbert had persuaded Godfrey to bestow upon him the port of Jaffa, the Tower of David, and the Sepulcher itself. To be sure, he held these places only in his spiritual jurisdiction, but

in his plans this carried with it the lawful possession of the
lands themselves. Daimbert cherished a dream of his own
—of a spiritual empire, wherein the lands were divided among
the abbeys and monasteries, and where the bishops ruled
the cities, and the patriarch ruled them all—a patriarch who
owed fealty only to Rome.

Bohemund might never come back from his captivity.
And Baldwin might never make the journey to Jerusalem
unharmed. Edessa was far off in the hills. And Daimbert, it
seems, had sent his secretary to Bohemund—before he
learned of the Norman's captivity—suggesting that Bohemund and Tancred restrain Baldwin by force from coming
to Jerusalem.[1]

In this way Daimbert made his plans. Whether he knew
it or not, he was opening a rift between the iron men and
the robed men. No longer were the priests and the men of
arms in full sympathy, as they had been during the ordeals
of the three-year march, or during Godfrey's leadership.

But he had not taken into account one thing. The Moslems
heard of the death of the splendid *Kundufry* and the im-
prisonment of *Maimoun*. They had looked on Godfrey as
the king of the Christians, and Bohemund as the sword-
arm of the conquerors. Now both were removed from the
scene, just when Raymond, count of Toulouse, had gone off
to Constantinople, and the great fleet of the Venetians disappeared. The news flew from caravan *serai* to mosque, and
the nearest sultans rode in to raid. Bands of horsemen beset
the roads, even between Jerusalem and Ramlah.

At this time, in October, Baldwin started down from
Edessa, leaving his great principality in the hands of his
youthful cousin, Baldwin du Bourg, to take up the reins
that Godfrey had let fall. And what happened to him is
related by the good Fulcher of Chartres.

Baldwin rode with a small army indeed, some two hundred

---

[1]What Daimbert wrote to Bohemund and what he said to Tancred has been
hotly debated by the historians. One account has it that he urged Bohemund to kill
Baldwin and to come himself to take the throne of Jerusalem. Nothing is certain.
It seems probable, however, that a letter was sent and that the letter fell into
Baldwin's hands—or he heard of it when he passed through Antioch. He reached
Jerusalem in a mood hostile to Daimbert.

mounted knights and men at arms, and seven hundred foot soldiers, pilgrims, and priests. From Antioch he kept to the coast road, and at Tripoli he was warned that the Moslems had assembled in the narrow passes where the red hills of Lebanon shoulder close to the sea. He kept on, but many of his following dropped out and went back without informing him. So says Fulcher:

Concerning the Trap the Turks Laid upon the Road, and the Admirable Courage of Count Baldwin

Not far from the city of Beirut there is a narrow pass on the highway, which we, and all travelers going that way, must cross.

We went on, nearly to that place. When our scouts approached the pass they beheld some Turks, apart from the rest, coming toward us and not watching out at all. When our scouts saw them, they thought that a strong body of the enemy might be in hiding behind them. Straightway they sent back word to Lord Baldwin by one of the riders. When he heard of this he ordered his men at arms drawn up in battle lines, and, raising up the standard, after a little while we advanced forward.

Then, straightway, the enemy came against our first group. Some of them were killed at once and four of our men, in truth, lost their lives. After both sides had drawn back from the struggle the order was given [by Baldwin] to pitch our camp and extend our lines on the spot to which we had advanced. Thus we would not seem so timid to the enemy, as if we had withdrawn from the place of fighting. Although we acted this way, we felt quite the contrary. We pretended to be fearless, but we feared death.

It was hard enough to go back, but worse to go on. We were hemmed in everywhere by our enemy. Along the shore in boats and unseen on the slopes of the mountains they crowded around us. That day brought us nothing good or quiet, nor could we water our thirsty animals. I, most certainly, would rather have been at Chartres or Arles—others also. All that night we wearied ourselves watching outside our pavilions.

At the first light, when sunrise began to lift the darkness from the ground, we took counsel together and decided that, live or die, we would go back the way by which we had come—the pack animals going before us with their loads, guarded by our followers. Thus the men at arms, coming after, would be able to cover them from the raids of the Saracens.

For those evil-doers, when they saw us turn back in this manner early in the morning, came down to pursue us immediately, like fugitives. Some along the sea with boats, others along the road, in truth, behind us, others, ahorse and afoot through the hills, they herded us like sheep to the fold—to a most narrow place where, cut off from the plain, they could intercept us for easy killing. But it did not happen as they thought.

Because our men made decision among themselves, saying, "If we were able to kill them in that open plain when we were going toward them, if we turn around now and fight bravely, it may be— God willing—that we shall break through them."

But at once they leaped out of their ships and cut off the heads of those of us whom they caught marching near the shore; now they rode down into the aforesaid plain behind us, and shot many arrows. Everywhere they reviled us, ululating like dogs or howling wolves. What shall I say? There was not anywhere a place to flee, or a hope of safety. Then God aided his people. The audacity of our men got the upper hand, so that the foes turned and fled.

Some, emerging headlong from the rocks on the heights, gave themselves up; others fled or were slain by the sword. Even their ships fled away over the sea—as if we could have caught them with our hands. So, exulting in this triumph, we returned joyfully to our followers who had guarded the pack animals meanwhile on the road. We were ordered to take out the tents and to pitch the camp.

There many rich Turks were brought alive, captive before Lord Baldwin, and they were laden with the spoils taken from the dead. We had also horses with saddles enriched with gold. When our lord had divided this spoil we rested quietly the following night in a deserted castle within a grove of olive trees.

At early dawn Baldwin, courageous as always, rode out with several men to the narrow pass, to find out if any Saracens were there to close the road to us. When he found no one, he climbed at once to the summit of a hill and made a fire for a signal. Where- upon we who had remained in the camp followed after him and the others who had gone ahead. We found the road open. That same day we came to the outskirts of Beirut, where the governor[1] sent food to Lord Baldwin, more from fear than love. In this fashion we passed by other towns.

Tancred was master of the town of Haifa at this time, because

---

[1]Beirut—Beritus as Fulcher writes it—was then in the hands of the Moslems. Fulcher speaks of Baldwin as the king for a reason that will presently appear. Tancred had not forgotten his first quarrel with Baldwin three years before at Tarsus.

the Jerusalem men had seized it. And because Tancred was ill-minded toward Baldwin, we did not enter in there. He himself was not in the town, but his people sold bread and wine to us outside, for they esteemed us like brothers and wished to see us. Passing by Caesaria and Arsuf, after a while we came to the maritime city of Jaffa. There our Franks gladly received Baldwin as their king-elect. Without tarrying there we went on to Jerusalem. And when we drew near the city, all the people came out toward him— the Greeks and Syrians also—with crosses and candles in their hands. They greeted him with joyful chants, and, going before him, led him to the church of the Sepulcher.

The patriarch, Daimbert, did not enter into this festivity because he had made accusations against Baldwin, and there was mutual dislike between them. The greater part of the clergy also was antagonistic to him [Daimbert]. So he remained in his house on Mount Sion, as long as his ill-will endured. But after six days of welcome quiet in Jerusalem had given us relaxation from toil, we took to the road again.

Concerning Baldwin's Sally into Arabia

Again Lord Baldwin collected his men, and set out toward Ascalon. When we reached it, we drove within the walls all those who sallied out against us. Then, because it was useless to undertake more than that, we returned to our tents. The next day we went toward the inland region where we found food for ourselves and grazing for our animals in a fertile country, and we laid waste the fields of our enemy. Then, passing on, we discovered villages whence the Saracen inhabitants had fled and hidden themselves and their animals in caverns because of us.

When we were not able to fetch them out, we built a fire in the mouth of a cave. Soon the smoke and intolerable heat drove them out to us, one after the other. Among them, assuredly, were the highwaymen who, lurking regularly between Ramlah and Jerusalem, were accustomed to kill our people. When we were told of this by some Syrian Christians who had been lying in hiding with them, we struck off the heads of the evil-doers who came out of the caverns. But we spared the Syrians and their wives. Of the Saracens we killed almost a hundred.

And when we had gathered up all their animals and as much grain as the beasts needed, and could find nothing more that was useful to us, we made preparations for the march into Arabia, led by some old men who knew all the cultivated and the barren lands.

And, crossing the mountains near the sepulchers of the patriarchs—that is, Abraham, Isaac, and Jacob—we came into the valley where the evil cities Sodom and Gomorrah were overthrown by the will of God.

Concerning the Dead Sea

Verily here is now the great lake which they call the Dead Sea because it does not rise. It is so salt that no animals will drink of it, nor will birds. I, Fulcher, made trial of it, climbing down from my she-mule and drawing some water up in my hand. I tasted it and found it more bitter than hellebore. Nor is it easy, even by force, to submerge anything in its depths.

I believe that this saltiness of the lake comes from one of two causes. Near it rises a solitary mountain great and high and encrusted with salt. Either rainfall, streaming down the ravines of the mountain, brings the salt, or an underground channel exists by which the great sea, which is salt, flows in.

Circling the lake on the south we found a village most pleasantly situated and abounding in the fruit of the palm, which they call dates—which we ate all one day, and enjoyed. We came upon other remarkable things there. For the Saracen inhabitants had fled, except some people blacker than soot whom we spared to carry loads of seaweed from the lake. Among the trees I saw some bearing apple-like fruit. However, when I gathered them, wishing to know what sort they were, I found when the shell was broken only a kind of black dust out of which puffed a lifeless black smoke.

Then we entered tne mountains of the Arabs, in the depths of which we halted that night. At dawn, when we climbed the heights, we came at once upon farms, but all quite deserted. So we took up our road elsewhere, our leaders always watching out. We found a valley most fertile in all the products of the earth, for in this place the holy Moses, God guiding him, twice struck with his staff the rock, whence a living stream of water flowed. In this stream I watered my horses.

We found, on the summit of the mountain above us, the monastery of Aaron where Moses and he were wont to talk with God. Whence we rejoiced greatly, since we had entered places so sacred and hitherto unknown to us.

And because the land beyond the valley was forbidding and barren and untilled, we were not willing to go farther. For three days we took our ease in that valley of all good things, fattening the animals upon the grazing and giving the pack beasts a needed rest. About the second hour of the fourth day the king's horn sounded, and he ordered us to start again upon the return road. . . . And so, upon the day in which the winter solstice begins, we reached Jerusalem.

Concerning the Incoming of King Baldwin, and the Dearth of His Kingdom

When the regalia needed for the coronation had been prepared —Daimbert being reconciled to Lord Baldwin—on Christmas day of the year of the Incarnation of our Lord 1100, Baldwin was crowned king, and hallowed by the sacred unction from the hand of the patriarch.

In the beginning, he was lord of few cities and people. Yet throughout that same winter he shielded his kingdom vigorously from its enemies. And because they found out that he was most able in war—although he had only a few men—they dared not attack him.

Up to now the path of our pilgrims had been full of obstacles. Franks, Angles, Italians, or Venetians had arrived at Jaffa under God's guidance, in great fear, after sailing in one or three or four ships through hostile pirates and past the cities of the Saracens. For at first we had no other port. As soon as we learned that they had come from our lands in the west, we hastened to meet them as joyfully as if they had been saints. Each one of us asked them earnestly for news of his country and kinsmen. They told us everything that they knew. When we heard good tidings, we were glad, and news of misfortune grieved us.

They went to Jerusalem and visited the *sancta sanctorum*—they had come all the way to do this. Thereafter, some stayed on in the Holy Land, others went back to their homes.[1]

Baldwin had saved Jerusalem by sheer audacity. The march of his handful down to the sea and over the desert

---

[1] At this time the land route was still practically closed by the hostility of the Byzantines and the Moslem armies. A small Genoese fleet arrived about the time Baldwin reached Jerusalem, but the ships of which Fulcher speaks were a scattered few making their own way out to the Holy Land—the advance guard of the first great pilgrim fleet which reached Jaffa in the next year, September, 1101. From that time pilgrim fleets came regularly in the spring and autumn. When he said Jaffa was the only port, Fulcher was thinking of the new Kingdom of Jerusalem. Already the crusaders in Antioch and Edessa were following out their own ambitions.

and back again put a stop for the time being to the aggressions of the Moslems. He found a new Genoese fleet anchored off Jaffa, and pressed it into service at once to capture Arsuf and Caesaria, thus gaining command of the coast from Acre to Ascalon. The Moslems watched his actions with increased respect. The new king of the Franks, they heard, rode abroad clad in the cloth-of-gold of a Byzantine emperor while attendants carried before him a shield of gold bearing an eagle with outstretched wings. Indeed this was a king, and a father of battles!

Turks and Arabs alike, they knew no power except that of the sword, and they understood *Bagh'dwan* as thoroughly as he understood them. They rebuilt their burnt villages, counted over their diminished herds ruefully, and sat down to await events.

Baldwin's character was as simple as the sword he wore. In the prime of his life, a brilliant soldier, harsh to his antagonists, he was just to his own people, and he was quick to demand all that was due him. No half-title, such as his brother Godfrey accepted, would content him. The men of Jerusalem had called him, and he meant to be king in all right.

Had not the coronation in the old stone church at Bethlehem been ceremonious and complete in every detail? The liegemen had thrice acclaimed him their choice, and his standard had been borne in by his constable. Mass had been sung, Baldwin emerging with the ring, symbol of his authority, the sword, sign of his justice, the crown, token of dignity.

Tancred left the field to him—going north to take command at Antioch in Bohemund's place, and leaving his fiefs around Jerusalem to Baldwin. Naturally, the new monarch came into conflict with Daimbert, who tried to build a papal state with him for a corner stone.

The struggle lasted for months. The single-minded king would not yield the lands of Jerusalem to the covetous patriarch. And in the end Daimbert had to withdraw from Jerusalem, and to seek the protection of Antioch. Eventually he carried his controversy to Rome, where after years of discussion the pope sustained him and sent him back to his patriarchate. But he died at sea, and with him vanished the dream of an ecclesiastical state ruled by a patriarch.

Meanwhile Baldwin was left, in that spring of 1101, to make the best of things in Jerusalem. In spite of his unceasing activity—he spent most of his time in the saddle—the watchful Moslems realized how small his army actually was. Tughtakin, lord of Damascus, agreed with the malik of Egypt to make a combined effort to crush Baldwin.

Reinforcements were coming out of Europe to aid the hard-pressed defenders of the city. Baldwin heard that a new wave of crusaders had passed Constantinople, under Raymond's guidance, and he awaited their arrival impatiently.

Jerusalem remained empty of men [Fulcher says] and we had no means of defending it from the Saracens, if they dared attack us. For we had no more than three hundred men at arms and as many foot soldiers. We dreaded that our enemies would learn in some way of our lack of men, and beset us suddenly from all sides. We would have lacked for nothing, if only we had men and horses. Yet they who came over the sea to Jerusalem were unable to bring horses. Over the land, in truth, no one came to us. The men at Antioch could not aid us, nor we them.

XXXV

THE PATH OF GLORY

WHILE King Baldwin held on grimly to Jerusalem, excitement spread through all of Europe. Even in the Far North people knew now that the crusade had been victorious.

For a time, three years before, the news had been ominous and disheartening—tales of the first massacres, and thirst and starvation. But now everyone was certain that Jerusalem had been captured, and the holy places regained. And the iron men were riding home.

They were coming back over all the highways in little bands, with new crosses sewn on the backs of their mantles, to show that they were returning from the Holy Land. They carried outlandish weapons in their packs, and the people of the hamlets thronged out to stare at their sun-darkened faces, and to fight for the privilege of holding their reins when they dismounted.

Tavern keepers hastened to set before them the best meats and wines, and proud esquires at arms thought it no shame to tend and groom the horses of these knights who had fought for God and had been victorious. Lords of near-

by castles sent down to bid the crusaders sup and sleep in
their halls. Old men and minstrels filled the benches when
tales of Jerusalem were told. This was a new day and a good
day.

Somehow, the people at home felt that these crusaders had
washed, as it were, a deal of sin out of the world. For one
thing, they brought back so many blessed relics, wrapped
up in clean white cloth or put in silver cases. Undreamed-
of relics. Splinters of the true Cross that had been found
buried securely under the shrines of the Sepulcher, water
from the stream that had sprung from the rod of Moses,
and fragments of the garments that had been worn by the
Virgin. There was even, in a colored vial, a bit of the darkness that had been one of the seven plagues of Egypt.

French and Rhinelanders, Provençals and Normans, the
iron men were coming home. They turned off from the highways to pass along the narrow forest roads that led to familiar, gray donjon towers. From the summits of the towers
hung the great banners that had not been seen since the
lord of the castle rode off, four years or more before. Children
ran out along the road, to climb the lookout trees and watch
for the first gleam of lance tip, or flurry of dust.

The halls of the castle had been fresh strewn with rushes,
and the long tables washed. Musicians were waiting with
harps and fiddles, and the esquires and maidens had put
on holiday garments, clean and bright. The lady of the castle
had seen to everything, and now she was waiting, in her
long blue robe with a white coif and embroidered girdle, to
greet her husband at the steps. Kinsmen and castellan had
mounted to go out and escort him in from the road, but her
place was at the steps, to give the welcome.

So she waited, with four years between them. She also had
had her ordeals, of sickness and deaths and failing crops.
Perhaps the specter of hunger had stalked over the fields
of the *mesnie*, or the mistress of the castle had to journey
to the money-lenders, the abbots, or the Jewish merchants.

Beside her waited the children, half fearful and half eager.
Would the stern lord, their father, have a kind word for
them? Had he brought back an infidel's helmet, or an Arab

horse, or a trumpet from Jericho? Would he wear gold armor?

Before the gate and in the courtyard clustered the women and the children of the lord's hamlet, herding together awkwardly in their coarse garments, their faces red with excitement. Their men, peasants from the huts, had gone out four years before with pike and broad-ax, and in all that time no word had come from them. The peasant women knew that most of them would never set foot within the courtyard again, or take plough to the fields. But some of the foot-soldiers and men at arms would return, and perhaps God had spared their Jacques or Pierre.

It was a joyful hour when the village boys ran up, and the women shaded their eyes and whispered prayers, and the heart of the lord's lady quickened at a familiar hoof-beat and jangle of steel. "They are home!"

So the crusaders reached the end of their road, in the homes of Christendom. But more often there would be only a hurried visit of strange men, a few muttered words, and a sword or perhaps a familiar cross and girdle left in the hands of the mistress of the castle. Words of courtesy: "Valiant he was, and honorable in all things—they pray for his soul at the Church of the Blessed Mary." And words hiding grief: "I give ye thanks, messires, for this your courtesy—God speed ye upon the road."

Then an empty hall that the kinsfolk cannot fill, a murmuring priest, and a woman left to care for hall and village and children.

The iron men were feasted, while the choirs intoned "*Salve Hierusalem gloria mundi.*" Richard the Pilgrim came back with his song of Antioch, and gained great favor thereby; Peter the Hermit drifted back, and people, remembering his preaching, hailed him as a holy man. But Peter did not preach again, nor did he say much, it seems, of the crusade. He brought with him many relics and he entered a monastery near Liége, where he became prior before his death, a dozen years later.

Quiet Robert of Flanders returned to his people without ostentation. Because he lacked a chronicler and because the song-makers cherished the names of the other leaders, the youthful Robert, count of Flanders, has been all but forgotten. Yet he fought from Nicea to Ascalon, and he claimed nothing for himself.

The Sleepy Duke came back—Robert Short Breeches—to Normandy, but he lingered on the way. The Normans in southern Italy had heard of his feat at Ascalon, and they feasted him. More than that, they remembered that he had forfeited Normandy to William the Red of England, since he had been away more than the three years given him to buy his province out of pawn. They were Normans and Robert was a great chieftain of the crusaders. They talked the matter over, and took up a kind of collection. One after the other they brought him gifts of money, and begged for the honor of a visit from the conqueror.

The great family of Conversano bestowed a bride upon him, the beautiful heiress of an Italian fief. With her dowry and the gifts, Robert had enough money in hand to redeem Normandy. He accepted everything, including his betrothed, with a good grace, and the splendor of Salerno made bright his wedding.

Then he heard that William the Red, king of England, had been slain. Not only was he free of his bond, but Normandy called for him, and the crown of England hung in the balance. If the Sleepy Duke had hurried his march he might have been king. But the feasts tempted him, he had more wealth than ever before, and his bride was fair. Robert lingered on the way, affable and unambitious as always, and if he lost England he found Normandy ready to make a hero of her duke.

Two other leaders of the crusade did not fare as well as Robert. Hugh the Great, count of Vermandois and brother of Philip of France, found it difficult to explain why he left the scene of the fighting—especially after he had boasted that he would not return alive from the crusade. And the pope, Paschal, issued a decree that touched Hugh narrowly:

We decree that they are disgraced who forsook the siege of Antioch because of lack of faith. Unless they assert, and give pledges, that they will return, let them be excommunicate.

Popular opinion forced Hugh to retrace his steps toward Jerusalem. He was joined on the way by his companion in the flight from Antioch, Stephen of Blois. The count of Blois was immensely rich, and lord of a hundred fiefs, and he was also eloquent. But all his reasoning could not convince his wife, the high-spirited Adele, that he was blameless. His actions did not match his letters, and Adele was daughter of a king of England. Her tongue harried the weak-hearted Stephen until he assembled his liegemen again and set out toward the east.

Already pseudo heroes were appearing in Europe, who claimed to have done great things in the crusade but who had never been south of Constantinople.

Ask of such [urges a chronicler of the day] by what route they journeyed to the Holy Land, in what battles they fought, and who were their leaders. They who have truly borne the cross will answer readily, and the false warriors will be confounded.

The veterans of Jerusalem found that the Church at home smiled upon them. Their sins of the past were forgiven, washed out. Their property was restored in most cases, as Urban had promised—Paschal insisted that this be done. And Paschal assumed the leadership of the crusading movement.

"The city itself of our Lord's suffering is opened to our men of arms," he said. "Our soldiers should earn forgiveness of their sins by hastening to the aid of the Church in the East. We should follow the divine Will by giving aid to our brothers who have remained there."

Paschal was an enthusiast, and he took full advantage of the popular exhilaration that followed the capture of Jerusalem. To the mass of the people this meant that God had aided them, and that salvation, in some way, was nearer at hand now that Jerusalem belonged to them. Many of them entered monasteries, or gave possessions to the Church. Feudal warfare lessened, because men were looking toward the East, where the new, greater war was in progress.

THE BASILICA OF ST. JOHN THE BAPTIST

The beauty of medieval design. The entrance to the basilica at Ravenna.

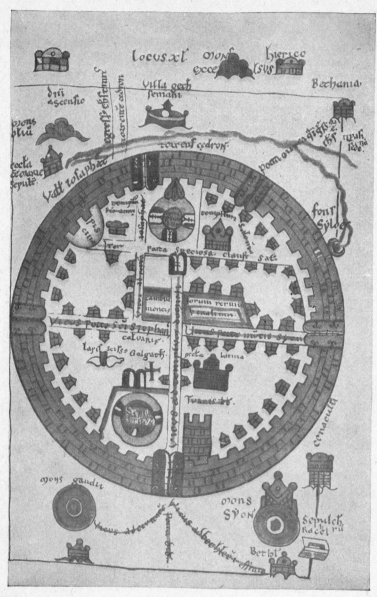

JERUSALEM

A plan made after the conquest by the crusaders.

Paschal pointed out that the Mother Church was there, in the East, and must be redeemed beyond all doubt.

His authority increased yearly. He could forbid Alphonse of Spain from going on crusade at the same time he ordered Hugh of Vermandois to do so. The kinsmen of his archenemy, the Emperor Henry, took the cross.

When Stephen of Blois and Hugh reached Constantinople they found there the bishops of Laon and Soissons; and Conrad, constable of the German emperor, with two thousand men. And they met there the wanderer of the first expedition, Raymond of Toulouse. Lombard princes joined them, under the count of Parma and the bishop of Milan. Gallant Josselin of Courtenay appeared, and the count of Vendôme.

This reinforcement of nobles and prelates probably numbered no more than forty thousand souls. This army of relief was the real crusade of the barons. Under joint command of St. Gilles and Conrad of Germany it set out in the early summer of 1101 to give aid to the hard-pressed garrison of Jerusalem.

Restless as the gray gulls that ranged the shore, and swooped up in circles to hover over passing ships and to dart down within the hollows of the sea swell, Raymond of St. Gilles, count of Toulouse, wandered among the palaces of the Imperial City. He was greeted with ceremony, and feasted and praised by the Byzantines, because he was the ally of the Basileus, their emperor. The Byzantines called him a warrior-saint, and the young knights who had just come out of Europe with fresh crosses on their mantles bowed to him with flattering respect, because he was a veteran of Jerusalem and a leader of the great first crusade. And yet St. Gilles found no solace in memory.

True, he had with him, encased in a silver reliquary, the rusted spearhead dug up at Antioch. Some of his men still lingered with him after the others left for Provence. Yet the years were passing, his young wife was about to bear him another child, and St. Gilles had conquered no fief in the Holy Land. The memories of the four years troubled him

—his ousting from the Tower of David when his own men, eager to go home, refused to defend his claim to the citadel of Jerusalem; the loss of Ascalon because he quarreled with Godfrey; the final estrangement with Bohemund at Laodicea on the way north. If he had been more patient!

But here he was, with not a foot of land to his name, with only a small following, and old age stiffening his sinews. Moreover, the troubadours who attended these new lords of the crusade sang of the deeds of Godfrey and Tancred. Seldom did they sing of St. Gilles or the Provençals. This hurt the pride of the fiery old warrior. Was he to blame that he had been absent from the field of Doryleum, and the Battle of the Lance?

St. Gilles was not content with the flattery of the Byzantine court. And presently he announced that he would guide the reinforcements now at Constantinople to Jerusalem. He would share the command with Conrad, the German constable, and lead the new host to victory in the Holy Land. Stephen of Blois and Hugh, the once proud envoy of France, would not oppose him as Bohemund had done. In fact, he knew that Bohemund was in the hands of the Moslems, far off in the East.

Alexis agreed amiably to his plan, because the honest old Provençal was a most valuable pawn and the German *pfalzgrafen* were plundering his suburbs, just as Peter's mob had done five years before. Outwardly the Basileus cherished this new brood of crusaders, inwardly he regretted that they had come, and he wished them anywhere but in Asia Minor, which he had just reclaimed by personal exertion and expense on the heels of the first wave of crusaders. And daily the sun telegraph, flashing from the bare blue hills, gave him news of Asia. Quiet Venetian cargo galleons, slipping into the Golden Horn, added their report of events on the southern coast. So Alexis knew that his fleet had fought with the Pisans—those dogged seamen from the barbarous little city republic. And down on the frontier of Antioch the fiery Tancred had driven his garrisons from Tarsus and Adana and Mamistra.

There was open war at last between Byzantine and Norman, and the stake was the mastery of the Near East, with its trade ports, the gateways of Asia. At the departure of the new crusaders he bestowed fresh gifts on St. Gilles—he wanted a friend in the south—and sent along a detachment of imperial troops to march with the cross-bearers and observe all that might happen.

XXXVI

MARCH OF THE BARONS

Just why St. Gilles turned east instead of south will never be known. Some say that he wanted to rescue Bohemund, and others say that he meant to march to Baghdad. Perhaps the inexperienced Lombards or Germans persuaded him to strike a blow at the heart of Islam in the East, or perhaps he planned to find a new route around the mountain barrier of the Taurus, down to the crusaders in Edessa, and thence to Aleppo.

It is clear that they marched due east. They stormed the little citadel on the height of Angora, and crossed the river Halys, and day after day they rode toward the rising sun. They entered a country of broken plateaus, where the roads were no more than trails through the willow and alder mesh in the ravines.

The new army did not move rapidly. The pikemen from the Hessian uplands swung along sturdily enough, hunting for deer and boar as they went, but the clumsy horses went heavily over the evil footing, and the pack animals were laden with useless trappings—immense pavilions for the noble ladies, and all the gear of their servants. They had to cut their way through brush and climb rocky ravines. And in the end they lost their way.

By chance they stumbled on a town, and killed all the inhabitants, and went on again, hoping that now they were near the edge of the wasteland. The country did change, but not as they expected. Smoke hung over the ridges in front of them, and they found wheat fields and villages burned to the ground. All the inhabitants had fled.

They passed over barren plains, shielding their heads from the sun glare, looking in vain for streams or open roads. The smoke rose up like a signal before them, and they felt the pangs of hunger. For weeks they pushed on toward the east, hoping to catch sight of the great cities that lay somewhere ahead of them. Instead of the cities, they encountered the Red Lion, who still remembered Doryleum.

At first they noticed nothing terrifying—isolated horsemen rode away from their scouts and they discovered tracks around the camp in the morning—tracks of small hoofs, unshod. And an invisible hand removed all provisions from the line of their march. It was necessary to kill and eat some of the horses.

Always the smoke hung in the air, over the blackened fields and the withered trees. The stout liegemen of the French bishops, the stolid Flemings and hardy Hessians did not lose courage easily, but they were bewildered by this strange enemy who harried them without being seen. Patrols rode off into the brush to look for the Moslems, and did not come back. Sentries were found at daylight lying on their posts stripped of armor and weapons, their throats slashed open and clouds of flies swarming over their heads.

Sometimes they heard owls hooting in full day from the ridges overhanging their road, and wolves howled at night in a strange fashion as if talking together. The Byzantines and St. Gilles knew that these were two-legged wolves—Moslems prowling around the camp and calling to each other. But the newcomers among the crusaders listened, and thought of the slain sentries and werewolves and vampires.

Then arrows began to drop through the tents at dusk, and to strike down men gathered around the fires. Horses vanished from the picket lines, and when some of the younger knights, enraged by the harrying, seized their weapons and rushed into the darkness to find the enemy, mocking laughter greeted them. They came back weary and empty-handed, convinced that demons had arisen in this barren land to beset them.

But it was only the Red Lion's advance guard of Turkish horsemen, keeping the crusaders in play until the army of the sultan, twenty thousand strong, could come up and surround them.

When the Red Lion arrived, with his veteran amirs and his kinsmen from the steppes, he rode out to look at this new host of Christians, and when he beheld the gaunt horses and stumbling men, he attacked at once, under a barrage of arrows—swift thrusts of mailed horsemen, throwing javelins before them and wheeling away from the bristling pikes of the steadfast German and Lombard infantry.

Now that they actually saw the enemy, the Christians fought calmly and kept firm in their ranks. They camped where they stood that night, within the barrier of their carts and piles of baggage, and they stood to arms the next day, smarting under the flights of arrows and the flying javelins.

The next night the Red Lion drew nearer, his camps hemming in the crusaders as if with a net, so that no one could go out to water the animals. And few could sleep, because the wailing flutes and clanging cymbals and the mocking ululation that rose and fell by the red fires gave them no rest. They did not know that the Moslems never liked to attack at night.

On the third day the Christians sallied out with all their strength and the Red Lion met them with saber and shield and the wild rush of Islam. The Christians found that they could not break Turkish cavalry, better mounted than they; for the Red Lion yielded and drew back, and wheeled and beset them again, until they rode in and dismounted among the haggard monks and the weeping women and the turmoil of a despairing camp. The leaders met in the Provençal's tent and talked together.

The next morning the surviving nobles, the knights and

mounted men at arms, and the noblewomen rode off in a mass toward the north, where the Byzantine captain Tzitas said they could find safety.

No sooner had they galloped off than the Red Lion's men surged in, snatching at the plunder, riding down the screaming servants, sabering the armed men.

Months later St. Gilles, with the count of Burgundy, Tzitas, Stephen of Blois, Josselin of Courtenay, and some three hundred survivors, sailed into the Golden Horn. They had fought their way to the Black Sea, and had boarded a ship at Sinope. Hugh the Great, count of Vermandois, was not among them, nor did any other prince or count emerge from those barren lands. At their request Alexis put them on a vessel bound for Jaffa. And when St. Gilles got as far as Antioch, he was seized and imprisoned by Tancred, who accused him of betraying the crusaders in the East. Later, Tancred was persuaded to release him.

Meanwhile a second army, more disciplined, commanded by the counts of Nevers and Bourges, had taken the direct road to the south—after failing to catch up with the first host at Angora. The Red Lion heard of it, and, flushed with victory, assailed it almost within sight of the Taurus and the protection of the mountain citadels. The Red Lion surprised it, smashed it, and only the débris of it drifted down into Antioch.

Still the human tide flowed out of Europe toward the Holy Land. It arose now in more distant regions where the exaltation of the new war was felt for the first time. Later in the summer Welf IV, duke of Bavaria, reached Constantinople with his liegemen, and Ida, margrave of Austria, with the archbishop Thiemo of Salzburg. There they joined the second wave from southern France, under command of the young William, count of Poitiers, and duke of Aquitaine and Gascony, who had been no more than a boy at the setting out of the great first crusade.

William of Poitiers was a warrior without fear, a maker of songs, and a joyous companion. He dared laugh at Alexis, whom he called a captain, and his men rioted with the Byzantines. Some took ship to go by sea, but the mass of the host accompanied the leaders upon the land road. Alexis gave them guides and a few soldiers. "He gave us thirty Turcoples," says Ekkehard, the chronicler of this army, "to lead us astray in regions unknown to us but known to them."

What happened then is told by an Armenian, a certain Matthew of Edessa.

From this moment the emperor began to carry out his plan of treachery. He ordered his officers to lead the Franks across barren lands. For fifteen days they led them through wastes without water, where nothing was seen but the desert in all its harshness—nothing but rocks and mountains. The water they came upon was white as if somebody had dissolved chalk in it, and salt.[1] Alexis had advised his people to put chalk into their bread, and to offer it to them [the crusaders] thus seasoned. So sickness broke out in their ranks. He did this because they had violated the oath they made him in the beginning, and they had not kept their promises. But the Greeks were not less guilty in the eyes of God, in making these men the victims of their treachery.

The great sultan of the west, Kilidj-Arslan[2], learned of the advent of the Franks, and wrote to Niksar to warn Malik Ghazi and the other amirs. Then at the head of a formidable army they advanced toward the Christians. These met the infidels in the plain of Aula. A bitter struggle followed for a great part of the day. The Franks, broken and lost in a country strange to them, saw no way out of their desperate situation. In their bewilderment they flocked together and stood like frightened beasts. This was a day bloody and terrible for them. Under these circumstances the general commanding the Greeks took to flight.

The count of Poitiers, making a stand on a near-by hill, around which the infidels surged, was forced to watch the defeat of his men. What a sight! Beholding his men exterminated and led off captive by thousands, the Frank prince wept bitterly. Hard pressed on every hand, the count fled with about four hundred men. He went to look for an asylum at Antioch with Tancred. His army, otherwise, was entirely destroyed.

The archbishop Thiemo met a death so horrible that his name was recorded among the most distinguished martyrs of

---

[1]Alkaline.

[2]The Red Lion. His homeland lay west of Armenia.

the Church. The margrave Ida, it seems, fell captive to the Red Lion. At least when Frederick Barbarossa came over that same road four generations later, he was greeted by a young Turkish chieftain, also Kilidj Arslan by name, who claimed that his great-grandfather had taken a German princess for a bride, and that he himself was kin to Barbarossa.

So the tide of living men was swept away and vanished in the wastelands of Asia Minor, leaving behind it only the débris of rusted armor and bones picked dry by the jackals. Perhaps a hundred thousand men died there in that summer.

From that time the land route was closed—by the treachery of Alexis, and by the aroused fanaticism of the Seljuk Turks, who were retaliating for the blow struck by the first crusaders.

Only the first host of the iron men, with Bohemund and Godfrey, got through to Jerusalem. The door they opened was closed behind them, and no Christian army ever marched after them over the land road to the Holy City.[1]

Not until the next year in the spring did the fugitives of the armies of relief set foot in the Holy Land. A few hundred of them sailed down the coast and disembarked at Jaffa. William of Poitiers had no heart for anything but a ride up to Jerusalem, to fulfil his vow. Then, with the first fair wind, he set sail for home.

Stephen of Blois made haste to follow him. He had redeemed his crusader's pledge, and not even his wife's tongue could dim his memory of that flight through the burning brush with the Red Lion's horsemen howling after him.

Then Stephen of Blois with several others [says Fulcher] wished to sail away. But a contrary wind rose and drove him back, and there was nothing for him to do but to return. He came back, out of the sea, into the port of Jaffa.

---

[1]Forty years later the hosts of the so-called second crusade attempted to cross Asia Minor, under Conrad and Louis VII of France. Most of them were massacred near Doryleum, some going around by sea. Frederick Barbarossa followed with an army of nearly a hundred thousand, and penetrated as far as the mountains of Armenia, where he was drowned in crossing a stream clad in his armor. His army was defeated and broken up, the survivors reaching Antioch.

He came back, and took refuge with King Baldwin. That enterprising soldier, however, was on the march as usual to repel a Moslem invasion with his skeleton army. For a year he had worked miracles by sheer daring; he had about two hundred horsemen with him then, and instead of being strengthened by reinforcements, he had to protect the newcomers. Straightway he impressed the departing guests, the worried Stephen, and the count of Burgundy, and a certain Hugo of Provence, to aid him.

They were on the march when misfortune overtook them. A powerful Arab army came out of nowhere, appearing on the heights around them. Outnumbered ten to one, the crusaders wavered, the newcomers on the edge of panic. Baldwin rode among them.

"Knights of Christ, and my friends," he said calmly. "Do not try to escape the battle. Anyone who flees will be lost. We will attack, and we may live."

They kept together and they charged the Arabs, who closed in around them. The Christian array was broken, and the knights became separated, cutting their way through the swarming Arabs who hung around them as dogs cling to the flanks of crippled wolves. The count of Burgundy went down. Some scores of Christians reached the gardens of Ramlah, but the exulting Arabs stormed the city. Three men on wearied horses rode into Jerusalem that night, and the great gates were closed, while the patriarch summoned the sick and the priests to watch from the walls.

Somewhere in Ramlah plain lay the body of Stephen of Blois, once lord of a hundred castles and husband of the beloved Adele. He had found at last the hero's death that he had avoided so earnestly for six years. Fulcher of Chartres made a note of his passing: "Then was slain Stephen of Blois, a sagacious man of noble blood." He did not call him brave.

Between Jerusalem and the sea the Arabs swarmed. Jaffa mustered its scanty garrison and prepared to defend itself. And men asked in vain for tidings of King Baldwin. He had vanished, in spite of thousands of eager Arab riders who ransacked the villages for a sign of *Malik Bagh'dwan*.

He had escaped from the massacre only after his men had

scattered, and with one man at arms and his young esquire, who clung to him like his own shadow, he hid in the neighboring hills. That night the three of them took shelter in an abandoned tower. They dared not light a fire, but even in the darkness they had been followed. A figure approached them, with arms uplifted and cloak waving, to signal a truce. The figure materialized into a Seljuk Turk of rank, who approached Baldwin.

"*Yah Khawand*," he said, "O my lord, there is no safety in this place for thee. Searchers will come and it is needful to go forth."

"Who art thou," the king asked, "and what words are these?"

The stranger made answer as bluntly. "I am one who hath sworn to render thee service, and now, verily, is the time of the service."

"And the reason?" Baldwin demanded.

"In the year before this," the Seljuk explained, "my family"—by which he meant a woman, probably his wife—"lay by the road in the pain of childbirth, and thy path lay also upon that road, for thy men were raiding. Thou gavest thy cloak to my family, and gavest command to thy men to bring water and fruit. So, no harm came to the mother, and my son was born under the shadow of thy protection. So I swore that I would requite service with service, and therefore am I here. Mount, O my lord, and ride to another place while there is time."

Baldwin never lagged in making decisions. He called to his men to bring up the horses, and the four of them made their way out into the hills. Later in the night the Moslem horsemen took possession of the tower. The king watched the hill trails all the next day, moving, when he could, nearer the coast.

They went down to water in the darkness, and sometimes they were able to find and slaughter a sheep, to stay their hunger. On the third night they lay motionless in the brush outside the land gate of Arsuf, until they heard a band of Moslems pass. Then they went up to the gate and called to the sentries.

He entered Arsuf [says Fulcher] amid the rejoicing of the people. He ate and drank, and went to sleep at once. For a king, like a common man, has need of all that.

The situation was bad enough, but Baldwin was alive. He sent a messenger with his signet ring to Tancred in the north, asking for aid. There was the shadow of the old quarrel between them, yet with the fate of Jerusalem in the balance, the king could not think of that. He got into a boat and sailed around to Jaffa, where his wife had taken refuge. At his coming the garrison grew bolder and he led a sally that drove the unsuspecting Arabs from their siege lines.

And then the first great pilgrim fleet, long overdue, sailed into the port of Jaffa and beached along the near-by coast. It landed its motley thousands: knights, monks, devout ladies, threadbare adventurers, merchants. Out of them Baldwin fashioned an army of sorts, and freed Ramlah.

A month later down from the north came Tancred and the younger Baldwin, now prince of Edessa, with fifteen hundred men. Here was power indeed. Within a few days King Baldwin had swept away the Arabs and was storming at the walls of Ascalon.

His worst moment of weakness had passed. Now that the road over the sea was open, the pilgrim fleets came regularly to visit him. His army grew from a skeleton to the semblance of an armed host. But the real safeguard of Jerusalem was the strong arm and the quiet courage of the man who had been once a brawler and a plunderer, and who was now *Malik Bagh'dwan*.

He had aid, in the next three years, from an old companion. White-haired St. Gilles returned to look again for his domain in the promised land, with a small following and a new-born son. The Provençal sought the sugar plantations and the fruit orchards of sun-warmed Tripoli again. And, stubbornly, he remained there, although Tripoli itself was no less impregnable than before with its walls rising from the sea.

If St. Gilles could not have the citadel, he meant to build one of his own. So he built a tower on the Pilgrim's Hill, a little way inland, and by degrees, in spite of the attacks of the Moslem governor of Tripoli, he enlarged the square tower and sheltered his people within a real castle. The Moslems called it *Kala'at Sendhjil*—St. Gilles' Fort.

There the old crusader held fast. A rather titanic struggle began between the citadel in the sea and the fortress on the hill. The Provençals guarded the roads, planted seed in the fields; the Moslems carried on their trade by ship with Egypt, but they lost their plantations. Syrian merchants set up shop under St. Gilles' walls, protected by his garrison, and soon a fair-sized town grew up on the hill.

It was harried and raided and burned from time to time, but it grew, and St. Gilles made himself master of one seaport after another. He watched his lands increase, and knew the day could not be far off when the old Tripoli must surrender to the new. Already the Moslem governor paid him tribute.

And then—a sudden sally of angered Moslems, a blowing of horns, a clash of steel; smoke spreading over burning buildings, and horses and men struggling in the streets of St. Gilles' Town.

The old Provençal mounted to a roof to direct his men, in spite of the flames in the building beneath him. The roof fell, carrying him with it, and—though he was saved from the fire—his aged body was broken, and life soon left it.

He was carried to Jerusalem and buried near Godfrey. Four years later Tripoli surrendered, and St. Gilles' son took possession of it, becoming prince of Tripoli.

XXXVII

BOHEMUND'S CRUSADE

FOR three years Bohemund had been a captive in a Turkish palace far in the east, beyond the scene of conflict. Even there, however, the presence of the mighty Norman was felt. Like that other adventurer, Cœur de Lion, prison did not subdue him. By messenger he gave advice to his principality of Antioch, and to those who were trying to raise his ransom.

Nor did Bohemund remain behind walls. It seems that he helped his captors to defeat Kilidj Arslan, with whom they had a quarrel of their own. And there is a story of a Moslem princess who loved him, and begged for his release. Meanwhile the Byzantine emperor made an enormous bid for him—offering the Turks two hundred and sixty thousand gold coins. Alexis considered it worth that much to have the turbulent Norman safe in a Byzantine prison.

But Bohemund persuaded his captor to set him free for the payment of half Alexis's offer. A friendly Armenian chieftain and Baldwin of Edessa raised the great ransom between them, and Bohemund rode out a free man after three years of confinement. Legends followed him out of the East, and he emerged as the comrade in arms of the Turk who had taken him, and the adopted son of the Armenian who paid his way. And he married the Moslem princess to someone else. "Bohemund," Anna Comnene wrote in her history, "was still Bohemund and not changed at all."

He was still intent upon welding an empire around Syria. And he wasted no more thought upon Jerusalem. If he could take Aleppo he would be master of one of the great trade routes.

Aleppo, however, was not taken, in spite of the powerful army that rallied to the Norman prince—something happened at the crossing of a river. The Moslems caught the crusaders half on one side and half on the other. Bohemund and Tancred got away safely, but Baldwin of Edessa and Josselin of Courtenay were taken prisoner.

This is called the Battle of Harran in the Moslem annals, and it marks a change in events. For the first time one of the main armies of the crusaders had been defeated in the field.

It did not dishearten the ambitious Norman. In fact, with Baldwin of Edessa off the scene, he took over the rule of the wide lands of Edessa, and he changed his plans entirely. Leaving Tancred to safeguard his dominion, he embarked on a ship and slipped through the watchful Byzantine fleets—legend has it that he hid himself in a coffin at one time during the voyage.

He landed upon the coast of southern Italy, among his Normans, and he was greeted by a tumult of rejoicing. After all, he was the prince of Antioch, the man who had saved the crusade, and had won the great Battle of the Lance. Tales of his daring had been told in all the halls of Norman Italy, and the legends of his captivity had not lessened his fame. Moreover, he brought a number of things with him—the great pavilion captured from the amir, Kerbogha, and precious relics. Even two thorns that were believed to be from the crown of the Seigneur Christ. These he bestowed upon a grateful church, and to another he made offering of silver shackles, as a token of his release from prison.

In the past Bohemund's towering figure and deep voice had been imposing enough, and he had not lacked for friends;

now he was a man exalted above others by the enthusiasm of the day. With Godfrey dead, Bohemund was the foremost leader of the victorious crusade, the mightiest of the mighty.

And this suited him well, because he had a part to play. He had left Antioch in order to attack Byzantium itself, not in Asia but in Europe. His shrewd eyes had seen the weak points in the glittering fabric of the empire, and he was ready to strike at Constantinople. Already, in Norman Italy and Sicily, his kinsmen had established their rule and were venturing to sea. If he could cross the Adriatic with an army and march to Constantinople, he believed he could overthrow Alexis.

Just now rumors of the emperor's share in the massacres of the crusaders were spreading throughout Europe. The prince of Antioch had only to feed the fire already kindled. Once master of Constantinople, he could push south, link his conquest with Armenia and his own principality of Antioch. Then he would be monarch of the Near East, and the Normans would rule from Rome to Baghdad.

So Bohemund planned. He needed two things—the sanction of the Church, and a mighty army.

To gain these he began a circus parade, himself the moving spirit of the show. Certain of the support of the Normans in Italy, he moved north with his relics. The pope, Paschal, was an enthusiast, eager to keep the crusading movement under the direction of the Church. Bohemund persuaded him to sanction a new crusade, and to bestow letters of authorization and the banner of St. Peter. Paschal did more—he added to Bohemund's procession a papal legate, to preach the new undertaking.

So far, good. The energetic Norman began the building of a fleet on the shore of the Adriatic. Then he went west to seek prestige and recruits. His march was really imposing, with the great warrior leading, the papal banner waving— the speeches telling of the conquest of the Holy Land, the legate's promise of indulgence to those who went on the new crusade. Bohemund even added several Betchenaks taken captive from the emperor's army—showing them as evidence of the pagans of Asia who served Alexis. Nothing was lacking.

The circus went to France, where Bohemund left it to journey more rapidly from monastery to castle, preaching his own crusade. He had in him the instinct of the showman, so often found in brilliant conquerors. Alexander had it, and Napoleon—who created a whole stage effect of varied uniforms, rewards, titles, the splendor of a victorious court and the bearskins of an Old Guard, the plumes of the *maréchals de France*—a truly gorgeous scene that vanished with the fall of the curtain.

Never had the excitement of the crusade been as widespread as then. Jerusalem delivered. Pilgrim fleets setting out. Bell towers ringing the new Angelus, and men's voices chanting:

> *"In regno tuo lumine,*
> *Gloria aeterna*
> *Maneat cum Patre*
> *In saeculorum saecula. Amen."*

Tall, red-haired Bohemund, rising from his seat at the end of the service to call for volunteers to go with him on a new crusade. Hundreds pressing forward to take the cross from his hand, or that of Bishop Bruno, the legate of the Apostolic See.

Bohemund wanted more. He visited the court of Philip, king of the French, and asked for his daughter Constance for a bride. At that moment the prince of Antioch was the heroic figure of Christendom, hallowed by the sanction of the Church—a figure that must have appealed to a woman's eyes. Constance was betrothed to him, and her sister to Tancred, the champion of the holy war.

Eleven years before, the two Normans had been almost landless adventurers. Now uncle and nephew were united to the royal house of France. Bohemund's wedding at Chartres had the solemnity of an imperial fête. Adele, the widow of Stephen, gave the wedding feast. The king and his son and the peers and prelates of France were at the church. The showman in Bohemund could not resist such a magnificent audience. After the service he climbed to the organ loft and urged the throng to join his crusade. Many did.

So the mighty Norman gained the support of the throne of France, and Constance. But he gained little from the kinsmen of Normandy and England—although he talked with Anselm, archbishop of Canterbury. Normandy and England were occupied with their own troubles.

After haranguing the men of Poitiers, who were still brooding over the massacre of the valley of Aula, he went back to the Italian seaports, Brindisi and Bari, to inspect his new fleet. He had money in his chests and promises of more. Bishops and knights escorted his banner down to the sea. The new recruits flocked in, and he housed them and fed them royally.

In the autumn of 1107, with nearly forty thousand men, Bohemund launched his crusade upon the waters of the Adriatic, in two hundred ships and barges guarded by a fleet of galleys. He left the flat green plain of Italy behind and headed toward the Dalmatian mountain wall and Durazzo, the citadel that was the western gate of Byzantium.

A Scythian galloper sped from Durazzo, killing horses along the highway through the mountains, past Salonika, skirting the Marmora to the white portals of the Golden Gate, and into the imperial palace. And the Byzantine courtiers, coming in from a hunt with Alexis, fell silent in fear when the words were whispered, "Bohemund has landed."

But Alexis, stooping over his hunting boots, said quietly, "Let us lunch first and see about Bohemund afterward."

The winter passed and spring came, and Bohemund still camped outside the wall of Durazzo. Alexis had done a remarkable thing—he had done nothing.

Nothing, that is, in the field against the Norman army. Bohemund's host was more formidable than any array of the Byzantine mercenaries, and Alexis knew this. He dared not risk a battle. So he drilled his army quietly enough through the winter, and apparently left Durazzo to its fate.

In reality, he watched every movement of the Normans. He sent false letters to Bohemund's camp, offered rewards to deserters, and arranged for his allies, the Venetians, to take a hand. Somewhat reluctantly a great Venetian fleet came down and blockaded Bohemund—playing, as the doges of St. Mark's so often played, a double part, pretending to aid the crusaders of Jerusalem, while they cut off the Normans at Durazzo.

Bohemund tried every trick of a besieger: building rams, digging tunnels, and moving up a massive wooden tower. But he had underestimated the strength of the great wall of Durazzo and Byzantine ingenuity. His rams were burned, his tunnels made a death trap by liquid flame, and his tower demolished by the inextinguishable Greek fire, while his armed men—who had had little chance to use their weapons—cried aloud in dismay.

Grimly, then, the indomitable Norman set fire to his own ships, drawn up on the shore. By destroying his only means of retreat, he wished to make certain that he would either break Alexis's power or go down to defeat himself. Curiously enough, neither fate befell him.

Alexis reached down into his treasure chests and bought contingents of cavalry from the Red Lion, far off in Asia; he persuaded the Red Lion to occupy Tancred, while Alexis withdrew the Byzantine fleet from the coast of Antioch. With all his mercenaries and his most wily generals, the emperor marched toward Bohemund and posted his divisions in the mountains and the passes in a circle around the Norman expeditionary force—which by that time had occupied most of the neighboring valleys.

So Alexis hemmed in the Normans by land, while the Venetians shut them off from the sea. In spite of all Alexis's maneuvering, battles were fought. A Greek division was routed by the Norman cavalry, and the Normans were worsted in other encounters. Stalemate followed. Bohemund held the valley lands, but could not get at the Byzantines—his cavalry could not ascend the mountain passes. Meanwhile his treasury was exhausted, food began to run short, and sickness and idleness slowly demoralized his men.

It was Alexis who first sent envoys to discuss peace, but so great was the poverty in the Norman camp that Bohemund went out beyond it to meet the Byzantine nobles. They began to reproach him with breaking his pledge of allegiance given the emperor ten years before.

"Be silent!" Bohemund cried. "If you have a message from the emperor deliver it and nothing more."

Schemer and adventurer the prince of Antioch might be, but he was not a hypocrite. He knew that his moment had passed—having failed at Durazzo, he could not hope to take Constantinople. He was undefeated, but his cause was lost, and nothing remained for him but to make the best terms possible. He knew this, yet somehow he managed to appear untroubled and unconcerned through all the interplay of diplomacy that followed—the exchange of hostages, informal discussion of points to be yielded, and the ceremonial to be observed when he met Alexis.

Bohemund wanted Alexis to rise from his couch to greet him, and the emperor actually did give the Norman his hand and allow him to stand at the head of his couch. Meanwhile the Byzantine ministers drew up one treaty after another until Bohemund was satisfied—until he went through the form of being persuaded to agree, for the sake of his men.

The treaty was voluminous, but the vital point was that Bohemund relinquished to Alexis all title to the principality of Antioch. He could occupy his conquests in the East until his death, but only as the vassal of Alexis, who would take possession after his death. (In the end Alexis gained little enough, because Tancred refused point-blank to yield Antioch.)

And then the signing of the parchment pages, before the court and the witnesses of the Church. The modulated Greek voices, reading over the treaty.

"This agreement with divinely crowned Majesty . . . I, Bohemund, son of Robert Guiscard, to be thy true man . . . to take up arms against thine enemies . . . the above-mentioned towns to return to the scepter of the Romans . . . moreover, I will make war on Tancred my nephew if he does not deliver the before-mentioned towns . . . I swear by the passion of Christ, by the God who is adored in the church of Antioch, by the crown of thorns and the lance . . ."

On the table beneath Bohemund's eyes lay the opened folios of the Gospels upon which he was to take oath. And there, too, lay a rusted lance-head upon a wrapping of white floss silk. It had been given to the keeping of Alexis by old St. Gilles, but Bohemund could not have known that.

He saw the lance-head that had been carried, bound to a standard, out of Antioch when he won his great victory over Kerbogha—the relic that he had mocked thereafter. Looking upon it, he uttered the words of surrender, and allegiance to the emperor. He signed his name.

The witnesses came forward and signed beneath him— prelates, an ambassador from the pope, Norman lords, Byzantine grandees, a eunuch, and a notary. Then he was handed a golden bull of the emperor, wherein Alexis's name was signed in red ink.

So Bohemund departed, and the curtain came down upon the play. But if he had taken Durazzo . . .

For more than a year the prince of Antioch remained quiet in the castles of southern Italy. His army had scattered, some returning to their homes, others making the pilgrimage to Jerusalem under Alexis's protection. Constance bore him a son, who was named Bohemund.

Ships put in to Amalfi, bringing word from the East. Pilgrims passed in a steady stream out of Brindisi, bound to Jerusalem. Venetian galleys swept past, their long oars creaking. Trade was coming out of the Eastern ports— camphor, spices, silk from Cathay. People were traveling to the Holy Land. Bohemund saw the fulfilment of part of his dream, as communication opened between Europe and Asia. But he himself remained a spectator. Alexis was reaping the fruits of the crusade, in trade and the recovery of Armenia. Byzantine governors were appearing in the cities of the Euphrates.

The Norman prince could no longer remain idle. He set about gathering a new army, assembling ships. He meant to go to the East again. Perhaps Aleppo would fall to him, and beyond Aleppo lay Baghdad. . . .

Before he could set out, he died, in the spring of 1111.

His principality, Antioch, remained in Tancred's hands, and prospered, extending more and more toward the east. Tancred never laid aside his sword, and his personal valor made up for his lack of statesmanship. He had separated almost entirely from the crusaders in Jerusalem, and he ruled the Armenians with an iron hand. For years he had chafed under Bohemund's restraint, and when he was at last master of the great city, he mustered his strength to go against Aleppo.

And then, a year after Bohemund, death sheathed his sword.

With the passing of the two mighty Normans, conquest ceased in the north. They had been the incarnation of the conquering spirit of the crusade; their courage had been a shield that the Byzantines, and Turks, and Arabs could not break. After a time the king of Jerusalem took over the rule of Antioch, until the coming of the rightful heir—the child Bohemund II, who was to sail to Antioch fifteen years later, and to be received joyfully by his people for his father's sake.

Meanwhile, of all the leaders of the crusade, there remained in the East only Baldwin, the king.

XXXVIII

THE LAST COMER

TIDINGS of the crusade were carried to the north by wandering monks and travelers. At first these tidings were little heeded—a new war, far from the world of gray seas and rock-bound fiords, where men put out to sea to fish and to pillage, where unbroken forests stretched to the white tundras. Then the tidings changed. All Christendom was marching to the war, to set free Jerusalem.

Giant Erik the Good, king of Danemark, was the first to take the cross. With his wife Bothilda—she of shining white skin—he betook him to the road, with three thousand ax-wielders and swordsmen tramping behind then. Jerusalem lay far away, but the Danes were a patient folk and they pushed steadily to the south through the forests of Russia where the church bells chimed a welcome to them, and the bearded priests chanted a blessing upon them.

By sled and by horseback they came south, and their road took them through Constantinople. Alexis gave them gifts and relics, and the Danes of the imperial Varangian guard—mercenaries long absent from the Northland—turned out to a man to worship their former king. Giant Erik feasted and

drank his fill, but Alexis could do nothing with his Scandinavian guardsmen until he rid himself of this monarch of the
north. He bestowed more presents upon them, and they
embarked at the quays of the Golden Horn to sail to the Holy
Land. Erik, unaccustomed to the heat, died on the way, but
Bothilda sailed on, and her ships joined the great pilgrim
fleet that reached Jaffa in time to aid the hard-pressed
crusaders in that summer of 1102.

For years the summons to the crusade did not reach Norway, up at the edge of the known world, near the last land
Thule. This was the homeland of the Vikings, the seafarers,
lords of the dragon ships, who cherished undying feuds, and
harkened to the songs of the skalds.

Then came the news of the capture of Jerusalem. The
berserks of the sea listened, and their young king Sigurd took
the cross. No ordinary viking-faring was this. To sail to
Mikligard[1] was a matter of years, but Jerusalem lay beyond
their knowledge.

None the less, they began building ships and outfitting
them. It cost a great deal, and before the sixty ships were
ready, years had passed. No matter. Ten thousand Northmen
were ready to follow their young king, a man of beauty and
mild manner, well loved.

The fleet was pushed into the water at Bergen, and the
masts were stepped. Sails were hoisted, and the Jerusalem-
farers left the shore, laboring at the oars, their storage casks
filled with dried fish and mead, corn and water and skins to
barter. They were fair men, blue-eyed, long yellow hair
hanging in braids upon their shoulders. They all had their
axes and heavy shields and sea-cloaks.

Many of them had not forgotten one-eyed Odin, or the
thunder-god Thor, but they were quite willing to go to war
for the white Christ. There would be a clashing of swords, a
breaking of shields—spoil to be gathered by those not summoned hence by the Choosers of the Slain.

They reached England and passed one winter there. They
heard of battles with the pagans in Spain and steered a course
thither, to land and encounter the surprised Arabs and

[1]Constantinople.

Berbers. They captured towns, and followed the elusive sails that plied between the Gates.

Then Sigurd called a halt and sailed toward Italy. Islands appeared in their course and they landed among barren rocks, to harry the Moslems again. The Normans of Italy came out to meet them, and feasted them from castle to castle—Duke Roger serving Sigurd with his own hands.

All this was pleasant indeed, and not until the spring of 1110 did Sigurd sight the low green hills of the Syrian coast. He followed the coast south and landed to ask for the king of Jerusalem. He learned that Baldwin had gone off to give aid to hard-pressed Edessa, but a Moslem fleet—taking advantage of that circumstance—was blockading Acre, now a Christian port.

Nothing could have suited the Northmen better. They turned their prows toward Acre, but when the Moslem seamen saw the lines of dragon ships moving toward them, with long oars swinging in cadence and shields dressed along the rails, they fled incontinent.

King Baldwin, hastening back to the relief of Acre, found the Vikings in possession of the sea. The crusader and the sea rover greeted one the other gravely and thankfully, and the exiles of the Holy Land feasted their guests in the royal pavilion.

Clad in their best garments, their long byrnies trimmed with sable and ermine, their gold arm rings gleaming, the Vikings went to pray at the Sepulcher, to gaze reverently at the stations of the cross. Then to Jericho and to bathe in the Jordan.

Baldwin received them in state at Jerusalem, and they rode on the king's horses through streets filled with gazing crowds, the ground covered with embroidered cloth. Sigurd had from the hand of Baldwin the most precious of all relics, a fragment of the cross discovered in Jerusalem, which they believed to be the true cross. His vow was accomplished, and he might now return home with a clear conscience.

But Sigurd wished to make a fitting thank-offering to Baldwin. He said he would take for the king any city of the sea that Baldwin wished. And the king of Jerusalem named

Sidon—the almost impregnable citadel, joined to the mainland by a causeway, the sister city of Tyre. Both of them were still in Moslem hands.

The Vikings manned their vessels, built catapults and mangonels, while Baldwin mustered an army at the land end of the causeway. The ships moved in toward the massive gray walls, pitted by the sea wash and coated with tar. No chance of breaking them down.

Sigurd set his machines to work and rowed in with the war galleys. With stones soaring and crashing over them, and javelins whirring from the catapults, the Northmen swarmed from the galley rails against the ramparts. Ax in hand, they leaped from scaffoldings, climbed ropes, passing from galley to galley to reach the wall.

The blond giants, fired by battle lust, were more than a match for the Moslems. Sidon surrendered, on the promise that the defenders might pass out with their lives and as much of their property as they could carry. The promise was kept, and the Northmen were rewarded by a rich spoil.

Not content with this, they joined a Venetian fleet in an attack upon Tyre, but here they failed. They bade farewell to Baldwin, and sailed to Constantinople, where they saw the marvels of Byzantium, and turned the games of the Hippodrome into a riot of swords. They left their ships and betook themselves to the long road to the North.

The survivors reached Norway after an absence of nearly ten years. And the skalds sang of Sigurd the Jerusalemfarer. He was the last comer of the crusade, and the first of the kings to journey to the Holy Land.

XXXIX

BEYOND THE SEA

ILGRIMS were landing on the new stone quays. They were leaving the hot decks of the galleys, stiff and weak, hoisting their packs upon their shoulders and looking around eagerly. Merchants in Frisian coats, monks in black hoods, ladies in bright cloaks and long trains waiting for their servants to lead up palfreys to carry them through the dust. Bold-eyed minstrels with gitterns slung on their backs, jesting youths in short cloaks and long striped hose. Plain and patient folk, grouping together like cattle, kneeling to give thanks that they were alive after weeks upon the sea.

In scattered bands they moved off toward the hills. Some of them were guided by sunburned men of arms, who wore white mantles and had their hair and beards clipped short. These were called soldiers of Christ—excommunicated knights for the most part who took upon themselves the task of guarding the pilgrims. Hugo of Payans and Godfrey of St. Omer were the leaders of these volunteer guards, who numbered no more than nine and had taken vows to keep their lives clean and to share their property in common.

King Baldwin had bestowed upon them a corner of his mosque palace, and they attended service at the Templum Domini. Not yet were they known as Templars, nor had the emblem of the red cross been awarded them.

Knights of another order met the pilgrims within Jerusalem's gates. They wore plain black robes with a white cross, and they weeded out the sick among the newcomers, leading them to the hospital by the Church of Mary. They washed them and gave them wine with bread, and beds of straw and cotton covers, and silver for their empty wallets. These Hospitalers prayed to St. John the Baptist, and soon they would don armor and arms and join in the fighting—to be known in time as the Knights of St. John of the Hospital, and some of them eventually as the Knights of Malta.

Meanwhile the pilgrims thronged the streets, like children hurrying between the booths of a May fair. For years they had listened to tales of Outremer, as the new lands in the East were called. This voyage to Beyond the Sea was the one miraculous event of their lives.

The streets of Jerusalem had changed in the twenty years since the conquest. Jews were at home again in their alleys under the Temple height. Moslem scribes sat on rugs near the wells; sallow-faced Armenian merchants erected their stalls in the old bazaar; children played among the sheep and horses near the gate of the caravans. Bells chimed from twenty towers, and at the sound groups of priests and cowled monks hastened toward the cloister doors. Bearded patriarchs, unchanged since the Kingdom of Israel, strode in at the head of their burdened women and the sons of their sons, pulling at the nose-cords of swaying camels.

On the height of the Sepulcher, the old Arnulf, once chapplain of the duke of Normandy and now—for the second time—patriarch of Jerusalem, watched the building of a new dome over his church. His authority was equal to that of the warrior-king, and the twain labored in friendship. To appeal to the patriarch, barons rode in from their castles along the frontier. They also had changed with the years. Over their armor they wore the comfortable Arab *jelabië;* their swift-paced horses were desert bred, and among the men at arms who followed them rode light-armed Turcoples, and archers from Lebanon.

With the lords of Outremer came their wives, veiled against the sun glare. While the men were disputing about a law-breaking, or a title to land, these wives would visit the Sepulcher, and then perhaps go to the booths for new camelots or silks, and somehow in so doing they would manage to hear the news from the West. Often these women were Syrians or Armenians, and their children would grow up in a new caste, the mixed blood of Outremer.

Already the men had written down the code of laws that Godfrey had begun. But the high court of the lieges passed upon the affairs of the gentle-born, from the election of a king to the satisfaction to be given for a blow. The people also had their tribunal, the court of the bourgeoisie.

For the first time the pilgrims could go, under safe guard, to the land beyond the Jordan. They found a citadel built by Baldwin on the King's Mountain, overlooking the Valley of Moses—a citadel with mighty double walls and towers copied from the Byzantine works, erected by Syrian and Greek masons while the crusaders stood guard. There were even a mosaic ceiling and marble flooring in the chapel, and a satisfactory bronze dragon spouting water through his nose.

They could, if they wished, go on and gain a glimpse of water far off—the Red Sea. More likely, they made the journey north, from monastery to monastery, visiting the crypt at Nazareth, passing prudently by the castle Baldwin had built to overlook the Moslems in Tyre. There were shipyards at Beirut, but beyond, at Tortosa—the object of the pilgrimage—the altar of Our Lady of Tortosa, with the ikon that had survived earthquake and flame and pillage.

"It is here," they were told, "that Messire St. Peter the Apostle, when he went preaching in the land, made a little church in honor of the Virgin who carried God the Son. And Our Lord hath wrought here many good miracles to honor His mother."

In later generations the crusaders would build here the simple and massive church of brown stone, with the sweeping arches over the old altar near the city wall. Already, near by, the strange monks of Lebanon and artisans from the pilgrim fleets were cutting out blocks of hard brown limestone for the new cathedral of St. John. But the men of Outremer were still too poor to do much more than repair and fortify.

The pilgrims returned to their homes content. Not all of them survived the two years' journey, but those who did passed through most of the Christian world, and beheld many marvelous things. They had broken away from the isolation of hamlet and town; they had been tossed on the waves of the Great Sea, and had seen outlandish peoples—crowded bazaars, black slaves, burning oil, transparent glass, soft gossamer fabrics. They brought back with them tales of armored beasts half fish and half dragon that passed from land to water—crocodiles, and water monsters as large as heavy bulls—hippopotami. Also of the great serpent Dracon who was to be found in Africa. They hinted at a glimpse of Pegasus, and the river Nilus.

They brought with them, as if they had just come from the doors of a gigantic theater, the after-spell of distant lands, the lure of strange names. And they brought home the reality of Jerusalem. It was all there, they had seen it. Jerusalem was Outremer.

The men of Outremer managed to guard the pilgrims along the roads, and the peasants working the fields—smocked Syrians followed the ox ploughs. Where the water wheels creaked, women worked the millstones. Christian laborers had immigrated from Moslem lands. Many Moslems joined them, for the reason that the masters of Outremer were less exacting than the Turk or Arab landholders. Their masters depended on the soil—on wheat and fruit and olives. Wine and honey they had, and sheep, but when the rains failed there was suffering, and numbers of the peasants drifted away to more fertile valleys. The crusaders watched their herds and learned the customs of the Eastern peasantry. They had Arab secretaries to help them in the management, and physicians to tend their children, and they began to forget the towns of Normandy and Lorraine.

It was more comfortable to wear slippers within doors

and the loose *khalats* of the East, to trim their long hair and to sleep in the heat of the midday. And it was hard to be summoned to arms by the king, when the fields must be left unguarded, and the men of the castle horsed and equipped.

We who were once the westerners have become like the Asiatics [Fulcher writes]. He who was once Roman or Frank is now a Galilean, or man of Palestine; whoever once inhabited Rheims or Chartres finds himself a citizen of Tyre or Antioch.

Already, we have forgotten the places of our birth; they have become unknown to many of us—at least no one hears mention of them. Some of us in this country possess homes and servitors which belong to them by hereditary right; someone else has married a wife who is not his country-woman—a Syrian, an Armenian or even a Saracen who has received the grace of baptism. And then he has at his house his kinsmen by marriage.

One cultivates vines, another fields. They speak different languages and are already capable of understanding all of them. Mutual confidence has drawn us all together. In truth, it has been written: The lion and the ox eat from the same manger.

Whoever was once a stranger is now a native. The pilgrim has become a citizen. From day to day our parents and our kinsmen come out to rejoin us here. To those who had nothing but a *mesnie*, God hath given a village; those who were poor, God hath made them rich. Why should any one go back to the West when the East is so kind to them?

Outremer had become neither a kingdom nor a church state. It was, at this time, a land of freedom, where king, patriarch, barons, merchants, pilgrims, and common people were making themselves at home among the elder Christians of the East.[1]

---

[1]Outremer, of course, was a popular name. In the records of the Church, the crusaders' conquest was still the *terra sancta*. Actually, it consisted of Armenia, the principality of Antioch, and the county of Edessa on the north, the long strip of the principality of Tripoli in the center, and on the south the Kingdom of Jerusalem. This in turn was divided into Jerusalem proper, the small principality of Galilee, and the counties of Jaffa and Cæsaria, the Ascalon region and the bordermarch of Montreal in the desert. Outremer had a continuous rampart on the east, protecting it from the Moslems—to the north, the Anisaris mountains, then the Lebanon, then the river Jordan and the Dead Sea. These principalities and counties were now the fiefs of powerful vassals, in hereditary right.

It had the rude strength of the young crusaders and the indomitable spirit of the crusade itself. But it had neither master nor plan. Year by year it was growing apart from the west. There remained one common bond, the city of Jerusalem, where the bells chimed now in the towers of the new churches.

Men in the West, listening to the bells of the Angelus at evening, thought of Jerusalem as something that, outside the familiar world, belonged somehow to them.

King Baldwin, at the end of seventeen years, had kept Outremer safe by his own effort. He seldom sat in his robes in the mosque palace on the Temple height. He had to watch all the frontiers, and to shepherd the pilgrims. In one year he had to break up an invasion from Damascus, and make a feint at Ascalon, to quiet the Egyptians; then he rode north again to protect that invaluable frontier buttress, Edessa, and came back to besiege Tyre. He built the outpost towers that the Arabs called the Watchers.

During one battle his cause seemed to be lost, when the crusaders were defeated on both flanks. Baldwin remained stubbornly in the field, and when one of the Moslem wings went off to plunder, believing the battle at an end, he returned grimly to the fighting and held his own. He was badly hurt while hunting, and remained in the mountains to keep the news from being carried to the Moslems. He was wounded many times, and when he fell ill during one summer the Egyptian fleet came and waited off the coast for tidings of his death, as vultures hover beside a fallen man.

Al-Afdhal of Cairo and Tughtakin of Damascus were content at last to buy a truce of him for a period of years.

In that year 1117 the observant priest Fulcher records a sign in the sky:

In the fifth night of the month of December, after the setting of the moon when darkness fell, we saw all the heavens flooded with fire—or with a glow the hue of blood. Considering this sign full of portents, we wondered much. For within the heart of that red radiance, which began to grow larger little by little, we beheld

KRAK DES CHEVALIERS

The citadel of the Hospitalers in Syria, sketching in the detail of the Twelfth Century.

THE EMPEROR MANUEL

Portrait of the Basileus of Constantinople
during the last crusade.

rays of a whitish color rising up in amazing fashion, now in front, now behind, now in the center.

Then in the lower part of the sky appeared a whiteness, as if it were the dawn of day in which light grows and the sun ought to rise. And in the forepart of this ominous thing we saw clearly a brightness as of the rising moon. By this the ground all around us, and the countryside, was brightly illuminated.

We wondered then whether this foreshadowed a great shedding of blood in war or some other not less threatening event; but what it would be we knew not.

So we awaited humbly the will of God. For this was a portent of the passing of men. At the beginning of the next year there died Paschal the pope, and the wife of Baldwin King of Jerusalem whom he had sent to Sicily, and Arnulf, patriarch of Jerusalem, and also Alexis of Constantinople and many other chieftains of the world.

That year brought sorrow to Jerusalem. King Baldwin was still far from well, but he set out across the Jifar to raid into Egypt with no more than two hundred mounted men and four hundred foot soldiers. He pushed across the sands, reached the Nile, and stormed the town of Pharam, where he let his men rest. They went fishing in the river with their spears, while the king kept to his tent feeling an acute inward pain and the renewed ache of his old wounds. When his men heard of this they thronged around his tent, and it was decided to start back at once.

Since Baldwin could not ride, a litter was brought him, made out of the strips of a tent. The king's horn gave the signal to march and they set out across the desert in anxious haste. Baldwin grew steadily worse and halted them at the first village.

The king had no hope of life, and he urged his officers to see that the patriarch and council of Jerusalem sent to Europe for his surviving brother, Eustace, to succeed him on the throne—his cousin Baldwin of Edessa could act as regent in the interval. He had one wish—that his body be carried back to Jerusalem and not left for the Moslems to dig up and dishonor.

Baldwin's men looked at each other without response. In that heat no body could be carried for a week over the sand.

Baldwin understood their silence, and roused himself to give them directions how to embalm him.

Within two days he died in his tent, with only his men and a chaplain to attend him. The little army, grief-stricken, tried to follow his instructions, cutting out and burying his entrails and organs, and washing the shell of his body with oils. Then they resumed their march. And they reached Jerusalem on Palm Sunday.

On that day the branches of palms are wont to be carried [says Fulcher]. Toward the procession of palm bearers which was descending the Mount of Olives, advanced the funeral cortège, mourning. When it was seen and known for what it was, everyone ceased singing. Instead of their song, they cried a lament. All who were there groaned instead of being glad. The Franks grieved, the Syrians wept and so did the Saracens who saw this. Who could contain himself and not yield to his feelings? Returning to the city again the people made the preparations that sorrow ordained. And they buried him in Golgotha, next Godfrey, the duke, his brother.

Godfrey, Raymond of Toulouse, and Baldwin lay in their tombs in Golgotha. With Baldwin, the men of Jerusalem buried the last leader of the great crusade. While he lived, the indomitable spirit of the crusade lived also. After his death, it passed, and it did not return again.

—

AFTERWORD

AFTERWORD

THE great crusade had been spontaneous. The men, summoned by Urban, had rallied to the cross of their own will. They came from all nations, and they marched under different leaders. Urban had summoned them, but he did not lead them.

Their indomitable spirit brought them to their goal. Perhaps a quarter million men died that thirty thousand should enter Jerusalem. They were sustained by the spirit of sacrifice, and of exaltation. When the leaders faltered the common people went on to final achievement.

When they gained Jerusalem no one was at hand to guide them. They did the best they could. While the spirit of the crusade lived the conquest went on. When it weakened, the crusade separated into the elements that had formed it in the first place—into the feudal barons, the servants of the Church, the transitory pilgrims, and the merchants. They had varying ambitions and differing needs. The mutual possession of Jerusalem remained the only common bond.

That, in brief, is the story of the great crusade. It did not end with the taking of Jerusalem, but it did end with the passing of the spirit of this crusade.

There never was another crusade like this.

After the Moslems recaptured Edessa another great expedition set out from Europe, in 1146-1149. It is worth looking at.

It began very much as the first[1] crusade had begun—Armenians appealed for aid to the pope, Eugene III; a French bishop preached a new crusade and found in the saintly Bernard an inspired orator. Louis VII, king of the French, took the cross, and Bernard persuaded Conrad III of Germany to do the same—a result that Bernard himself called a miracle.

Everything happened differently. The two kings were the sole leaders of the movement; disciplined armies made up the mass of the crusaders, one third the strength of the host of the first cross-bearers. Both armies were cut up by the Moslems in Asia Minor, the survivors going down to Jerusalem by sea.

There, being too weak to attempt the recapture of Edessa, they united with the host of Outremer in an attack upon Damascus, which accomplished nothing. Louis became estranged from his queen Eleanor, whom he had left at Antioch, where the luxury-loving court proved too agreeable to that self-willed lady.

This expedition is called the second crusade. It did not have for its purpose a settlement in the Holy Land. It aimed at restoring Edessa, and it failed in this. After the failure

---

[1]History has spoken of the six or more crusades for so long, as if they were six different movements of the same kind, that it is impossible to mention them otherwise. In reality, the first crusade, by capturing the Holy Land and occupying it, started anew a religious war between Christian and Moslem, at first in Outremer and then along most of the frontier of the two faiths. The succeeding crusades were the most important offensives in this war. Minor attacks and counterattacks went on between whiles.

It is no more logical to say that there were six crusades than to say that the Battle of the Marne, the Battle of Verdun and the Campaign of Gallipoli were three different wars.

And it is misleading to call the host led by Godfrey, Bohemund, and the others the Crusade of the Barons. The barons were the leaders, as they had been the leaders in the countries of Europe, before the journey. But they were not more numerous in the crusade itself than the other classes, and their authority tended to diminish. It was really the Crusade of *the People*.

The reinforcement of 1101 had more of the barons, in proportion to the lower classes, and this might be called the Crusade of the Barons, just as the second crusade might be christened the Kings' and the third, the Emperors'.

the remnants of the two armies went home, almost without exception.

For years a steady movement of pilgrims and individual barons with their followings kept on, to Jerusalem. These also returned home when they had visited the holy places. The next great expedition followed the capture of Jerusalem by Saladin in 1187. And this is known as the third crusade.

The scenes at its start were very like those when men set out upon the first voyage of God. The loss of the Holy City sent a stir of religious fervor through all Christendom. The popes declared a Truce of God for seven years, and feudal strife was almost abandoned, while the lords of Europe prepared to take to the road. People fasted and held public prayers. Cardinals made vows of poverty, and pledged themselves to walk afoot until the Holy Land should be regained. Sometimes willingly, sometimes reluctantly, the sovereigns made up their quarrels—the pope, Clement III, and the German emperor of that generation, Frederick Barbarossa, being the first to do so. Philip Augustus of France and Henry II of England exchanged the kiss of peace, before Henry died and his impetuous son Richard the Lion Heart succeeded to the throne and a crusader's cross.

At an assembly in Cologne Frederick Barbarossa refused to preside, saying that Christ Himself was present among them. Genoa even made peace with Pisa, and the Normans of Sicily with the Byzantines.

Noblewomen took the cross in numbers. Great gifts were made to monasteries, and most of Christendom joined in the mobilization. Fleets prepared in Sicily, and up along the cold Northern coasts. The Danes put to sea with the Scandinavians.

The multitudes that set out were as great as in that first march of a century before. The enthusiasm was as great. The object, in effect, was the same—the capture of Jerusalem.

What made the difference?

This third crusade, instead of being a movement of the common people, began as the mutual undertaking of the sovereigns. It was the Crusade of the Sovereigns.

Diplomacy played a hand in it. Before setting out, treaties were drawn up, an *entente cordiale* established. In this arming of Christianity the pope did not lose sight of the interest of the Church as a growing temporal power. The enthusiasm had been spontaneous, but the mobilization became a matter of bargaining.

Strategy played a hand. This would be no blind march toward Jerusalem. It would be a duel between armed Christianity and armed Islam. So the points of attack ran all the way from Spain through Egypt and Asia Minor. Some of the fleets landed on the Granada coast, and Frederick Barbarossa drowned himself in a river near Armenia.

Statecraft accompanied it. The monarchs who led the armies could not forget their affairs at home. All the world was in arms, and wary. The Lion Heart was drawn into quarrels on the way at the strait of Messina, and at the islands. In fact, he was almost the last to appear at Acre. The king of Sicily, the Templars, the emperor of Byzantium all had great stakes on the board.

Quarrels divided it. There had been quarrels along the line of march of the first crusaders, but these had been caused by different men wanting different things when they made their conquest. The kings and emperors of the third crusade brought their differences with them, and Philip Augustus could not agree with the Lion Heart; Guy of Lusignan hated Conrad of Montserrat.

The third crusade was the greatest military effort of medieval Europe. And it failed.[1]

The scenes at the end are utterly unlike the scenes of a century before—Philip Augustus hastening back to reap advantages in France, Leopold of Austria following him, Richard of England delaying to bargain with the Moslems, and finally to arrange a treaty permitting Englishmen to visit the Sepulcher as pilgrims, while he sold Cyprus for one hundred thousand pieces of gold to the Templars. And the Genoese and Pisans bargaining for the commerce of the Levant.

In reality the third crusade was one of the great crises of

---

[1]The failure of the great undertaking is discussed in a note at the end of the book.

the new world war between Christian and Moslem that would soon spread along the line of the Mediterranean, and would enter Europe. As a military undertaking it gained much, and the great pageant, colored by the prowess of the Lion Heart, is breath-taking.

The fourth crusade, in 1202–1204, almost upon the heels of this great mobilization, did not enter Asia. It was diverted by Venetian statecraft—which made capital out of the needs of the crusaders—to an attack upon Byzantium. It landed, in spite of the objection of the bulk of the common soldiers, on the Dalmatian coast, took Zara, and marched upon Constantinople. With the aid of a great Venetian fleet it forced its way into the Queen City, and there ensued a massacre of the Byzantines that drew down upon the crusaders a sentence of excommunication from the pope, Innocent III.

So it became a purely military expedition, that ended before it crossed the frontier of Islam.

In all this century the spirit of the first crusade had not reappeared. Little by little the great expeditions had begun to change into armed undertakings called crusades, but used for political purposes in Europe. On the other hand, there had grown up the world conflict between Islam and Christianity, in which the possession of Jerusalem was only one stake among many on the board. Like a vast conflagration, put out in one place, it sprang to life in another, dwindling down at times but always threatening.

What of the kings of Jerusalem? How did they fare in the interval between the death of Baldwin and the coming of Saladin—nearly sixty years?

They did not measure up to Godfrey, or to the great Baldwin. Eustace, the third brother, did not succeed to the throne. He was on his way to Outremer when he heard that the barons and prelates had chosen the younger Baldwin du Bourg, prince of Edessa, and had crowned him king. Whereupon Eustace turned back, leaving the throne to Baldwin II.

Of the first Baldwin, Matthew of Edessa says this: "He was a worthy man, a friend of holiness, and humble in heart." Of the new Baldwin, he adds: "This prince was one of the most illustrious of the Franks by rank and by valor, and pure in his habits, but his character was tarnished by a craving for silver and a lack of generosity."

The second Baldwin kept Jerusalem safe, and in his reign, which lasted until 1131, the Venetian fleet came again and captured Tyre at a price. But the tide of conquest had reached its full; only along the frontier was there ebb and flow. Meanwhile the spirit of the Moslems was growing more aggressive, especially in the north. Men came forward to devote their lives to the struggle with the Christians— Maudud and Ilghazi, and finally Zangi, who made a battle-field of the north and retook Edessa.

Baldwin II had taken part in the first crusade, and he followed the traditions of the older men; he tried to keep Antioch in the north united to Jerusalem in the south. His successors were content to remain within the borders of Jerusalem itself. So, Baldwin III saw Edessa lost, but captured Ascalon, the "bride of Syria."

The spirit of the great crusade was leaving Outremer. The spring and autumn pilgrimages grew larger, but gave less aid than at first. Adventurers appeared in numbers, and the pilgrims found the situation in the Holy Land hard to understand, with the king often living on friendly terms with the Moslems of Damascus. So the pilgrims sometimes forced the king to undertake a war on their behalf or they broke the truce of their own accord, and thereafter went home. Twice Damascus was attacked in this way with unfortunate results.

Meanwhile the military orders were growing stronger. Men of valor who wished to serve overseas did not now take the cross. They entered the Temple or the Hospital, vowing lifelong service in arms in the Holy Land. Within the preceptories of the Hospital and the commanderies of the Temple they found what they desired most, in that age—the privilege of bearing a sword, the companionship of their brethren, the quietude of the cloisters.

The symbol of the red cross was awarded to the Templars.

Wealth began to flow into their coffers. Fathers who had

sons—and few noblemen did not—wearing the white cross of the Knights, bestowed gifts upon the Hospital overseas. Money being scarce, these gifts usually took the form of real property, lands and castles in Europe. So, with amazing swiftness the two orders found themselves great landholders in Europe as well as in Outremer. And naturally enough— being disciplined, experienced, and willing—the frontier posts, the Watchers, and the new citadels, were given to them to guard. Eventually they became actual owners of the castles.

So likewise prospered the monastic orders. The Augustinians held the great church on Mount Sion, the Sanctuary of the Ascension, the basilica of Bethlehem, and the tombs of the prophets by the Dead Sea. Alms and gifts flowed out to them. The Church of Mount Sion now held lands in Provence and Poitiers as well as in Outremer. The Templars and Knights of the Hospital guarded them.

Inevitably, the merchant cities prospered. The Genoese, Pisans, and Venetians gained their third of everything along the coast. They built warehouses where the caravans came in from Aleppo and Damascus, and they diverted into their ships the trade that had once passed through the hands of the Byzantines. The kings of Jerusalem, being dependent upon the support of the fleets, had to yield them privileges that grew more important as trade increased.

The kings of Jerusalem actually owned no more than their personal fiefs in and around the city. Their one unquestioned privilege was the right of calling their outlying barons to arms, but if their vassals did not respond nothing much could be done about it.

Nor could they command the forces of the Temple and the Hospital, which were subject only to the authority of the distant popes, and were privileged to make treaties and declare war on their own account.

In the reign of Amalric, an Armenian prince visited him and noticed the skeleton force of armed men around the king. All the strongholds of Jerusalem, except three, belonged to the Temple and the Hospital. And the Armenian asked Amalric a question.

"Tell me, where do you find warriors when the Moslems come against you?"

"I hire them," the king responded.

"Whence do you draw the money—for I do not see that you have revenues that will yield money."

"I borrow."

In these years from the death of Baldwin I to the coming of Saladin, the power in Outremer passed from the hands of individual men to institutions. The military orders and monastic orders held the lands of Jerusalem, supported by the merchant fleets. And this was the period of splendor in Outremer.

New churches were rising over the earthquake-shattered basilicas of the older days. The great piers of cathedrals were going up—limestone columns, massive and simple, standing out against the brown earth and the blue sky. Before Notre Dame of Paris was roofed over, the smaller but beautiful cathedral of Our Lady of Tortosa stood erect.

At the coming of Saladin, a Moslem chronicler cried:

Islam gained back a territory that it had left almost without inhabitants, but which the infidels have transformed into a garden of paradise . . . those accursed ones defended with lance and sword that city which they have rebuilt with columns and slabs of marble, where they have erected their churches and the palaces of the Templars and Hospitalers, and fine fountains in which water always runs. Their columns are like flowering trees, and they have even bent iron into gates, and made their gardens white with marble.

In this year the Moslems marched as one man, united under the brilliant leadership of Saladin. And he was fired by one purpose, to take and hold Jerusalem. It was the *jihad* at last, the holy war of the Moslems.

At the same time the Christians in Outremer found themselves divided. A too-hardy adventurer had embarked on a war of his own, down by the Red Sea; there were two rivals for the throne of Jerusalem, and the patriarch and the grand master of the Temple shut the gates of the city against one named Raymond of Tripoli. The last king of Jerusalem had been Baldwin the Leper. In Constantinople there was chaos, because the Byzantines had massacred the Franks.

The spirit of the crusade had passed from the West and entered the East. And conquest went with it.

In these years the power of the popes had grown, largely through the crusades.

Urban had taken the reins of authority in his hands, in calling Christendom to arms that afternoon in Clermont. The apostolic lords who came after him did not release the reins.

The first crusade had bred new fervor throughout Europe. The Truce of God gained adherents, and men looked now, more and more, to the popes for leadership. In their piety they gave freely to the monasteries, and these grants of land grew into great holdings. Crusaders who had borrowed from the churches and had died before returning forfeited their security.

Later popes offered the privilege of buying exemption. A man who took the cross might offer a substitute to go and fight in his place. In this case he paid a sum to the Church, not to the substitute.

The clergy also began to administer the property of crusaders left in their hands. Often the churches declared that no interest need be paid on the debts of crusaders, and that questions affecting the property should be tried in ecclesiastical, not in feudal, courts.

And the papal legates, wielded, during the period of a crusade, extreme power in both hands. On one side they could excommunicate a crusader who failed in his vow; on the other they could grant dispensation—they could condemn or absolve.

The pope had become apostolic lord of a growing kingdom, but not the Kingdom of God that Urban had preached. At the conquest of Constantinople, a hundred years after the first crusade, Innocent III reigned in effect over a mighty dominion extending from the Northern seas to the coast of the Holy Land.

But Saladin held Jerusalem.

It was in the year 1212, during the pontificate of the great Innocent III, that the spirit of the crusade awoke again in Europe.

Among the shepherd folk of the Vendôme fields it stirred. A boy named Stephen took to the St. Denis road, carrying a cross, and many followed him. But they were all children, and they did not know why they went. They left the sheep and they marched, with makeshift wooden crosses, and when good people asked whither they went, they responded, "To God."

In the forests boys left the sheep, and girls came from the hamlets. Spring had made fair the fields and joyous the roads. From the Rhinelands the children thronged with bundles and candles and staffs. Here and there youths and grown people joined the processions. They sang when they passed through villages. Women carrying babies at suck, barefoot girls running from the herds they tended, boys holding to the hands of younger ones—leaving behind them the cold and the hunger of the farmlands, they searched for the sea.

"We shall pass the seas," they said, "and we shall find the Holy Land."

They were thronging together and they were marching toward the Great Sea. They were going to find the city of Jerusalem, where the Seigneur Jesus lived. They were going to follow the armed men, and set Jerusalem free.

Through the forests their thin voices rang; they filled the mountain roads, and the good people of the villages stared at them, and gave them food. Down to the cities on the sea they marched, straggling along with their wooden crosses and their hymns.

To the quays of Marseilles they came, and down the steep alleys of Genoa—into the canals of Venice, and the hot shore of Brindisi. But among them and behind them came the human wolves, slave-seekers and girl-despoilers.

At Brindisi the bishop would not let them embark. Elsewhere ships were offered them, ships of the slave-traders. Some of the children were carried to the Moslem slave markets of Kairuwan and Córdoba. The rest of them wandered among the dark quays, waifs of a vain crusade. God had once opened a way through the waters for those who sought Him, so the children said. But they saw no road for them to walk dry-shod through the sea. The remnant of them turned back into the alleys.

Tired, they made their way home. Heavily walked the young girls who had been raped. Sad were the children when honest folk mocked them because they came back without their crosses and their songs. They did not sing because they were lost, and ill and alone.

They did not look any longer for Jerusalem. Because, in their childish hearts, they had sought not the Jerusalem yonder in Outremer, but that other City of God, lying unseen and unknown to men, beyond all the seas of the earth.

NOTES

I

THE NUMBERS OF THE CRUSADERS

WE WILL never know how many men took the cross in the years 1095 to 1110. Nobody kept any records, and the leaders of the crusade had no muster rolls. The chroniclers wrote down their guesses at various times, and most of the figures they give are fantastic. Moreover, they used Roman numerals, which do not deal gracefully with anything over a thousand. As a matter of fact, an army of five thousand was large for Europe in that age, and the great masses of the crusade baffled the worthy chroniclers.

The Arab historians do not help us, because they content themselves with the usual "as multitudinous as the sands of the shore," or "as many as swarming locusts."

Still, the figures given in the chronicles remain the only evidence. A letter attributed to Urban II states that 300,000 men were ready to march east in the spring of 1096. And Tancred is quoted as saying a month before the capture of Jerusalem that only one man in ten had survived. Now we can estimate the army at that time as about 35,000. (Raymond the chaplain says there were 1,500 knights and the proportion of knights to others was usually one to twenty. Two other sources give 40,000.)

The Byzantine princess, Anna Comnene, had neither head nor memory for figures. She says Godfrey brought 80,000 men with him, while the Western chroniclers say 40,000 and 20,000. But Anna leaves us with the impression that she saw at least four divisions of the crusade larger than any Byzantine army. The Byzantines did keep some records and 20,000 would be a large army in that empire. Granting that Godfrey had 25,000 men, the total under the command of the barons when they reached Constantinople might have been 125,000.

At Constantinople they were joined by the remnant of Peter's mob, and by some Lombards and Taticius's Byzantine division, which seems to have numbered no more than 3,000. Other smaller contingents were arriving steadily, and the crusaders may have assembled 175,000 men at Nicea.

A German historian calculates, by the time taken to cross the bridge beyond Nicea, that the host numbered 105,000. This does not help much, because no one knows whether the crusaders marched in close or open ranks.

At Antioch the bishop Adhemar reports that 100,000 armed men still survive. The casualties here were frightful. During the pestilence after the Battle of the Lance, two hundred a day are said to have died at times. After that the army divided, many turning home, and some staying with Bohemund in Antioch and Baldwin in Edessa.

Raymond the chaplain says that 12,500 armed men survived when the siege of Jerusalem was begun, and that 1,200 mounted men and 9,000 foot were at Ascalon, while Daimbert says Godfrey's army at Ascalon numbered 5,000 horse and 15,000 foot. From this point on the numbers were so small that all the estimates agree pretty well.

So it is possible that a quarter million crusaders started from Europe by land in 1096, and 30,000 reached Jerusalem three years later. But this is not all. The numbers that sailed on the Frisian, the Pisan, Genoese, and Venetian fleets are given as about 45,000; the reinforcements under Conrad and the Lombard princes, 70,000; the count of Nevers, 5,000; the count of Poitiers and the Germans, 60,000.

In Bohemund's crusade of 1107 there were some 35,000, and in Sigurd's fleet, 10,000.

So the total of the figures selected from the chronicles approximates 465,000 in the main military divisions. These figures may well be exaggerated; on the other hand unnumbered throngs made the journey toward Jerusalem in the years 1095–1110.

II

URBAN AND THE CRUSADE

UNTIL the last century Peter the Hermit was thought to be the inspiration of the first crusade. It is now clear that he only preached the crusade after Urban's summons at Clermont—although the Hermit did lead the vanguard of the cross-bearers.

To-day the evidence is plain that Urban planned the crusade, and announced it and directed it, as long as the marching hosts were in Europe. His legate, Adhemar, represented him with the army, and to Daimbert—or Dagobert, as the name often appears— he outlined a plan, the details of which have been lost, for affiliating the churches recovered in the Holy Land with the churches at home. This project always held a place in his thoughts. A little before his death he sent a papal legate and priests to the East, to reëstablish the churches in the battle area, but they found the lands in Asia Minor devastated by fire and troubled by the Red Lion's raids, and Alexis did not smooth the path of the Latin priests.

Urban, as his epitaph states and as the cross-bearers themselves wrote, was the single author of the crusade.

It is impossible to read the chronicles of the time without realizing this. Years after the crusade comments like the following, upon his speech at Clermont, are encountered: "*Si amonestoit a granz sopirs le pople et les Barons que la terre d'Outre mer fut secourue. Sa parole qui volontiers fu receue es cuers des boens Crestiens par la vertu don S. Esprit, fit grant fruit.*" His message, which was willingly received, bore great fruit.

After discarding Peter, a number of historians find the cause of the crusade in the renewed onsets of the Moslems in Spain and Asia Minor during the decade from 1085 to 1095, in which the Emperor Alexis appealed for armed aid.

To say that is to mix things up. The situation is clear when we look at Spain during that time. The Berber Almoravids persecuted Christians and gained a number of cities, but the actual warfare was casual and of the usual border type, without threatening the line of the Pyrenees. To say that the crusade was planned by Christian military leaders to check the Moslem advance here is to lose sight of the fact that the crusade drew away the strongest military unit from the Pyrenees—the Provençals. We find in the ranks of the cross-bearers veterans like William the Carpenter who had come out of Spain. One historian believes that the Christian leaders were so ignorant of geography and so carried away by the enthusiasm of the moment that they hoped to defeat all the Moslems by invading Jerusalem. This disregards the fact that the leaders set out with the idea of forming a new kingdom *at* Jerusalem. The crusade was migration as well as war.

Looking at Asia Minor, we find the Byzantine emperor at truce with the Seljuk sultans, although worried by them. He was actually at war then, not with the Moslems, but with the nomad peoples along the line of the Danube, and when a contingent of knights came out to him from Flanders a little before Urban's speech, they were pressed into service there, not in Asia.

And looking at Urban just then, we find in a prelude to one of his Acts, "our armed people have driven back and defeated the Saracens in Spain in the west, and the Turks in the east."

The struggle for military supremacy between Christian and Moslem was a constant factor in events of that century. Urban invoked this factor in his speech at Clermont, and it aided in launching the crusade, but it did not cause the crusade to be launched.

Why did Urban undertake the crusade?

It is possible [states Professor Munro, the American authority upon the period of the crusades] that he foresaw the gain in authority that would accrue to the papacy from the leadership in a universal movement which would arouse religious enthusiasm and be conducted under the guidance of the Church. It is also possible that he was influenced mainly by the spirit of the age, with its kindred virtues of asceticism and valor. As most of his letters concerning the crusade have been destroyed, there is not enough material to make it possible to dissect and weigh his motives.[1]

The motive of the apostolic lord can never, probably, be established.

Most probably Professor Munro's first suggestion comes nearest to the answer. At the time of the Clermont speech the weight of existing authority was against Urban in the schism. He emerged from the launching of the crusade in a dominant position.

Count Riant, a penetrating thinker, has this to say:

Is it not, in fact, the splendid success first of the preachings of 1095, then of the expedition itself, that carried the lawful papacy to unwonted greatness, and reduced to impotence a schism triumphant until then? Is it not at Clermont in 1095 that Guibert was really conquered? The driving-out of the schismatics ought to be viewed only as the forced consequence of the great gathering at Auvergne.[2]

One or two circumstances seem to confirm this viewpoint. Urban worked intensively for the crusade until the final speech for the

[1]"The Popes and the Crusades," an article by Dana C. Munro.

[2]*Un dernier Triomphe d'Urbzin II*, in the *Revue des questions historiques* XXXIV, 1883.

bella sacra at the Lateran in January, 1097, at which time all the armies of the first crusade were well on their way. After that little appears in the documents of his pontificate concerning the holy war. After the crusade became an accomplished fact the pope assuredly did not have the same interest in it. The crusaders had vanished into the East, and Urban was occupied with affairs at home—except for the appointment of Daimbert and the plan for restoring the churches in the East, after the tidings of Adhemar's death and the capture of Antioch reached him.

In fact, Urban apparently made no effort to communicate with the expedition. After his death Paschal II, on hearing of the capture of Jerusalem, took an active interest in the conquest as long as he lived.

The present writer was struck by the curious circumstance that Urban made some attempt to have the crusade preached in the hostile countries of England and the German states, but did not, apparently, endeavor to enlist his own military supporters—the Norman duke Roger in southern Italy, the Countess Matilda —in the crusade. While after his death Welf and the Lombard princes took the cross with the Germans in that ill-fated attempt to reinforce the men in Jerusalem during 1101 and 1102.

Bohemund and the Normans of Apulia and Sicily had been on friendly terms with Urban, who had visited them at Salerno and consecrated a church for them in Bari before the speech at Clermont. But he did not seem to notify them of the crusade; the chronicles say that Bohemund and his men first heard of it from passing cross-bearers, and—although Bohemund enlisted at once—they were the last to set out. The chronicles add that Duke Roger did not approve of their going.

However that may be, two things are certain—Urban organized the expedition to the Holy Land for his own purpose, whatever that may have been, and once the cross-bearers had passed beyond Italy they were left to their own devices.

III

THE CASE AGAINST THE BASILEUS

ALEXIS, emperor of Byzantium, was charged long ago with conspiring against the first crusaders, led by Bohemund and Godfrey and the others. Time has cleared him of this—except for the minor counts that he was careful to conciliate the Red Lion of the Turks, and that he abandoned the crusaders to their fate in Antioch.

But there is a blacker charge pending against him—the accusation that he betrayed to their destruction all three armies of reinforcements passing through Constantinople in the summer of 1101 to go to the relief of Jerusalem.

The accusation is made point-blank by Ekkehard of Aura, the chronicler who accompanied the crusaders to Constantinople, and went from there by sea to the Holy Land. So, evidently, Ekkehard did not himself witness the massacres but repeated the tale of some survivors.

This accusation is strengthened by the chronicle of Matthew of Edessa, the Armenian who was living at the time not far from the scenes of the massacres. His testimony has been quoted in Chapter XXXVI.

Alexis's daughter, the Princess Anna, was also living at the time and in touch with what went on at the court of Constantinople. Here is her testimony:

The Emperor repeatedly advised them to travel by the same road as the armies that had gone on before, and to reach Jerusalem by the coast, and thus join the rest of the Latin army. But he found they would not listen, as they wanted to travel by another route more to the east and march straight to Chorosan[1] in the hope of taking it.

The Emperor knew that this plan was quite inexpedient and as he did not wish such a large crowd to perish—for they were fifty thousand horse and a hundred thousand foot[2]—he tried the next best thing when they would not listen to him. He sent for Isangeles [St. Gilles] and Tzitas [a Byzantine officer] and asked them to accompany the Normans, to advise them to their advantage and to restrain them as far as possible in their mad enterprises.

After crossing the straits of Cibotus they hastened on to Armenia and on reaching Ancyra [Angora] took it by assault; next they went over the Halys [river] and reached a small town. This was inhabited by Romans [Byzantines] and consequently the citizens feared nothing; the priests clad in their sacred vestments, and carrying the gospels and crosses, went out to meet their fellow-Christians. But the Normans in an inhuman and merciless fashion slaughtered not only the priests but the rest of the Chris-

---

[1]By Chorosan (Khorasan) Princess Anna means the Eastern lands of the Seljuk Turks, with the cities of Rayi, Baghdad, Mosul, etc.

[2]An exaggeration.

tians also, and then quite heedlessly continued their journey, moving in the direction of Amaseia [Amasiya].

But the Turks, long practised in war, seized all the villages and food supplies, and burnt them, and when they caught up with the Normans they attacked them at once. . . .

Isangeles and Tzitas with the few surviving knights reached the capital [Constantinople]. The Emperor received them and gave them plenty of money, and after they were rested asked them whither they wanted to go; and they chose Jerusalem. Accordingly he lavished more presents upon them, and sent them by sea.[1]

The princess says nothing of the other two divisions of crusaders that were destroyed, but Ekkehard says of the third army: "He gave us thirty Turcoples to lead us astray in regions unknown to us but known to them."

Princess Anna wrote this some years later, when the accusation had already been made against her father. She is a biased witness, faithful to the Basileus, and not too truthful in any case. Our eye is caught by the words "as he did not wish such a large crowd to perish." And her story of the slaughter of Christians can be ignored. The crusaders never did what she described. Why did she invent this, unless possibly to make out a case for the subsequent massacre of the crusaders by the Turks of the Red Lion?

A third point—the Byzantines with the doomed army apparently knew where they were, since they mentioned Amasiya, a city far in the northeast of Asia Minor. But the crusaders did not know where they were.

The princess is telling the truth when she says that her father offered ships to the survivors, as he did a few months later to Ekkehard and others. But the crusaders who went by sea were few; the main bodies perished on land.

Now consider the relations between the sultan who annihilated the Christians, and the emperor who gave them guides. Just before the first crusade set out, Alexis had called upon the Red Lion for aid in getting rid of a rebel who occupied Smyrna; he paid the Red Lion a subsidy every year or so, and took many of the Turks into his army—these are the Turcoples of the chronicles. When the crusaders besieged Nicea, Alexis was careful to protect the family of the Red Lion in that city.

Three years after the massacres we find in the chronicle of Ibn Athir, "The Emperor sent to ask aid from Kilidj Arslan [the Red

---

[1] *The Alexiad*, translated by E. A. S. Dawes. Brackets by present writer.

Lion] against the Franks." (Bohemund was then loose at Antioch, hostile to the Byzantines.) And eight years later we learn from the same chronicle that the sultan of Aleppo received an agent of the emperor, who urged him to make war on the Franks.

And another Moslem, Mirat ez-Zamen, relates that in 1106 "Kilidj Arslan went then to Nisibin where he halted because he had with him only a weak detachment, the rest of his army being engaged in Asia Minor *in defending the king of Constantinople against the Franks.*"

It is evident, then, that Alexis held communication with the Red Lion at intervals, and drew aid from him.

Now consider the situation that confronted Alexis in that summer of 1101. His fleet had been at war with the Pisans, on their way to aid the crusaders at Antioch and Jerusalem. Tancred was endeavoring to oust the Byzantines from the coast of Antioch. Bohemund had refused to yield Antioch to Alexis, who was then trying to gain possession of the person of the Norman leader by buying him away from his captors, the Turks.

Alexis, of course, did not want these new armies of crusaders at Constantinople, where the Germans were causing him trouble enough, and where the nobles of Poitiers accused him of treachery to the Germans. Nor could he have wished them to reinforce Tancred.

The story persists that the first of the doomed armies, led by St. Gilles and Conrad, turned east in order to rescue Bohemund. That would have been a mad undertaking, but it is possible that if things had gone well they could have forced the Turks to yield him up. At all events, their army was destroyed somewhere between Amasiya and Sivas, or within forty or fifty miles of Niksar, where Bohemund was imprisoned. If they had actually set out—and remember that Anna speaks of their "mad enterprises"—to rescue Bohemund, that was the one thing Alexis wished to avoid, above all others. To have Bohemund free, in command of a large army in Asia Minor, was unthinkable, for him.

But if they did not go to rescue Bohemund, why did they turn north of east after leaving Angora, crossing the Halys into barren, waterless country, when they could have followed the Halys southeast down toward the Taurus and Armenia and Tancred's support? The only answer is that they lost their way.

But the Byzantine guides knew well enough where they were—at least they knew that Amasiya lay near and that Sinope, on the coast to the north, was the nearest point of safety. In all the massacres the Byzantine guiding parties withdrew from the scene early and in safety.

The only remaining possibility is that the Christian leaders in both cases—ignoring the small division of the ill-fated count of Nevers—insisted stubbornly upon turning off the road into desert country. And this is very hard to believe.

There is one other point. The three armies were within a few weeks' march of each other. If Alexis had really desired their safe passage through to Antioch he would have advised them to unite, as he advised Peter's host in the first place.

After the massacres St. Gilles would not remain in Constantinople, and the Christian armies ceased coming there.

To sum up: The crusaders accuse Alexis directly of betraying them into the hands of the Turks; Princess Anna denies this without offering any tangible confirmation of what she says; the weight of probability is that the Byzantine guides did lead the crusaders astray, and that Alexis planned the destruction of the armies.

The facile statesmanship of Alexis so wrought upon the pope, Paschal, that he actually endeavored to have the Basileus proclaimed emperor of the Holy Roman Empire, instead of Henry V, his enemy.

Alexis's policy of claiming the conquests of the crusaders was followed by his successor, the emperor John, who marched down upon Antioch, taking possession of the Taurus region with a large army, after the death of Bohemund II of Antioch. The crusaders in the north were compelled to acknowledge his overlordship, but when John called upon his new vassals to take the field with him—he had donned a gold helmet for the campaign—they spent all their time rolling dice in their tents.

Ill feeling between the crusaders and Byzantium grew steadily, and when Barbarossa came through during the third crusade he wrote back to Europe advising an attack upon Byzantium. Meanwhile the Venetians had partially strangled the Byzantine trade with the Moslems by their new shorter routes to the coast of Syria.

The thing came to a head when the Byzantines rioted and massacred the Venetian and Frankish merchants across the Golden Horn, embittering the Normans beyond remedy, and breaking forever the alliance with Venice. This resulted in the fourth crusade's being turned aside, against Constantinople, following the road Bohemund had dreamed of nearly a century before.

IV

GREEK FIRE

FLAME, as a weapon, was well known to the Arabs and the Byzantines from the Seventh Century. Just what use they made of it at first is not clear, but by the Tenth Century the Byzantines had developed it to a really remarkable extent.

And they guarded their secret with jealous care. Privileged visitors who asked about the "Greek fire" were taken to the laboratories of the arsenal at Constantinople and shown curiously shaped clay and porcelain vessels, and bronze tubes, and casks of various liquids, but were never allowed to see how the ingredients were put together.

Igor, prince of Russia, came out of the Black Sea with thousands of open war boats manned by a multitude of barbaric swordsmen in heavy iron armor, to attack the wall of Constantinople. His flotilla drew near the sea wall, and was spattered by liquid flame shot out of long tubes upon the parapet. The Russians were so terrified by this apparition of fire that the men in the nearest boats leaped into the water and drowned in their armor rather than await burning. "The Greeks have a fire like the lightning of the skies," they said when they returned home. "They cast it against us and burned us, so that we could not conquer them."

The stories of the day exaggerated the effect of the fire, which was said to follow swimmers in the water, and to start conflagrations that could not be quenched. "Flaming oil" and "sea fire" and "liquid fire" were some of the names given it. Men could not understand how fire, which always rises up, could be projected downward, or why the Byzantine liquid flame could not be extinguished.

We are not certain of the formulas used by the Byzantines. They had more than one. Probably they mixed niter, saltpeter, sulphur, and carbon in various ways. They used clay and pottery bombs, cast by the mangonels. Either a slow match was inserted in the bombs, or they ignited when they burst, with a searing rush of fire and strangling fumes of smoke.

The most dreaded form was the liquid fire. Naphtha went into this, but they had something else as well. On the *pyrophores* or fire-bearing ships, the prow-head was a metal lion's head, or dragon or serpent, always rearing high in the air with open jaws.

Within these jaws projected a moveable metal tube that could swing from side to side, or up and down. The rear end of this tube, or a hose connected with it, rested in a vat of the liquid, which was siphoned or pumped up through the tube. At the muzzle of the tube was placed some smoldering material that ignited the liquid as it passed out into the air.

The Byzantine war galleys stood high in the water, and the tubes in the elevated figureheads were able to throw the liquid fire on the decks of hostile ships, among the crowded men, with devastating effect. Other tubes were placed along the side and on the high stern. Apparently they could not project the streams very far, but this was not necessary.

Anna Comnene, the princess-historian, gives an account of an action at sea between the Byzantine fleet, commanded by Landolph and Taticius, and the first Pisan fleet that went out with Archbishop Daimbert to the relief of Jerusalem. The Pisans were rivals of the Byzantines, and they seem to have plundered the islands of Corfu and Cephalonia on their way down. Landolph's ships were ordered to retaliate.

On the prow of each ship he had a head of a lion or other land animal fixed, made in brass or iron with the mouth open, and gilded over so that their mere aspect was terrifying. And the fire which was to be directed against the enemy through tubes he made to pass through the mouths of the beasts, so that it seemed as if the lions and the other similar monsters were vomiting the fire. . . . When they heard that the Pisan fleet had sailed past, they heaved up their anchors and hurried after them toward Cos, reaching that island in the evening, after the Pisans had reached it in the morning. . . . So they loosed their cables and overtook them between Patara and Rhodes. When the Pisans caught sight of them, they immediately arranged their fleet in battle order.

The Roman[1] fleet did not venture upon a regular sea-battle with the Pisans, but made a series of swift, irregular attacks upon them. Landolph himself first of all drew close to the Pisan ships, and threw fire at them but aimed badly, wasting his fire.

Then the man called Count Eleemon very boldly attacked the largest vessel at the stern, but got entangled in its rudders, and as he could not free himself easily he would have been taken, had he not with great presence of mind had recourse to his machine and poured fire upon the enemy. Then he quickly turned his ship round and set fire on the spot to three more of the largest barbarian ships. At the same moment a squall of wind struck the sea. . . .

The barbarians now became thoroughly alarmed firstly because of the

[1]Byzantine.

fire, and secondly they were very much upset by the storm, and consequently they fled.

Bohemund also ran into the liquid fire at Durazzo, some eight years later.

The Normans started to tunnel under the wall of the Byzantine city, and the defenders dug a counter-tunnel, at right angles to the approach. They stationed sentries along this counter-tunnel to listen for the sound of the Norman picks. As soon as the Norman workmen were heard the Byzantines sent a detachment of flame-throwers to the menaced point. When the digging almost reached the Byzantine tunnel the watchers opened up a little hole, about the height of a man, and thrust through their flame projectors.

Now this fire is prepared from the following ingredients. The readily combustible rosin is collected from the pine and other similar evergreen trees and mixed with sulphur. Then it is introduced into reed pipes and blown by the man using it with a strong continuous breath[1] and at the other end of it fire is applied to it and it bursts into flame and falls like a streak of lightning on the faces of the men opposite.

This fire the men of Durrachium used, directly they were face to face with the enemy, and burned their beards and faces. And the enemy could be seen, like a swarm of bees which has been smoked out, rushing out in disorder from the place.[2]

As with the Pisans, terror did more harm than the flame itself. But Bohemund's great tower was burned down by the liquid fire, which probably saved Durazzo from capture by the Normans.

The crusaders in the East did not encounter more than flaming oil and projectiles saturated with oil and set on fire until long after the conquest of Jerusalem. Then they had to feel at the hands of the Arabs the full effect of flaming naphtha, and hand grenades that took fire as they burst.

V

THE BELFROI AT JERUSALEM

As MIGHT be expected, there are many stories of how Jerusalem was first entered. The Unknown says a knight named Lethold gained the wall from the summit of a ladder; another account

---

[1] Probably bellows were used.

[2] From *The Alexiad* of the Princess Anna Comnene, translated by E. A. S. Dawes.

speaks of Lethold and his brother, while Raymond the chronicler relates that Godfrey and his brother Eustace were in the tower, that the Rhineland men drew up to the wall, and that the count lowered the tower drawbridge to the wall when the Moslems had left the spot on account of the flames on the wall. According to him the duke of Lorraine and Tancred were among the first to cross the drawbridge.

William of Malmesbury gives an interesting detail or two:

The Franks threw faggots flaming with oil on a tower of the wall, and on those who defended it; which, blazing by the action of the wind, first seized the timber and then the stones, and drove off the garrison. Moreover, the beams which the Turks had left hanging down from the walls in order that, being forcibly drawn back, they might, by their recoil, batter the tower in pieces, in case it should advance too near, were by the Franks seized and drawn to them, by cutting away the ropes; and being placed from the engine to the wall, and covered with hurdles, formed a bridge from the tower to the ramparts. The enemy, dismayed by the smoking mass of flame, and by the courage of our soldiers, began to give way. These advanced upon the wall and thence into the city.

It seems fairly clear that Lethold gained his footing somewhere else, and that Godfrey and Eustace were in the tower, or near it. The beams mentioned by Malmesbury—if they were there at all —must have been resting on the top of the wall, or slung there from a frame, if they were to batter the besieger's tower.

William of Tyre mentions the presence of a drawbridge on the tower. This would have been placed high enough to descend on the ramparts, when lowered. The crusaders were pretty accurate in describing such details, and it is quite possible that when the drawbridge was let go it caught on the out-thrust beams, and the crusaders ran across before the Moslems could man the ramparts again.

At all events, it is clear that Godfrey and his men crossed to the wall from the tower and were the first actually to force the wall of Jerusalem.

VI

THE LEGENDS

ROBERT, COUNT OF FLANDERS, returned home and occupied himself there quietly. He died still young, being drowned in the river

Marne in 1111. This silent leader of the crusade was not extolled in the later chronicles, but he was always known as the Jerusalemite.

His cousin, the doughty Robert, duke of Normandy, "whom neither pagan nor Christian could unhorse," engaged in long wars with his brother Henry who had seized the crown of England in his absence. Eventually he was defeated, losing lands, followers, and prestige, and he died in prison in 1134, an old man, the last surviving leader of the great crusade.

But before then the legends were beginning to form. The victories of the crusaders had fired the imagination of men in Europe, and *chansons* were made of their deeds—the popular songs of the day, sung from hall to hall by troubadours. The "Chanson d'Antioche" became a favorite, and it grew more picturesque and imaginative as time went on.

The chronicle of the Anonymous was copied over and over in Jerusalem, and Fulcher's narrative found its way from monastery to court at home. Out of these, partisan writers fashioned revised narratives praising their favorite leaders—the *gesta*. These new narratives, rather naturally, tended to ignore the sufferings of the crusaders and the actual course of events. In the spirit of the time, they dwelt upon the prowess of the leaders in battle. In the "Gesta Tancredi," the author waxes poetic as he describes the charge of the crusaders who saved the day at Doryleum:

> *Advolat ante alios regum clarissima proles*
> *Magnus Hugo, galeis conte tus ferme trecentis.*
> *Irruit in medios non ut qui pugnet in hostes,*
> *Sed qui post pugnam fugienta terga sequatur.*
> *Sic rapidus, sic intrepidus, sic undique tutus*
> *Aggreditur, lacerat, fugat, insequitur, premit, arctat,*
> *Fulminat, exsultat, fremit, exclamat, furit, ardet.*

Hugh the Great, rushing into battle as if he were pursuing the fleeing, is shown as a true marvel of animation. And when Godfrey appears, the chronicle invokes the classics:

> *Dux Godefridus homo totus bellique Deique*
> *Cujus non fervor, non vires, non animosus*
> *Spiritus Hectoreis cessit; praefuit armis,*
> *Laetus adest. O quas acies, quae pectora ferri*
> *Quam longum calybem lateris munimina laevi*
> *Cernere erat comitata ducem! quis flatus equorum,*
> *Quis fremitus hominum, quae gloria Lotharidarum?*

At the same time the song makers began to improve on the early narratives, and to insert imaginary conversation between the Moslem amirs and sultans. Some of these were based on actual incidents—as when Rudwan of Aleppo warned Kerbogha before the Battle of the Lance that the crusaders were more formidable than they seemed, in hand-to-hand fighting. But most of them were quaint concoctions. The chronicle of the Unknown had several of these inserted in it.

Another alteration took place The actual written chronicles were scattered among the monastic and episcopal libraries; most of the people in Europe heard of the deeds of the crusaders from the songs, or the stories told by men returning from Jerusalem. Tradition, as usually happens, began to give one man credit for another's deeds. Peter the Hermit loomed up more and more as the preacher of the crusade, and Godfrey as its leader, while the single authentic spectacular feat of arms performed by Robert of Normandy multiplied into many. He had overthrown the Moslem standard bearer at Ascalon, but in the "Chanson d'Antioche" he appears as the vanquisher of the mighty Kerbogha:

> *Kerbogha came on with close-drawn ranks,*
> *When the Count beheld him and came against him,*
> *Smiting his shield so great a blow*
> *That he was cast down with flying legs. . . .*

This same song adds the slaying of the Red Lion to Robert's list of honors. And even before the middle of the Twelfth Century, as Professor David points out,[1] the Sleepy Duke figured in the chronicles of William of Malmesbury and Henry of Huntingdon, as the victor in purely imaginary battles, and as declining the offer of the throne of Jerusalem. Almost before his death, in obscurity, Robert had become a popular hero in legend.

Perhaps because the Normans of Italy lacked such fervent chroniclers—the "Gesta Tancredi" being an exception—Tancred and Bohemund and Richard of the Principate did not achieve such a place in the legends. Tancred's personal deeds of valor appear often enough, but the part played by Bohemund was not enlarged upon after the first few decades. Unlike the Sleepy Duke and the lord of Bouillon, Bohemund was never very popular— probably because of the failure of the crusade that he led against the Byzantines.

---

[1] *Robert Curthose, Duke of Normandy*, by Charles Wendell David.

During the latter part of the Twelfth and all the great Thirteenth Century these legends of the first crusade took their place in the epics and songs of the day, and in the case of Godfrey grew into a veritable cycle, more and more romantic, beginning with the "Gesta Godefridi" and reaching its climax in the "Chanson du Chevalier au Cygne et de Godefroi de Bouillon."

And they colored the later work of Tasso, the "Gerusalemme Liberata." By then Godfrey had been exalted in the legends to the actual leadership of the crusade, to equality with Raymond of Toulouse in the council, and with Tancred in feats of arms.

> *Veramente è costui nato all 'impero,*
> *Sì del regnar, del commandar sa l'arti;*
> *E non minor che duce è cavaliero;*
> *Ma del doppio valor tutte ha le parti.*
> *Nè fra turba sì grande uom' più guerriero,*
> *O più saggio di lui potrei mostrarti.*
> *Sol Raimundo in consiglio, et in battaglia*
> *Sol Rinaldo e Tancredi a lui s'agguaglia.*

Suffice it that for centuries the early chronicles of the men—the Unknown and Raymond and Fulcher—who had taken part in the crusade were overshadowed by the poetic legends, and that these legends dwelt upon Peter the Hermit, and Godfrey, and to a less extent Robert of Normandy.

Whereas the early narratives make it clear that Godfrey did almost nothing to direct the course of the crusade, and that Peter the Hermit actually had less share in controlling his men toward the end of his unfortunate march than Walter-without-Wealth, and the Sleepy Duke, for all his valiant fighting, rendered less service than his cousin of Flanders, who figured in almost every enterprise.

The legends have obscured the memory of Raymond of St. Gilles, whose devotion helped the crusaders through the stress that followed the struggle at Antioch, and of Bohemund, who was the only one to take actual command in the field, and Baldwin the king, who saved Jerusalem at the end.

One thing is clear. No single man led the crusade or aided it to final achievement. It was the spirit of the Unknown and his comrades the unnamed men of lesser rank, that brought the crusaders through and captured Jerusalem.

VII

THE FIRST AND THE THIRD CRUSADES

IT HAS often been said that the first crusaders succeeded in reaching Jerusalem only because the Muhammadan powers were too occupied with internal war to oppose them. That is a dangerous half-truth.

The great Seljuk sultan, Malik Shah, had just died, and rival princes were contending for the portions of his empire. This strife, however, extended around Baghdad, and to the east. And large armies were in the field at all points. The Seljuk Turks, in 1098, did not lack numbers or fighting ability. What they lacked was a leader.

At least four times in that generation they formed alliances against the crusaders—at the battle of the Arak, under Kerbogha at Antioch, at Harran in 1104, where Jakarmish and Sokman and the Turkomans defeated the crusaders of the North, and in 1114 when Temirak, Ayaz, and Tughtakin joined Maudud of Mosul. In every case they outnumbered the crusaders, as at Ascalon. But they lacked the aggressiveness of the Christians and they had no single leader they trusted.

Bohemund was only occasionally general-in-chief of the first crusade, but the Christians had something that often makes armies victorious without a skilled commander—an unbreakable spirit. For a time, at Nicea and Doryleum, they were almost powerless, but they learned their lesson. At Antioch and the Battle of the Lance they kept on in spite of ghastly losses. So at Jerusalem and Ascalon the remnant of them were able to cope with the Moslems and to win speedy victories. Under Baldwin, a handful of them withstood odds of five to one. Men like Bohemund, Tancred, and Baldwin adapted themselves quickly to the new method of fighting in Asia.

At least one early historian says that the crusaders failed in the great expedition led by the sovereigns a hundred years later—called the third crusade—because the Moslems had learned military science from them in the interval. That is nonsense. It was the Christians who learned from the Moslems. No one can read the detailed chronicles of both sides, from the Unknown's first tribute to the fighting ability of the Turks, without realizing this.

The flank attack, the concealment of troops, the feigned retreat, fire weapons, portable siege engines, water sacks, lighter armor and weapons, and more serviceable horses—the crusaders gleaned more than this from their experience in the East. Above all, they learned scouting and maneuvering. Eventually they mounted their archers on horses in Outremer, so that they could maneuver with the knights and men at arms.

On their part, the Moslems seem to have adapted nothing from the first Europeans. Their armor—frequently made of fine steel rings, in Damascus and Cairo—was lighter and usually better, and often included arm, thigh, and breast pieces, which did not appear in Europe until the beginning of the Thirteenth Century. Their helms had the adjustable nose-pieces of Persian invention, that could be pulled down or thrust up out of the way, long before the movable vizors were in use in Europe. The curved eighteen-inch Turkish knife proved more serviceable in the hand of a skillful horseman than straight poniard or short battle mace. And it must not be supposed that the scimitar of that time lacked either weight or length. It was light only in comparison with the great Norman sword.[1]

Nor did the Moslems avoid hand-to-hand fighting with the invaders—although they fared better in open combat at long range. Anna Comnene says of the annihilation of the reinforcements in 1101 by the Red Lion:

Now the Turks had them in their power. They [the Turks] put aside the spears and arrows with which they had been fighting; drawing their swords they made a hand-to-hand fight of the battle, and soon drove the Normans back to their camp.

The so-called third crusade, led by Philip Augustus of France, Richard the Lion Heart of England, Frederick of Swabia, Henry of Champagne, Leopold duke of Austria, Conrad marquis of Montserrat, the duke of Burgundy, and others, assembled the greatest armament of the medieval years.

Accompanied by fleets from Scandinavia and England and Flanders, strengthened by the experienced Templars and Knights

---

[1] Few sword blades of the Eleventh Century have survived. The present writer was fortunate in being shown in Asia Minor a beautiful Arab blade with a Kufic inscription dating from that time. The hilt pieces and the sheath were more recent. The blade measured a full three feet, of the type of the reinforced head, being three and a half inches wide a foot below the point, and narrowing toward the center of the curve. It weighed more than the American cavalry saber of twenty years ago.

of the Hospital, it landed on the coast of Outremer more than a quarter million strong—more than half being disciplined fighting men. They had adequate siege engines; they had command of the sea behind them, and fortified ports—Tripoli and Tyre—from which to disembark. More or less regularly they were supplied with food by the Italian fleets. Hundreds among them knew intimately the country they intended to invade.

Moreover, they faced different conditions than did the first crusaders. The war had gone on for a hundred years; quarter was given frequently in battle, and long truces afforded respite to both sides. Moslem amirs and Christian princes negotiated one day, and fought the next.

Why did it fail of final success?

The story is long and most interesting. It did not fail as utterly as the Gallipoli venture of the late World War. It captured Acre and Ascalon, won battles, reduced Saladin almost to the end of his resources, and drew up a treaty before it sailed away.

It was the Verdun of the crusades—the greatest military effort of the Christians and the most terrible check. Saladin won, in the end, and the invaders never came within sight of Jerusalem's walls.

In Saladin the Moslems at last had a leader, brilliant, victorious, and earnest. He devoted his life to the war, and under him it became for the Moslems a *jihad*—a holy war.

Richard the Lion Heart was a glorious fighter, and the whole crusade became a setting for his inimitable personal valor. He could jump from his sleeping robes and ride out without armor to repel a night attack, he could wade ashore with a few knights in the face of an army, but he could not direct a campaign. And this is what he tried to do. The result was quarreling—men and time wasted in the wrong places—delay, uncertainty, and finally retreat when victory at last became possible. Richard played the knight-errant to his heart's content, and lost the cause for which he fought.

The parts played by Saladin and Richard were important, but for the Christian soldier in the ranks, the third crusade was just another—although different—war. He knew the meaning of discipline, and his morale, especially at first, was good. But the campaign led him over islands and along a strange and arduous coast, and Jerusalem became, in his thoughts, no more than his objective—after which everyone would go home. When the leaders failed to gain more than a foothold along the coast, the men in the ranks were ready to go home.

VIII

BOHEMUND AND THE LION HEART

ONLY the figures of Bohemund and Godfrey, of the first crusaders, are distinct after the lapse of the centuries. And Bohemund, thanks to the half-fearful admiration he aroused in the Byzantine princess Anna, is the clearer in the records—the Ulysses of the first crusade.

Inevitably, he invites comparison with Richard the Lion Heart. The Moslems admired them both, *Maimoun* and *Malik Ric*, the little god of the first Franks and the sword-arm of the later invaders. Both were indomitable Normans, living for battle and conquest—leading figures of their centuries and the greatest of the crusades. They left everything to go with the crusades, while more prudent brothers, Roger the Counter and John Lackland, profited by their absence; and both, taken captive, were bid for with huge ransoms. And in the end both had to acknowledge defeat at the hands of lifelong antagonists, the politicians their erstwhile friends, Alexis of Byzantium and Philip Augustus of France.

They had in them the cool daring that seems little less than clairvoyance. Bohemund, in a sea battle, his galley crushed by two Byzantine dromonds, leaps into the water and swims to safety; with fifty men, he climbs the wall of Antioch in the darkness; besieged in his turn, he holds the backbone of the city almost single-handed against the Turks. Captured, he volunteers in the army of his jailer, and at Durazzo he burns his ships behind him.

The twain shared equally the vices of their age—a craving for spoil, sheer cruelty, and callousness in shedding blood. Richard grew up in court and tournament and hunting field, and the minstrels have left us a deathless record of his gallantry. Much less is known of Bohemund. The full tale of his deeds might rival those of the Lion Heart.

Richard was one of the bravest men, and the worst kings, ever to rule England. He entered the crusade as the leader of a people, while Bohemund went forth as an adventurer, with a following of some five thousand men. He established a dominion in Syria that endured for two hundred and fifty-odd years in the hands of his descendants. He made himself the marshal of Christendom, the equal of kings. Playing for higher stakes than that other Norman, William, who conquered England, he overreached himself.

Joined as he was then by marriage to the royal house of France, with the pope, Paschal, in leading strings, with his brother governing southern Italy and Sicily, his nephew Tancred holding Syria and Edessa—if Bohemund could have made himself master of Constantinople he would have been the dominant figure of his century. He failed, and his effort weakened the crusading spirit.

IX

THE WHITE MANTLE AND THE BLACK

For the first decade of their existence the Templars-to-be remained less than a dozen knights, until their leader Hugh, or Hugo of Payans, sailed from Outremer in the year 1128 and applied to the papal council of Troyes for recognition of his "poor soldiers of the Temple." He was granted that, and also a rule for his new military order and certain privileges such as immunity from taxation. And when he followed Bohemund's course and toured Europe for recruits he gained an immense following. Distinguished knights, younger sons of the nobility, and men who wanted to make their peace with God followed him back to the Templars' quarters.

His order—in the beginning a kind of military police for the highroads behind the battle area—was now devoted to service in the battle line. It combined the two ideals of the men of his age, the shelter of the cloister and the career of the sword. It called for sacrifice and devotion, and the renunciation of "human favor." It held the inducement of a lifetime spent in the Holy Land. And it was very far from being a sinecure.

In their quarters within the courtyard of the Temple corner at Jerusalem these new Knights were bound by lifelong vows to give implicit obedience to their master and his seneschal and marshal. They kept silence at meals; they slept in their clothes on beds that were no more than carpets spread over the stones, with a light burning in the dormitory, to be ready for any call to service. Women and hunting and hawking were denied them—although they could hunt down lions if they wished.

Forty days of fasting was the penalty for a blow struck, and if two knights quarreled they must eat their meals together, apart from the others, on the ground without tablecloth for a month. Anyone who raised a weapon against a brother, or deserted his comrades during battle, was stripped of his habit in public and driven out of the order. They could no longer hold or receive property of any kind, and they were fairly certain of ending their lives sword in hand in the struggle with the Moslems.

The rule of the Templars was modeled upon the rule of St. Benedict, and it was enforced.

Most of the Templars were novices on probation, or serving brothers. The Knights alone could wear the white surcoat over their linen coifs and the casing of ring mail that covered even their arms and feet. Under the surcoat they had wide belts with the long swords inserted. On their close-clipped heads they wore red skull-caps, but their beards were allowed to grow rough.

The Moslems called them servants of God's House, adding that they had nothing to do with women, and swore lifelong enmity against Islam and did other strange things. Hundreds of them began to appear in the highways of Jerusalem, and the white mantles, beside the black mantles of the Hospitalers, became the flower of the army of Outremer.

Nothing was more natural than that the Templars should take over the guarding of the frontier strongholds called the Watchers, and that in due course of time they should acquire title to these citadels.

At the same time the Knights of the Hospital of St. John of Jerusalem were building other hospitals in Jaffa, Tyre. They were the older order, devoted in the beginning to giving first aid to the pilgrims and warriors. They followed the rule of St. Augustine, and gained recruits in growing numbers from the nobility of Italy and the North—the Templars were mostly French and Burgundian. They had clerics as well as laymen, and Paschal adopted them in 1113, freeing them from obedience to any power other than the Holy See. For a long time only noblemen served in the ranks of the Hospital, and not until the Templars went out against the Moslems did the wearers of the black mantle and white cross take to the sword. Immediately men thronged to the hospitals, to be trained in arms and led against the infidels.

These two fraternities were the outgrowth of the crusade. The strange order of St. Lazarus had for its object the care of the lepers as well as the defense of the Holy Land, and many of its members were lepers. The order of the Teutonic Knights was not created until later.[1]

---

[1]The period of the great political power of the Temple and the Hospital in Outremer came much later than the events related in this volume. Not until 1170 did

X

THE TALES OF OUSAMA

AN ARAB amir, Ousama by name, lived in Shaizar, in Syria, during most of the Twelfth Century, from the time when Tancred was lord of Antioch to the coming of Saladin. He wrote down anecdotes of the crusaders and of his own experiences in curt, vivid words that offer us almost the only clear picture of the men and the country at that time. These anecdotes were grouped together in a manuscript which is now in the royal archives of Spain, and which has been translated by a French orientologist, M. Hartwig Derenbourg.[1] The following incidents, translated from M. Derenbourg's version, show the crusaders at war with the Moslems after the first conquest.

The praise be to Allah, creator of all things. I will relate something about the Franks, who are superior in courage and in ardor for battle, but not in other things.

They comprehend not the niceties of honor, nor of jealousy (in regard to their women). If one of them, walking with his wife, meets another man, the stranger takes the woman's hand and talks with her while the husband stands aside and waits. If the woman talks too long, the husband goes away, leaving her with her companion.

Think, then, of this strange contradiction. Here are men, not jealous or susceptible to honor, yet they are possessed of great courage.

Here is an instance. We had in our household a bathman, Salim by name, who came from Ma'ara an-Nouman, and who was employed by my father (may Allah grant him mercy). Salim said one day, "I put in order some baths at Ma'ara an-Nouman, to make a living out of them. A Frankish knight visited them. Now these Franks do not like to bathe as we do, with a robe. My visitor stretched out his hand and pulled my garment off. In so doing he noticed that I had just shaved my body. He called out, 'Salim!'

"I came over to him. He touched my skin with his hand and said,

---

the Hospitalers begin the building of the castle-forts for the defense of the Lebanon region. In 1201 they finished the mighty Krak of the Knights, that the Arabs called the "Flame of the Franks." In 1220-1240 they were supreme masters of the Lebanon region. In 1260 the reigning king of Jerusalem—the title meant little except an honor by then—sold the whole city of Sidon to the Templars for cash. At that time the Templars had the largest bank in France.

[1] *Souvenirs historiques et recits de chasse par un emir syrien du douzième siècle.* Paris, 1895.

'Salim is splendid. By the truth of my faith, do likewise to me.' He lay down on his back and I shaved all the hair from his body. Then with his hands he felt how smooth he was all over. He said to me, 'Salim, by thy faith, do likewise to madame.' Now in their speech they call their wives madame. He actually meant his wife. And he sent one of his servants to bid his wife to come to the bath. The servant sought her out and brought her. And her husband ordered me to shave her also—he watching while it was done. Then he gave me thanks and the price of my labor."

At another time they brought into the house of my father (may Allah grant him mercy) several girls, captured from the Franks. They (may Allah curse them) are an accursed race, and they will never intermarry with another. My father selected from the captives a girl both beautiful and in the most delicious youth. He said to the elder women of his house, "Bathe her and give her new garments, so that she shall be ready to go upon a journey."

They did so. My father gave the girl into the care of one of his armed men, bidding him take her to the amir Malik ibn Salim ibn Malik, lord of Kala 'at Jabar, a friend, and he wrote: "We have taken spoil from the Franks and I send thee part of it." The girl gave pleasure to the amir and he favored her. He kept her himself, and by him she bore a son who was named Badran.

His father made this son his heir-to-be. The boy grew up and the father died. So Badran became lord of the town and the men in it, his mother insisting, however, upon giving orders and prohibiting certain things.

She arranged with some men to escape, climbing down by a rope from the rampart of Kala 'at Jabar. The men accompanied her as far as Sarudj which was then in the hands of the Franks. Although her son was lord of Kala 'at Jabar, she married a Frankish cobbler.[1]

This took place before Schaizar in September of the year 1111. The commander-in-chief Maudud (may Allah grant him pity) was encamped in the outskirts of Schaizar. Tancred, lord of Antioch, made preparations to attack him, but—being hemmed in by greater forces—had to retire. He went toward Apamea. Three days later our army cut the Franks off from water, blocking the sources of water so they could not get at it.

A horseman came out of their ranks. Alone, he attacked our men and cut a way into the midst of them. They killed his horse, and riddled him with wounds. He fought on foot and managed in the end to rejoin his comrades. The Franks retreated into their own lands.

Some months after, a letter from Tancred reached us, carried by a warrior who was escorted by esquires and companions. The letter said:

[1]Both the indifference and the loyalty of the Westerners puzzled the Asiatics, who could better appreciate their fighting qualities. After the conquest, individual duels often took place—the single combat on horseback in which the Arabs and the crusaders were equally at home.

"The bearer is a knight much esteemed by the Franks; he has started on the pilgrimage to Jerusalem, and to return to his own country. He has prayed me to introduce him to you, so that he may see your knights. I have commended him to you. Have him in your care."

He was young, handsome and elegant in attire. Only, he bore the scars of numberless wounds. His face was cleft by a sword-cut from the line of the hair to the cheek. I asked who he was. They told me: "He is the one who charged all alone against the men of the commander-in-chief Maudud, and who, when his horse was killed under him, fought so desperately to rejoin his comrades." Praised be Allah, to whom all things are possible.

The father of one of my companions, Magrabin al Oukab, the poet, left Palmyra to go to Damascus. He took with him four horsemen and four men on foot, leading eight camels which were to be sold. During the journey a Frank came up, at the edge of the desert, crying out as he rode to meet them: "Give up your camels to me!"

We answered him by shouts and insults. He reined his horse at us, and overthrew and riddled with wounds one of our horsemen. We pursued him, but he outstripped us, and wheeled again to charge. Thus he put two of our men out of the fight.

This time one of us stopped him with the blow of a lance. The blow struck upon his saddle horn and the lance broke. Then the rider, our enemy, gave our companion a lance thrust and wounded him. After that he attacked us again, striking one of us with his lance, and casting him to the ground. He cried out again, "Give up your camels to me, or I will make an end of you."

We said, "Come—take half of them."

"Pick out four," he responded, "and leave them here. Take the other four and go on."

And that is what we did, hardly being able to believe that we were safe with what was left to us. He led off the four camels under our eyes. We were powerless and without spirit against him. He led off his spoil—he who had come forward alone against eight armed men.

A deed of the same sort took place when Tancred, lord of Antioch,[1] marched against the city of Schaizar, where he carried off large numbers of pack animals, after killing or taking prisoner many of our men. His camp was near to Zalim, where inaccessible caverns stand in the face of

---

[1]This happened in 1108 when Bohemund was absent in Europe. Ousama's brevity leaves much to the imagination. Apparently the knight in the basket wrought such havoc among the Moslems in the caverns that they surrendered and lowered themselves down by ropes.

It is interesting to see how conditions have changed in the decade since the capture of Jerusalem. The crusaders can talk with the Arabs now, there are frequent truces, and the knights are as well mounted as the Moslem warriors. The time of the following anecdote is about a generation later.

a cliff which forms the side of a hill. No one can reach them by any path leading down from the summit or up from the plain. If a man wishes to take refuge in these caves, he can only do so by lowering himself on ropes from the height above.

It was the twentieth of the month of the second *rabi* in the year 502 of the Hegira. A devil among the Franks came to Tancred and said to him: "Make me a wooden basket. When I am placed in it, lower me from the summit of the cliff, down to our enemies who have taken refuge in these caverns. Be careful to use iron chains strongly bound to the basket, so that they cannot cut the fastenings with swords and make me fall."

They made him his box, grappled with iron chains, and lowered it against the mouths of the caverns. He captured every place and brought back to Tancred those whom he found within. That happened because the interiors of the caves were no more than straight galleries without hiding places, and when this man shot his arrows he struck someone with each shaft—so narrow were the places and so crowded.

I visited Jerusalem, going into the al Aksa mosque. Beside this stood a little mosque which the Franks had changed into a church. The Templars occupied the al Aksa, and they were my friends. When I visited their quarters, they pointed out the little mosque to me, for a place to pray. One day I entered it and glorified Allah. I was in the midst of my prayer when a Frank rushed at me and grasped me, turning me about to face the east,[1] saying, "This is the way to pray!"

Some Templars went up to him, seized him, and put him outside. I began my prayers again. But this same man, when they were not looking, ran back to me and again turned my face to the east, crying, "This is how to pray!"

The Templars again made for him and put him outside. Then they apologized to me, saying, "He is a stranger who has only just come from the land of the Franks. He has never seen anyone praying without turning toward the east."

I answered, "I have prayed enough for to-day."

I went out, and was truly astonished to notice how chagrined this demon was, how he trembled, and how much he had been affected by seeing anyone kneel toward the *Kibla*.

And I saw one of the Templars go up to the amir Mou'in ad-Din (May Allah grant him mercy) when he was within the Dome of the Rock. "Would you like," the Templar asked him, "to behold God as a little child?" Mou'in ad-Din responded, "Yes, certainly." The Templar led us before an image of Mary, with the Messiah (may he be saved) upon her lap. "Here," the Templar said, "is God as a little child." (May Allah exalt himself above those who utter such impious words.)

---

[1]Ousama had followed the custom of his faith, kneeling toward the Kaaba at Mecca, which lies more south than east of Jerusalem.

SELECTED BIBLIOGRAPHY

I

THE SOURCES

Note: The author of this book does not presume to give a full bibliography for the crusade during the years 1095–1110. The titles given below are of the works he found most useful in his search for information. The epics and songs of the period which he read in part are not listed because they do not bear directly upon the crusade. On the other hand, the existing histories of the crusade, by earlier and modern authors, are not included because he has not read them—with the exception of Hagenmeyer's *Chronologie* and the portions of Chalandon's work dealing with Byzantium.

It was the intention of the author to work directly, according to his ability, from the sources of information. In this work he has been aided greatly by the modern authorities upon the special subjects listed in the last division of this bibliography.

THE most valuable chronicles of the first crusade are those of the Anonymous, of Raymond the chaplain of the count of Toulouse, and Fulcher.

The account of the unknown Norman is shorter than the others, and more accurate. Its author was present at all the critical events in the crusade, and being an unprejudiced soldier, his testimony is invaluable. On the other hand, he knew little about what the leaders were doing, and he was not intelligent enough to grasp more than what happened under his eyes. This is at once his great virtue, and his lack. His point of view is that of a company commander in a modern army. His narrative, the *Gesta Francorum et aliorum Hierosolymitanorum*, was written down before 1101, and a manuscript copy of the Twelfth Century exists in the Apostolic Library of the Vatican—Reg. Lat. 572. The various manuscripts have been compared and edited by Louis Bréhier—*Histoire anonyme de la première croisade*, Paris, 1924.

Raymond's chronicle is half argument and half narrative. Apparently he wrote with the help of another man, one Pontius,

who was killed at Arkah. Raymond goes to great lengths to prove
that the Provençals did not lack courage, and that the discovery of
the lance was not a fabrication of Bartholomew's—in reading his
version, you are left with the impression that Bartholomew died
months after the ordeal by fire, simply because Raymond does
not mention his death until later. Disregarding these two points
of bias, his chronicle gives invaluable detail all through the march
of three years. He sympathized with the common men, and he does
not forget the men of the sea, while he understands the actions
of the leaders. From the capture of Antioch to the end of the
battle of Ascalon, his account is the fullest and clearest. Judging
from the character of the work he wrote it from memory, and from
some notes a little after that battle. His chronicle—*Historia Francorum Qui Ceperunt Jerusalem*—is printed in Migne's *Patrologia*, CLV. And in the *Recueil*.

Fulcher, unlike the other two, was absent from the march after
the passing of the Taurus, since he followed Count Baldwin to
Edessa. He was less intelligent than Raymond, but he observed
the country he passed through, and even made his own investiga-
tions into natural history, with curious results. He followed Baldwin the king faithfully, and his account of the years 1100 to 1126
is most valuable. By that time he had learned a good deal about
the Muhammadans, so his chronicle gives almost the only clear
picture of the crusaders at home in their conquest. It is included
in Migne CLV—*Historia Hierosolymitana*.

A later work, but hardly less valuable—*Gesta Clarissimi Ducis
Godefridi Fratrisque Eius Balduini Regis Hierusalem* of Albert of
Aix gives some detailed descriptions of the country the crusaders
passed through, and incidents in the battles, and mentions many
Rhinelanders who do not appear in the other chronicles. Judging
from the fine Thirteenth Century manuscript in the Vatican—
Vat. Lat. 1999—it is pieced together from earlier chronicles, by a
man who heard many narratives from the crusaders. He gives
names to the mountains in Asia Minor that are not found elsewhere, and mentions incidents rather than great achievements in
the battles.

A fourth chronicle, the *Gesta Tancredi*, was written apparently in
Syria about 1115 by a Norman who exulted in the deeds of Bohemund and Robert of Normandy, but especially of Tancred. It is
interlarded with long speeches and longer fighting, but it is interesting in its revelation of a crusader's character. The writer, one
Raoul or Ralph, was a knight and a follower of Tancred. While he

lacked Raymond's keen mind and Fulcher's observant eye, he reflected the spirit of the leaders at the end of the crusade. His narrative is printed in Migne, CLV.

The "Chanson d'Antioche," composed first by Richard the Pilgrim and after him by a certain Graindor de Douai, gives the legends as well as the incidents of the crusade. It speaks of the women and the ribalds, and at times—as in the Battle of the Lance —it is fine indeed. Historians may have little use for such a song, but it yields intimate details and touches of color that are not to be found in the narratives of the priests and the chroniclers. It has been edited and published in modern French, "Le Chanson d'Antioche," Paris, 1848.

Then there are the letters; Stephen, count of Chartres, to his wife Adele, Adhemar and Simeon to the faithful in the north, the leaders of the crusade to Pope Urban II, and Anselm of Ribemont to the archbishop of Rheims—published in the *Recueil des historiens des croisades—Historiens occidentaux*, Tome III, Paris, 1864. As well as the letter of Alexis to Cardinal Oderisio, which is preserved in the library of Monte Cassino, and two letters of Urban addressed to the faithful in Flanders and to the inhabitants of Bologna. This is published in Migne, CLI, with other letters of Urban.

The history of the reign of Alexis written by his daughter, Anna Comnene, resembles the "Chanson" in that it is unreliable as to facts. The princess Anna was no more than fourteen years of age when the crusaders first passed through Constantinople and she wrote her history some twenty years later. Nearly everything she says is distorted in one way or another, but she draws a splendid portrait of Bohemund, and gives an impression of Godfrey and of the other leaders. Above all, she has left us an immortal record of Byzantine life, and of the statecraft of Alexis. Her work is published in the *Recueil* in Greek, and has been translated into English by Elizabeth A. S. Dawes, London, 1928.

The chronicle of Matthew of Edessa was written by an Armenian who was living at the time of the crusade, but is only interesting in its account of happenings in the northeast—the affairs of the Moslem amirs and the local Armenian princes. It is published in the *Recueil*, and separately, edited by M. Edouard Dulaurier— *Chronique de Matthieu d'Edesse*, Paris, 1858.

The Moslem chronicles have little to say of the crusaders until after their settlement in the East. The most useful narrative, giving a summary of events each year, is that of Abulfeda. It is in the *Recueil*, Volume I. The work of Ibn Athir, the *Histoire des atabegs de Mosul*, is also in the *Recueil*, Volume II.

II

OTHER WORKS OF THE TWELFTH AND THIRTEENTH CENTURIES YIELDING INFORMATION ABOUT THE CRUSADE, IN MOST CASES AFTER THE CAPTURE OF JERUSALEM

CAFFARUS, *Annales. Monumenta Germaniæ Historica—Scriptores.* XVIII.

Chronicon Syriacum, Gregorii Abulpharagii, sive Bar-Hebraei. Lipsiae 1789.
> (A chronology of events in the Near-East during the Twelfth and Thirteenth centuries by an Armenian who often gives interesting anecdotes. A Latin translation.)

EKKEHARDUS, *Hierosolymita.* Edited by Hagenmeyer, Tubingen, 1877. (A brief account of the peasants' march, and the betrayal of the expedition of 1101.)

ITINERARIO DI LA GRAN MILITIA A LA PAVESE—*Recueil*, Volume V.

LUPUS PROTOSPATUS, *Chronicon Anonymi Cives Barensis—Rerum Italicarum Scriptores*, V, Mediolani. 1724.

NICETAS DA CHONE—*Historia Degli Imperatori Greci dal MCXVII fino al MCCIII—*Venetia, 1562.
> (A translation of part of the long history of the Byzantine (emperors, that treats of some amazing personalities.)

ORDERICUS VITALIS, *Monachi Historia Ecclesiastica. Recueil des Historieus des Gaules et de la France*, XI.

PASCHAL. *Patrologia*, Migne CLXIII.
> (Letters, privileges, and notices of the pope Paschal who succeeded Urban.)

ROBERT REMENSIS, *Monachi historiae hierosolymitanae—* (A Twelfth Century manuscript is in the Vatican, 2000 Vat. Lat.) Migne, CLV.

URBANUS II. *Patrologia*, Migne CLI. (Letters, life, and privileges.)

WILLIAM OF TYRE, *Historia Rerum in Partibus Transmarinus Gestarum.* (A Thirteenth Century manuscript is in the Vatican, 2002, Vat. Lat.) In the *Recueil*.

III

DESCRIPTION

FRETELLI, *Liber Locorum Sanctorum Terre Jerusalem.* Migne CLV.
IBN JUBAIR, *Extrait des Voyage. Recueil* III.
WIRZBURGENSIS JOANNIS, *Descriptio Terræ Sanctæ.* Migne CLV.

IV

MISCELLANEOUS

ACCOLTI, *Benedetto degli. De Bello a Christianis Contra Barbaros,*
    Venetia, 1539.
BARONIS. *Annales Ecclesiastici.* Rome, 1593.
BREHIER, LOUIS. *L'Eglise et l'Orient au moyen âge. Les Croisades.*
    Paris, 1928.
DAVID, CHARLES WENDELL. *Robert Curthose, Duke of Normandy.*
    Harvard University Press, 1920.
DIEHL, CHARLES. *Byzance, grandeur et décadence.* Paris, 1926.
    Figures byzantins. Première série. Paris, 1925.
    Figures byzantins. Deuxième série. Paris, 1927.
ENLART, G. *Les Monuments des Croisés dans le royaume de Jéru-*
    salem. Architecture religieuse et civile. Paris, 1925–1928.
HAGENMEYER, HEINRICH. *Chronologie de la première croisade.*
    Revue de l'Orient latin, VI–VIII.
HEYD, WILHELM. *Histoire du commerce du Levant au moyen âge.*
    Leipzig, 1923. (A French translation.)
Histoire littéraire de la France. Par des Religieux Bénédictins de la
    congrégation de S.-Maur. Tome VII–VIII. Paris, 1746.
JAFFE, PHILIP. *Regesta Pontificum Romanorum.* Lipsiae. 1885.
KREY, AUGUST C. *The First Crusade—Accounts of Eye-Witnesses*
    and Participants. Princeton University Press, 1921.
LE STRANGE. *Palestine Under the Moslems.*
MUNRO, DANA C. *The Popes and the Crusades.* 1916.
    The Children's Crusade.
NEUMANN, CARL. *La Situation mondiale de l'empire byzantin avant*
    les croisades. (Traduction française par Renault et Koz-
    lowski). Revue de l'Orient latin. Tome X, 1903–1904.

PAULOT, L. *Un Pape français, Urbain II.* Paris, 1903.

POTTHAST, AUGUST. *Bibliotheca Historia Medii Aevi.* Berlin, 1896.

RAMSAY, W. M. *The Historical Geography of Asia Minor.* London, 1890.

REY, EMANUEL. *Monuments de l'architecture militaire des croisés en Syrie. Documents inédits sur l'histoire de France, VI-6.* Paris, 1871.

Les Colonies Franques de Syrie aux XII et XIII siècles, 1883.

RIANT, COMTE PAUL. *Inventaire critique des lettres historiques des croisades. Archives de l'Orient latin. Vol. I* Genoa, 1881.

Expéditions et pélerinages des Scandinaves en terre sainte au temps des croisades. Paris, 1865.

Un Dernier Triomphe d'Urbain. Rev. des Quest. histor. XXXIV. 1883.

RUINART, DOM. *Vita B. Urbani II.* Migne, CLI.

SCHLUMBERGER, GUSTAVE. *Récits de Byzance et des croisades.* Paris, 1922.

STEVENSON, W. B. *The Crusaders in the East. A brief history of the wars of Islam with the Latins in Syria during the Twelfth and Thirteenth Centuries.* Cambridge University Press, 1907.

YEWDALE, RALPH BAILEY. *Bohemund I, Prince of Antioch.* Princeton University Press.

Special bibliographies are given in Bréhier's volume, in Stevenson's, and in Yewdale's.

And Professor Munro gives in his fine article on the children's crusade the sources of information for that little-known event.

NOTE

MR. LAMB's next book will deal with the story of the later crusades in the years between the fall of Jerusalem, the crusade of St. Louis, and the coming of the Mongols; years in which Saladin, Richard Coeur de Lion, and Baibars (the Panther) loom as the great dramatic figures.

INDEX